T0309820

THE KINGDOM SUFFERETH VIOLENCE

Other Titles of interest from St. Augustine's Press

Rémi Brague, *Eccentric Culture*

C.S. Lewis & St. Giovanni Calabria, *The Latin Letters of C.S. Lewis*

Josef Pieper, *Happiness and Contemplation*

Josef Pieper, *The Christian Idea of Man*

Josef Pieper, *The Platonic Myths*

Roger Pouivet, *After Wittgenstein, St. Thomas*

H.S. Gerdil, *The Anti-Emile: Reglections on the Theory and Practice of Education against the Principles of Rousseau*

Seth Benardete, *Archaeology of the Soul: Platonic Readings in Ancient Poetry and Philosophy*

Gerhart Niemeyer, *The Loss and Recovery of Truth*

Ralph Hancock, *Calvin and the Foundations of Modern Politics*

Alexandre Kojève, *The Concept, Time, and Discourse*

Roger Kimball, *Fortunes of Permanence*

Pope Pius VI, *The French Revolution Confronts Pius VI* (in 2 vols.)

Gabriel Marcel, *Man against Mass Society*

Gabriel Marcel, *The Mystery of Being* (in 2 vols.)

Peter Augustine Lawler, *Homeless and at Home in America: Evidence for the Dignity of the Human Soul in Our Time and Place*

James V. Schall, *The Regensburg Lecture*

Roger Scruton, *An Intelligent Person's Guide to Modern Culture*

Peter Kreeft, *Summa Philosophica*

Edward Feser, *Last Superstition: A Refutation of the New Atheism*

Jacques Maritain, *Natural Law: Reflections on Theory and Practice*

Joseph Cropsey, *On Humanity's Intensive Introspection*

Leo Strauss, *Xenophon's Socrates*

Leo Strauss, *Xenophon's Socratic Discourse: An Interpretation of the* Oeconomicus

Philippe Bénéton

THE KINGDOM
SUFFERETH VIOLENCE

The Machiavelli / Erasmus / More Correspondence
And Other Unpublished Documents

Translated by Paul J. Archambault

ST. AUGUSTINE'S PRESS
South Bend, Indiana

Copyright © 2012 by Philippe Bénéton

All rights reserved. No part of this book may be reproduced, stored in a retrieval system, or transmitted, in any form or by any means, electronic, mechanical, photocopying, recording, or otherwise, without the prior permission of St. Augustine's Press.

Manufactured in the United States of America

1 2 3 4 5 6   18 17 16 15 14 13 12

Library of Congress Cataloging in Publication Data
Bénéton, Philippe.
[Royaume souffre violence. English]
The kingdom suffereth violence: the Machiavelli/Erasmus/More correspondence and other unpublished documents / Philippe Bénéton; translated by Paul J. Archambault.
p. cm.
Translated from the French: Le Royaume souffre violence.
Includes bibliographical references and index.
ISBN 978-1-58731-415-5 (hardbound: alk. paper) 1. Political science – Philosophy. 2. Political ethics. 3. Christianity and politics. 4. Rhetoric. 5. Machiavelli, Niccolr, 1469–1527 – Correspondence – Fiction. 6. Erasmus, Desiderius, d. 1536 – Correspondence – Fiction. 7. More, Thomas, Sir, Saint, 1478–1535 – Correspondence--Fiction. I. Archambault, Paul J., 1937– II. Title.
JA71.B4615 2013
320.01 – dc23   2011045684

∞ The paper used in this publication meets the minimum requirements of the American National Standard for Information Sciences – Permanence of Paper for Printed Materials, ANSI Z39.48-1984.

ST. AUGUSTINE'S PRESS
www.staugustine.net

To Catherine (†)

Contra spem in spe

TABLE OF CONTENTS

Prologue   1

Preliminaries   6

    Section 1. The Readers, The Readings   6

    Section 2. The Authors, The Strategic Context   15

    Section 3. The Authors, The Historical Contexts   31

    Section 4. The Texts, The Writing   42

Book I. Morality and Necessity (July 1517–March 1518)   51

    Ch. 1. The Tender Commerce of Friendship   51

    Ch. 2. *Institutio Tyranni*   60

    Ch. 3. *Liber Necessitatis*   85

Book II. Realism and Utopia (April–November 1518)   101

    Ch. 4. Prince Atecratos's Island   101

    Ch. 5. Nowhere and Elsewhere   125

Book III. The Hidden Prince (1519–1525)   149

    Ch. 6. *Quia Nominor Princeps* (1)   149

    Ch. 7. *Quia Nominor Princeps* (2)   168

    Ch. 8. Addenda   176

Book IV. The Registers of Writing (1535–1536)   182

    Ch. 9. The Languages of Friendship   182

    Ch. 10. *Apte dicere, apte tacere*   201

Epilogue   227

Appendices   232

Acknowledgments   252

Index   253

PROLOGUE

"Writers, if you only knew with
what frivolousness books are read."
—L. Moria, 1782

"The adventurers of the mind are
delivered to professors. Professors
are not adventurers of the mind.
Sometimes they get their revenge."
—A. Sapiens, 1872.

I.

Fortune can favor the undeserving. It was quite fortuitously that
we discovered, deep in the archives of the Palazzo Tuttofare in Florence, a sheaf of autographed letters exchanged between Niccolò
Machiavelli, Desiderius Erasmus, and Thomas More in 1517 and
1518. There followed a systematic exploration, allowing us to discover
other precious documents. How these texts had gotten there, ignored
for five centuries, remains an enigma. But as we know the history of
manuscripts is often a weave of unlikely events. In any case, the authenticity of these letters and other documents, which was questioned
for a time, can hardly be questioned now. The problem was resolved
in part after a day's colloquium organized in June 2007 by the Institute
for Utopian Studies on the Island of Abraxa. It was definitively
resolved at the *Congresso Internazionale di Scienza Machiavelliana*

1

held in Florence in March 2008. Thanks are due to our eminent colleagues, Professors R. Hellish and A. Sbagliato.[1]

We are publishing here the entire corpus of these documents, minus a few editorial omissions, which are self-explanatory. All of the texts are from the Tuttofare archives, except for the last two letters, the sources of which cannot be revealed, until further notice, for reasons that will be obvious to the reader.

These texts, for the most part, were written in Latin, the main exception being the textual explication given by Machiavelli, written in Italian. I shall gloss over a few technical questions, to be treated in the Appendices. As for the principles which guided these translations, they will be made explicit in a note. Translation, as we know, is a heroic adventure and a problem without a solution.

The order of the letters is chronological. Most of the documents are dated. The undated ones have been dated with a reasonable approximation.

All notes are by the translator.

II.

First and foremost, these documents are letters. Most of them are letters exchanged between Erasmus, More, and Machiavelli; the others, for the most part, are late letters by Erasmus wherein, among other things, he clarifies certain points of his Folly. To this correspondence are added texts of a different crafting which are, as it were, annexes to the *Prince* or to *Utopia*, or annotations to their content.

These writings were not revealed to the public by their authors. For some it appears certain that they were not destined for publication;

---

[1] See *Proceedings of the Institute for Utopian Studies*, Vol. 666, R. Hellish, ed., Abraxa University Press, 2007; *Relazioni del Congresso Internazionale di Scienza Machiavelliana*, LC (452), Firenze, 2008, especially the paper delivered by A. Sbagliato, "Contributi all' epistolario Machiavelliano," pp. 212–328. The Machiavelli/Erasmus/More correspondence has been catalogued and is accessible to all, with the authors' authorization (Palazzo Tuttofare, Signora T. Stultitia, Via del Loco, Firenze, 35000).

for others it happens that, for some reason or other, they were never published. In all cases, they belong to the domain of personal correspondence, or are closely related to it, in that they are addressed above all or exclusively to one or several individuals in particular. We know, of course, that personal correspondence is the most flexible of all literary genres. It follows that from one text to another, the manner of writing can change entirely. Much depends on who the letter is addressed to.

An initial examination of the documents shows that the questions raised or disputed are of two orders that can be clearly distinguished: the art of governing on the one side; the art of writing and the art of reading on the other. However—and this is what makes things difficult—these same questions are interwoven like substance and form. Let's try to clarify this. The first questions, the most predictable ones, bear upon the art of governing. Whatever their differences in status might have been, Erasmus, More, and Machiavelli were all participants in the political affairs of their time; all three played, or played at playing, the role of counselor to the Prince. In so doing, they would seem, in appearance at least, to have pleaded in opposite directions, Erasmus and More on one side, Machiavelli on the other. It is not surprising, then, that in their letters they battle or argue about the best manner of governing. They clash in particular on two grounds: on morality and necessity in politics, and on the political forms of necessity. In the background to the quarrel looms the problem of the political power of Christianity, perhaps that of its truth.

As to the second questions, those concerning the art of writing and the art of reading, they are by right preliminary questions, since they govern the interpretation, and therefore the discussion, of texts on the art of governing. Erasmus, More, and Machiavelli are not unaware of this, surely. They are accomplished writers, each has several styles at his command, and they know and practice the resources of the art of writing. They also intend to read as they should, which means not to be prisoners of the letter. So, alongside the general discussion, they argue about the significance of their respective works; they interpret, rightly or wrongly, the way of writing of the other; they explicate their own writing or avoid explication; they reveal themselves or they lead into error. What is at stake is the meaning of these enigmatic works called the *Prince* (1513), *Utopia* (1516), and to a lesser extent the *Praise of Folly* (1511). The problem, one sees clearly, rebounds upon itself: assuming that these authors speak in covert language in their works, can one assume that they speak in un-covert language in these letters or in other documents assembled here? Or do they write in one register, then another, according to the case? These very famous works we are discussing have at least one thing in common: they are not clear; they have been tugged right and left. Can we say that these unpublished texts are without pitfalls and equivocations? And if some of them are, do they tell the whole story? In short, what is the best way of reading them? If it is true that Erasmus, More, or Machiavelli can proceed with masks on, how does one manage to remove the mask when the author is hiding his true face, and not provide him with a mask when he shows his face? We shall see what can be suggested by tones, variants, precautions, circumstances. It is not for the translator to decide the true meaning. At best, the translator might do well to recall this rule of thumb: guard against concluding too fast.

The texts speak more or less for themselves to the careful reader. In another sense, however, they can be clarified by data that are external to the discourse itself: contemporaneous history, proximate events, particular circumstances, personal experiences, the conventions of the milieu, the mental equipment of the times, the state of the mores. . . . Between the text in the strict sense and what is external to the text in the broad sense, relations are regulated by a general law, the most certain, surely, of all the human sciences: it all depends.

What about the present case? Erasmus, More, and Machiavelli are inserted into their time in several ways. It would be unwise to proceed with them as Heidegger did with Aristotle: he was born, he worked, and he died. What must be granted to the history in question, however, can be determined in several ways, and particularly these: either this history defines above all the strategic framework within which the art of writing takes place (the author, for example, intends to oblige a Protector or to save established ideas), or it does far more than that by tracing the circle of what is thinkable (every "truth" belongs to its time). In the former case, the writers know what they are doing; in the latter we know it better than they do. Except that, if one considers that history always keeps thought on a leash, this is no less true for the reader than for the author. We cannot understand one another from one "intellectual matrix" to another, or from one *episteme* to another. It becomes an impossible game.

This is all very complicated. Let the reader be the judge. We shall merely attempt to clarify these documents, first of all by inserting each of them into its proper context, then by giving a preliminary presentation of established things, which are never more than reasonably established. As to the works in question, we shall attempt to speak of them without prejudice of any sort, even allowing ourselves a liberty that many scholars deny themselves, that of saying "I don't know," or "I have not understood." One of the difficulties is this one: these writings come to us accompanied by a great renown and overloaded with interpretations. How can we read them with an open mind, with simplicity, with a fresh eye, when there are so many reasons to be intimidated? One has to do violence to oneself to avoid any *a priori* judgment.

Notes on References and Endnotes

Occasional references are given in footnotes, main references in the Appendices. The letters of Erasmus, More, and Machiavelli cited in the introductory texts are all letters already published. They are accompanied by their date and their addressee: the collections used are indicated in the bibliography. At that time, the year began generally at Easter, but in Florence it began on the day of the Annunciation [March 25]. Each time there is a discordance we provide the year corresponding to current usage. On the other hand, a date is given according to the Julian calendar (reformed in 1582). It is therefore ten days earlier than our calendar.

The existing translations—whether of these letters, or of the works themselves—are very unequal. We relied on those that seemed to us the surest while taking the liberty of modifying them on occasion (see the Appendix).

PRELIMINARIES

SECTION 1.
The Readers, The Readings

On the one side, then, the authors: Erasmus, More, and Machiavelli; on the other the mass of readers, including ourselves, spread over five centuries. In its purest form, the game is played between each author and each reader, each in his context. At stake is the image of the work, its significance, its influence. This relation can assume a thousand shapes: the author convinces the reader, seduces him, leaves him indifferent, fools him, irritates him. . . . The reader reads correctly, reads wrongly, pays for his innocence, opposes his bad faith, adheres, leaves the game. . . . Practically speaking, the game is played largely between the author and his important readers, those who contribute to fixing an image of the work. Who are they? In the present case, they are a mixed or colorful assortment—admirers, detractors, pilferers, Doctors—among whom several illustrious names stand out, especially around Machiavelli: Jean Bodin, Francis Bacon, Marlowe, Frederick II, Rousseau, Hegel, Mussolini, Kamenev, Croce. . . . (The Prince is surely of all the works of political thought the one that most captured the interest of men of government: a few have commented on it; how many have read it in secret!) The posthumous interlocutors of Erasmus are hardly less impressive: Montaigne, Bayle, Voltaire, Sainte-Beuve, Stefan Zweig . . . as are those of More: Bodin, Swift, Morris, Kautsky, Chesterton. . . . In our own time, Professors have stepped in and taken over. The overall result has been an enormous cacophony. Reading follows upon reading in a constant succession and opposition, works change their configuration entirely, authors change camp and change position. One doesn't know who is right, or whether anyone is right; one knows only that many are wrong. The relation between the author and the reader, like any human relation, lends itself to misunderstanding—here the misunderstandings, or what appears as such, pile up. If the authors protest from beyond the grave, or if they snigger, one doesn't hear them. The author gets the ball rolling, and then the game is played without him. Great works are delivered to us, as Péguy said, and we readers are not perfectly reliable, any more than are editors and translators. Cioran thought it strange that the prospect of having a biographer never dissuaded a man from having a life. One might ask how the prospect of delivering oneself over to so many strangers did not incite more authors to give up writing.

It is true that writers can play the game by their own rules. Can we really believe that Erasmus, More, and Machiavelli are nothing but gentle writers facing bad or nasty readers? Perhaps they sinned through obscurity or incoherence, or . . . perhaps there was something else? Does the famous "Erasmus mystery" owe nothing to his intentions? Or the "Machiavelli problem," which is sometimes said to be similar to that of the squaring of the circle? Or the "More question," which has raised so much perplexity?

At the heart of this free-for-all, as one might call it, one finds the *Prince*, the *Utopia*, and the *Praise of Folly*. Now if these works had a destiny which has something incredible about it, one cannot deny that their authors had something to do with it. Why so many enigmas, detours, ambiguities? Many readers have maneuvered no doubt, through some political, religious, theoretical passion or other; but didn't the authors themselves do their own kind of maneuvering? If these works seem somehow to have escaped them, we don't know to what extent. It is not certain that each of the three cases is the same.

I.

This posthumous history is therefore made up of readings coming from all directions. Here is one episode, no doubt the most bizarre. It takes place in Moscow in 1934–1936, and secondarily at the Vatican during the same period.

In Moscow, during Stalin's reign, Machiavelli is an object of infamy and More is on the honor roll. In November 1934, Lev Kamenev, an old "comrade" of Lenin and Stalin, publishes a new edition of the *Prince*. In his Preface, he reads Machiavelli as he is supposed to, that is, from the heights of truths established by Marx, Engels, Lenin, and Stalin, and he gives Machiavelli a high grade. No doubt the Florentine Secretary remains a stranger from the real sociology of power, but he has the merit of lifting a corner of the veil on the politics of his time: "an oppressive class of masters struggling among themselves for power over the laboring masses" in a period of transition from feudalism to capitalism. The cynicism is not Machiavelli's; it is in the class reality which he describes.

Whether Machiavelli was being cynical or not, there is no doubt that Stalin knew how to be so. On the first of December, Kirov was assassinated. Several weeks later, Kamenev and Zinoviev were arrested. In August 1936, both were the principal defenders in the first of the great Moscow trials. Vyshinski inaugurated his role of prosecutor, that is as executor of the Master's base judiciary chores. He tore apart the *Prince* and its Preface, presented Machiavelli as a Machiavellian and Kamenev as his disciple:

> You had a good teacher, Kamenev, but you, and you must be given credit for this, you have surpassed your teacher. [. . .] Machiavelli was a puppy and a yokel compared to them [Zinoviev and Kamenev], but he was their spiritual preceptor. Machiavellianism and Azefism were the sources of your criminal activities [. . .]: murder, cunning, deception and masquerade.

The comrade-prosecutor denounced Machiavelli while acting in keeping with the image he gave of him. Kamenev was surely not in a position to defend his reading of the *Prince*. He confessed everything that was expected of him: "My defective Bolshevism became transformed into anti-Bolshevism, and through Trotskyism I arrived at

Fascism." His retribution was in keeping with his "crimes": he was condemned to death and shot.[1]

At the same period, R.W. Chambers finished his great biography of More. He received a letter from the Marx-Engels Institute of the Central Committee of the USSR seeking information on the great communist Sir Thomas More. The *Utopia* had become a "people's classic," and its author a "precursor of scientific communism." Edition had followed upon edition: 1918 in Petrograd, 1920 in a review called *The Flame*, 1923 in Kharkov. In 1935, while Kamenev's edition of the *Prince* is being withdrawn from circulation, a new translation is published by the Academy of Sciences. More's editors read him the way Kamenev read Machiavelli: his book is a milestone on the road that leads to those great heights everyone knows. The honors rendered to More are even engraved in stone. Since 1918, in the gardens of the Kremlin, a monument to the glory of the pioneers of communism bears his name, and in good company: Marx, Bebel, Campanella, Meslier, Proudhon, Tchernychevski. . . . Kamenev should have known that in the land of the Soviets, the pious More was a safer author than the "impious" Machiavelli.

That same year, 1935, on the 19th of May, Thomas More was canonized in Saint Peter's basilica, with all the magnificence of Roman pomp. Pope Pius XII pronounced this solemn declaration:

> We declare Saints the Blessed John Fisher and Thomas More.
> We define them as such. We inscribe them in the Catalogue of
> the Saints and we proclaim that their memory will henceforth
> be celebrated in the universal Church on the anniversary date
> of their birth in heaven.

At the end of the ceremony, the bells of Rome pealed out joyfully.

---

[1] Kamenev's Preface was published in an English translation in the New Left Review 15, May-June 1962, pp. 39–42, with a presentation by C. Abranski: "Kamenev's Last Essay," pp. 34–38. The report on the trial was published in an English version by the Commissariat of Justice of the Soviet Union: The Case of the Trotskyite-Zinovievite Centre (Moscow: People's Commissariat of Justice of the U.S.S.R., 1936). The excerpts cited are taken from the morning session of 20 August.

This adventure is unique in its way: No one except More had the "fortune" of entering into the Bolshevik pantheon while at the same time being elevated upon the altars of the Church. Of course it was not the same Thomas More being honored. The canonization consecrated the martyr of the Catholic Church, condemned by Henry VIII for his opposition to the schism; the Soviet laurels were directed to the author of *Utopia*, read according to the regime's official terms. The work is detached from its author. The Papal Bull of canonization does not mention the *Utopia*, nor does the *Motu proprio* of John Paul II (31 October 2000), which makes of More the holy patron of politicians. The Soviet texts in turn do not glorify the Christian's fidelity to Rome. More generally, history has dissociated the writer's glory and the statesman's image, as well as his glorious death. Bringing these two glories in harmony is not a simple matter.[2]

II.

Let us now consider all the roles played by Erasmus, More, and Machiavelli throughout the long history written by their readers. Seen in small print, things seem complicated and confused. But seen from a distance, two main roles can be distinguished in each case.

The most spectacular metamorphosis is Machiavelli's. To put it briefly: he was infamous; he became honorable. For centuries, the dominant tradition retained from all his work the *Prince* and only the *Prince,* making of the author of that work an impious, deceitful blasphemer, a counselor of tyrants par excellence, in short "the most evil and villainous of men" (Frederick II, *The Anti-Machiavelli,* 1740). Toward the end of the XVIth century, or shortly before, Machiavelli's

---

[2] See especially R.W. Chambers, *Thomas More,* London, 1935; pt. 1945, p. 374; Igor N. Osinovski, "Thomas More's *Utopia* in Russia," *Moreana* 22, 1969, pp. 33–37; W. Bubenicek, "L'Utopie: du latin au russe," *Moreana* 63/1, 1979, pp. 100–104. One might add that in 1935, the state of Great Britain had not forgotten that More had been condemned as a traitor to the Crown. When the canonization ceremony took place, the ambassador of the United Kingdom was conspicuous by his absence.

reputation was already made, the Church placed him on the Index (1559), the Protestant Innocent Gentillet made his case against him (*Anti-Machiavelli*, 1576), the Jesuits went to war against him. The political and moral vocabulary added two words to its lexicon: *Machiavellianism* and *Machiavellian*.

For a long time, then, the prosecutors and detractors set the tone. Yet once in a while discordant voices arose to plead in his favor. Some of them praised his realism on the basis of a softened or tempered reading of his ideas. Most of them declared him innocent by virtue of a double meaning: the *Prince's* real intention was hidden; it is just the opposite of its apparent intention. What is it? According to one version, the author would deliberately be giving bad advice to the Medici in order to lead them to ruin (the idea was developed on several occasions in XVIth-century Italy). Another version would have Machiavelli indirectly giving good lessons to the people by unmasking the Prince (this thesis, put forward as early as the XVIth century, was upheld by Spinoza with precaution, and by Rousseau with his habitual peremptoriness).

The great reversal, begun in the XVIIIth century, took place in several directions. New readers in new contexts provided Machiavelli with new certificates of honorability. With what justification? The theses diverge, but they have a common ground: the Florentine is not masked, but that doesn't make him a villain. Who, then, is this real Machiavelli, who doesn't hide and who has taken so much time to be discovered? His principal faces are the following: 1) an Italian patriot; 2) the systematizer of the politics of his time; 3) a Republican humanist; 4) a pioneer of modern political science. Except for the first interpretation, the interpreters base themselves preferably on the *Discourses on the First Decade of Titus Livy*, the second of the great political works of the Florentine Secretary.

The thesis on Machiavelli's Italian patriotism came from the countries in search of national unity: first Germany (Herder, Hegel, Fichte, Ranke), then Italy, especially at the time of the *Risorgimento*. Toward the end of the XIXth century began the period of scholarly research. Since that time, Machiavelli has generally been read in a way that saves his reputation while down-grading him. Historians underline the historical roots of his thought. A first version makes of him the mirror of the Italian politics of his time (F. Chabod, 1926; A. Renaudet, 1942). The contemporary version considers him as the spokesman for a Florentine humanistic tradition which allies civic virtue and political freedom (J.G.A. Pocock, 1975; Q. Skinner, 1981.) On the political science side, he is generally presented as a precursor of the scientific attitude, his work as a first step in the right direction.

The "Machiavelli question" remains, of course, subject to controversy, and the philosophers remain attachèd to the atemporal significance of the work (Leo Strauss, 1958; Claude Lefort, 1972; Harvey Mansfield, 1996). But if one sticks to the dominant image, it is clear that Machiavelli has greatly changed: the great blasphemer, the perverse counselor is nothing more than a good republican or an amateur political scientist. Much ado about nothing.

Thomas More the writer—let's leave aside More the statesman for the time being—has also played the posthumous role of two main characters and of several secondary characters. Even more than Machiavelli, More owes his glory to one book only, the *Utopia*, a work less important than the *Prince*, surely, as a political work, but with an extraordinary literary fecundity. The title itself attests to its reputation: it has become a common noun, denoting one of several literary genres. The ransom of this glory has been a great confusion. *Utopia*'s posterity is composite beyond description, and the word *utopia*, surcharged with meaning, is enough to discourage the most obstinate of intellectual historians.

Let's return to the readers, the interpreters of the text. They belong, generally speaking, to one of two traditions. The first makes of More a man of imagination, blessed with a highly imaginative or satirical pen. What is More doing, if not walking in the footsteps of Lucian of Samosata, the Greek writer of the second century who told tales in order to mock everything: More had translated him as a pleasurable exercise in Erasmus's company! *Utopia* was written above all to entertain us: it is a work of "such wit," as Antoine Clava wrote, it shows "such a wealth of invention," said Nicholas Harpsfield, both in the

XVIth century. This tradition is still with us: after G.K. Chesterton and C.S. Lewis, it has been maintained in England by literature professors, but it has nonetheless given way to other interpretations.

The most influential tradition, and one might say the richest, says something entirely different: one cannot seriously doubt the seriousness of this work beneath its superficial pleasantries. More must take his place in the gallery of writers who have theorized about the best regime. His isle of *Utopia* offers a model, the model of the perfect city in itself, or of the perfect city under certain conditions or with certain reservations. But if there is a model, what is it? That is where the shoe pinches and where the arguments begin.

These arguments have increased since the end of the XIXth century. Let's attempt a summary. More the Christian presents the best regime on a basis of reason alone; if he does so it is so that his pagan utopia will put Christian Europe to shame (R.W. Chambers, 1935). Not at all: More draws the picture of a real Christian Republic (J.H. Hexter, 1952). You've understood nothing: More's greatness resides in the socialist inspiration of his work (K. Kautsky, 1890; W. Morris, 1893). You're way off the mark: More is not a socialist but an imperialist, anticipating England's colonial enterprise (H. Oncken, 1922; G. Ritter, 1940). Let's be serious and give science and history their due: *Utopia* is first and foremost a product of Renaissance humanism, or more exactly a humanistic critique of humanism (Q. Skinner, 1978). Of course, but in another way (G. Logan, 1983). In an aside, Max Beerbohm jokes: "*Utopia*? Oh, excuse me, I thought it meant hell!" If model there is, it is not that of a good society, but of its opposite (R.S. Sylvester, 1977). How to make heads or tails of all this?

Finally, Erasmus. He had the same fate, or the same misfortune, tossed back and forth from one camp to another. His readers did worse; they deserted him. Placed on a pedestal during his life, he was quarantined after his death. His immense production fell victim to the Reformation and the Counter-Reformation (he was placed on the Index in 1559). It lost much of its prestige before lying dormant on library shelves. Erasmus has become more of a great figure than a great author (Marie Delcourt). Only one of his works has remained living, that *Praise of Folly* whose importance is due mostly to its prodigious literary fecundity, undoubtedly surpassing that of *Utopia* because of the greatness of those whom it inspired (Cervantes, Shakespeare, et al.).

Like his friend More, like Machiavelli for a time, Erasmus has therefore become a man of a single book, or almost. This book was read in the XVIIIth century as an attack on the Church prefiguring those of the Enlightenment. The following century echoed this opinion, resulting in this image, which prevailed until the middle of the XXth century and beyond, of a skeptical, mocking Erasmus. A "moderate Voltaire," said Sainte-Beuve. The "Voltaire of the XVIth century," added Dilthey. In our contemporary period, the professors of literature, basing themselves on Erasmus's complete works and on his correspondence, have broken with this interpretation. Erasmus is not a free-thinker, one of those "non-believers of the Renaissance"; his Christian faith is above all suspicion (J.Cl. Margolin, J. Chomarat, A. Godin). Is the question resolved? There seems to be a broad consensus in this direction, but difficulties of interpretation remain, including those raised by the text of the *Praise of Folly* itself. How must this text be understood? As "a travelling scholar's pastime" (Pierre de Nolhac, 1936)? As a literary exercise where irony is in charge from beginning to end (Clarence Miller, 1979)? As "a praise of happiness in creative joy and vital energy" (Joel Lefebvre, 1968)? As "a fundamentally Christian religious pamphlet" (L. Halkin, 1987? . . . Perhaps some works (M.A. Screech, 1980; M. Fumaroli, 1988) lift the veil, or a corner of the veil? Here as elsewhere, we can only refer to the documents that follow.

To conclude, the present situation is the following: the readers who set the tone are the professors. The professors don't all say the same thing, but they agree in general on this: Machiavelli doesn't teach Machiavellianism, he doesn't deserve the reputation he has been given; More isn't a Utopian, a dreamer, or a joker, he is more serious than we had thought; Erasmus is not an unbeliever, one might discuss his way of being a Christian, one cannot doubt that he is one. The debates aren't closed, but the positions are drawing closer together.

SECTION 2.
The Authors, The Strategic Context

Whatever might be the right interpretation of our authors, they have been seriously mistreated; unless, that is, they intended to be so. What do we know of these men that might shed some light on their intentions? Erasmus, More, and Machiavelli have given their readers three enigmatic works par excellence. They have equally provided other texts. What do these texts say? Can their total meaning be brought in harmony? If not, what do their incoherencies or their contradictions mean? Has the author changed his mind, or changed his pen? Desiderius, Thomas, and Niccolò (if we may be allowed this familiarity) have more than one string to their bow. What can we conclude from that?

On the other hand, what is the status of our authors? What constraints might be likely to paralyze their pens, what incitements might point them in a certain direction? The moment an author publishes his writings, he risks saying to all what should be said only to a few; he incurs the favor or the disfavor of readers known and unknown, and everything that follows. And what follows could ultimately change his life. There are opportunities to seize, there are risks to take. If he clashes with accepted ideas, the risks go up. The possible sanctions range from the most violent (the stake, the firing squad) to the most gentle (silence, ostracism). But the writer is rarely left without resources: prohibition or pressure can invite deviousness. Brutal or oblique censure calls for a subtle writer.

What about Erasmus, More, and Machiavelli? The readers, or the readers who count, might be (without mentioning posterity): a restricted public, a larger public, a certain Prince, a certain Pope, censors. The stakes follow: the opportunities, to win over minds, renown, the Prince's favor, the Pope's protection; the risks are those of confusing minds, incurring reprobation, the censorship of the theological faculties, the disfavor of the mighty and the diverse forms of persecution. Otherwise said, each writer performs in a strategic context made up of constraints and incitements. Does their writing vary accordingly?

To what extent? All these questions demand too much of us; we can provide only fragmentary answers. They open paths of investigation, but are they the right ones?

Must we seek help elsewhere? Authors have a life beyond writing. What does it tell us? The first pitfall here is that the connections between the author and what the man is in other respects are more or less tight, or more or less loose. The personal history of the political or religious writer can follow a course of its own. It is made up of the spirit's autonomous life, or marked by certain experiences or by certain singular encounters. It might also be that the writer's life outside of his writing tends to authenticate the work or contradict it. In any case one never knows until the end. Things exterior to the author are best known approximately (one biographer of More's bases an argument on More's sexual life. . . . Was he in the bedroom?). As for the writer's interior life, we usually examine it with a blind man's eye. We cannot see the human heart, as Alceste puts it, nor are we better at seeing the human spirit. And those of our authors are well guarded. These men knew how to remain aloof. How we wish they had kept us in mind, we who sweat blood trying to understand them, especially Machiavelli, the most elusive of the three.

I.

In a sense Erasmus the author is a case apart. He is a writer and only a writer. He is, because he wants to be, in the margins of the institutions, and he becomes an authority. This is something new. Erasmus is a man of the pen through and through. He is neither a professor, nor a preacher, nor a man of government, nor a grey eminence. His entire activity is writing. It isn't that Erasmus is uninterested in his time, but if he acts to reform it it is always with pen in hand.

At the height of his fame, Erasmus was portrayed by three great painters, Quentyn Metsis (1517), Holbein (1523) and Dürer (1526). All three captured the same image on canvas: the scholar, the man of letters, the thinker at work "in that magic instant when invisible thought appears on paper" (Stefan Zweig). The frail body is wrapped warmly in a fur cloak, or something like it; the head is muffled in a thick bonnet, the fine hands hold the pen, the gaze is directed to the paper or turned inward. Near the writing case books are scattered helter-skelter. We hear the pen scratch against the paper; we sense that great thoughts will be inscribed there. Erasmus in his majesty breathes reverential silence, gravity, perhaps resolution. There is no trace of his mocking spirit, or so little.

This man, so admired, so feared, is to a certain extent a man in the margin. He belongs to no circle of power; he is foreign to this powerful institution which is the university; and if he is a priest and respectful of his estate, he leads an independent life and dresses like a layman. Even famous, he dwells apart. His favorite company is composed of friends, or their letters, a few students, and of course his books. His solicitations are many, but he wants to be obliged to no one, so as, he says, to preserve his precious freedom without which "a life is not a life."

The price to pay for this (relative) independence was the money problem that plagued him his entire life. While the scholastic theologians keep warm in the University, humanists like Erasmus, devoid of charge or fortune, were out in the cold. Until the age of 40–45, his life was a harsh existence: periods of indigence, living by his wits, the race for prebends from place to place, promises without consequence, a shaky religious status. Erasmus was born in obscure conditions between 1466 and 1469 in Rotterdam. He was a nameless child born of illegitimate parents. After his parents died, his tutors directed him toward the convent. He remained there five years and was ordained to the priesthood, though he seems to have been unhappy. In 1493 he was able to leave. Going from permission to dispensation, he never returned. His situation would only be regularized in 1517, by Pope Leo X. These difficult years were heroic ones for Erasmus. After a hard-fought struggle he achieved his status as a man of letters, made educationally valuable trips to Italy and England, met remarkable people such as John Colet, Thomas More, and Jean Vitrier. This frail, sickly man was the hardest of workers. He complains, he groans, he curses his "damned poverty," he is ironic in describing his "beggar's rounds." He never gives up. From 1510 onward, with glory comes a certain life of comfort, and Erasmus disdains neither. His success provides him a new status: he lives from his pen, for the most part, or more exactly from his publications. He is the first man to do so.

Erasmus lives in the margin in another sense as well. He is a citizen of nowhere. Nothing is more foreign to him than the idea of national prestige. He was born in Holland, studied in Paris, finished his formation in Italy, made several trips to England, settled at Louvain, then in Basel, then Frankfurt, finally in Basel. He had no other attachments than the "Christian Republic," and, at the heart of it, the Republic of Letters. He wandered as a pilgrim throughout Christendom, on his horse, with his portable reading and writing materials and his books, which accompanied or followed. Everywhere he spoke and wrote in Latin, the common language of learned men. He had readers and correspondents in the four corners of Latin Europe.

Finally this European glory made an authority of him. From 1510 onward, he was recognized as the most eminent member of that Republic of men of letters which had set itself up in opposition to the University. Erasmus became the "Prince of the humanists," the party leader of a current of ideas calling for the reform of the Church, of knowledge, of politics. He has no institution backing him up, and a great influence: through him, the author asserts himself, he rises in people's eyes. In this sense one might say, although the expression is somewhat jaded, that Erasmus is the first "intellectual" of European history. For better or worse, his line of descendants is a prestigious one.

The great friendship between Erasmus and More has come down to posterity as equal to that of Montaigne and La Boétie a few years later. They became friends from their first meeting in London in 1499, in spite of their age difference: Erasmus was about thirty, More was slightly more than twenty. A thousand reciprocal services followed, of a material order on More's part, of a literary order on both sides, but especially on Erasmus's. There also followed a correspondence spread over nearly thirty-five years. Their contemporaries often likened them to twin brothers.

More's status as an author is nonetheless very different from

Erasmus's. Thomas More is, of course, more than just a writer in his spare time, yet he is a writer in hours taken from other activities and from sleep. He has made other choices. His life is burdened with tasks of all sorts. He is careful to preserve his quiet moments, yet he is infinitely more anchored in the social world than his elder. He is an established man, who plays for stakes of a different order than Erasmus.

Thomas More was never portrayed as a writer. Holbein's portrait (1527), the most famous, depicts him as a man of government, with the gold chain of the Order of Knights around his neck. He has a serious pose, with something sad about it, the gaze is the surprising, intense look of a man taking his distances. In any case, More as portrayed majestically is More the statesman.

More, then, had a great political career. He took the leap that Erasmus always refused to take, agreeing to serve the Prince. This happened in stages during the years 1515–1519. Before that he had, like his father, practiced the law. His studies had been serious, he had had enough leisure time to further them. For a time he had felt a calling to the cloister, then worn the robe of lawyer, then of judge. Everywhere he went More exhibited qualities of ease, of mastery, of integrity that impressed everyone. His dry wit could be disconcerting. In 1519 he joined the privy council of Henry VIII. The King loved his company, responded to his cultured manner, his sense of humor, no doubt his uprightness, which was not the most widely shared virtue in the Court. Things were to end badly.

Why did More accept this political role, with such great risks of wasting his talent? In Part I of *Utopia*, he stages a dialogue based on the question: "Should the philosopher join the counselors of the Prince?" and presents the arguments for and against. Did More enter the circles of power reluctantly? He says so, Erasmus confirms it. His biographers are not all in agreement. He had no illusions, in any case, judging by the dialogue in *Utopia* and by what his son-in-law William Roper said of him:

"I thank our lord, son, quoth he [soon after being named Knight of the duchy of Lancaster] I find his Grace my very good lord indeed [. . .]; howbeit, son Roper, I may tell thee. I have no cause to be proud thereof, for if my head would win him him a castle in France (for then there was war between us), it should not fail to fall." (The Life of Sir Thomas More, III).

More's other great burden was his large family. His first wife had given him four children. When he became a widower, he remarried and took charge of his second wife's daughter. The household grew with the arrival of sons- and daughters-in-law and grandchildren. More was a considerate father. He followed the humanistic education of his sons and daughters with great care. Erasmus had fond memories of his sojourns in his dearest friend's family. Life was pious, studious, and gay. More governed his world with a smile, always with a teasing remark at the tip of his tongue.

And yet More found the time to write and entered easily into the Republic of letters with the publication of *Utopia*. Taken in its entirety, his literary production was abundant and diverse. While Erasmus is a European writer, More is both European and English. As a humanistic author of *Utopia* he is European; in other writings, particularly in his violent polemic against his Reformed compatriots, he is English. England and Christendom are his two countries, and corresponding to them are the two languages in which he wrote. His Latin and his English are not aimed at the same addressees.

Machiavelli was also both a man of letters and a man of action, but the former never experienced literary fame, any more than the latter experienced political fame. A second rank function in the Florentine government, a career brutally interrupted by the return of the Medici, literary works which, with one exception, circulate in manuscript form only—Machiavelli's life and works remain in the background of history. He did of course acquire a certain renown as a political and military writer, more broadly as a writer of comedies, but always on a small scale.

What do we know of him? Scholarly research has made use of everything available, but Machiavelli remains a question mark in spite of everything. Outside his political years, the material is rare. Even his face escapes us. The outlines which adorn the editions of his works, the most famous being the portrait of Santi di Tito (1564), are posthumous.

They provide an image of the images of Machiavelli, but we cannot ask for more. The most obscure part of his life is that of the thinker and writer. His work exhibits exceptional qualities of analysis and writing. Could he have been unaware of it? If he knew it, how was he planning to make use of it? The life and the work intersect: to what extent are they linked? The weight of circumstances is uncertain, as is that of their interconnectedness. Like More, Machiavelli has a double allegiance: he is a citizen of Florence at a time when the Italian nation does not exist, but he is an Italian writer and he speaks in Italy's name. If he is a patriot, what is his patriotism like? What we know complicates matters even further, since in his writing, as in his life, the Florentine Secretary appears as a man full of ambiguities and complications.

Machiavelli's life was conditioned by the political agitations of Florence. It is comprised of two phases and one abrupt interruption: the phase of political action, then the phase of forced inaction and of attempts to return to action. Machiavelli served the Republic from 1498 onward; with the return of the Medici (1512), he offered them his services with insistence; with their departure (1527), he aspired to serve the Republic again. But the Medici in power were wary of him—they were not choirboys—and the Republicans were on guard. Equivocations can serve a man, but they can work against him.

The years prior to 1498 are couched in shadows. Machiavelli was born in 1469, roughly the same year as Erasmus, take away one or two. He comes from an honorable but modest family, or modest but honorable. Young Niccolò was taught the elements of a humanistic training, but apparently did no advanced study. He seems to have been largely self-taught, very much as a result of contemporary events. Machiavelli grew up in a tormented period, a time of conspiracy in Florence, the armies of Charles VIII descending upon Italy (1494), the expulsion of the Medici, the Republic, Fra Savonarola with his austere, other-worldly regime.

In 1498, shortly after Savonarola's execution, Machiavelli appears on the scene. He is named Secretary of the Second Chancery, then attached to the Council of Ten charged in part with external affairs. What are his duties? Things in Florence are confused and overlapping.

He is something like a bureau director or an embassy secretary. In 1502, his position is reinforced by the election of Soderini as Gonfalonier for life. Machiavelli becomes his confidence man or, as his enemies call it, his factotum. His trenchant, precise reports enhance his reputation. He also makes enemies. Alamanno Salviati, one of Soderini's chief opponents, calls him "rabble" [*ribaldo*] (letter of B. Buonaccorsi to Machiavelli, 6 October 1506).

In and around Florence, history is on the move. The city on the Arno, prosperous and weak, is caught in the turmoil of the Italian wars. Machiavelli is dispatched from one front to the other. He is charged with diplomatic missions, four at the court of Louis XII, two in Romagna at the court of Cesare Borgia. He follows the campaigns against a rebellious Pisa, he forms a militia of peasant-citizens (at its head the accursed soul of Cesare Borgia, Miguel Corella). One threat follows upon another, the Secretary gets through a great deal of work. He is an ardent man of action, known to favor radical means. He is never bored.

In 1512, the militia organized by Machiavelli is routed by the Spaniards at Prato. The Medici follow and return to Florence. Now begins for Niccolò a long period of retirement and writing. He complains of his poverty, makes offer upon offer to his new masters, dedicates the *Prince* to the young Lorenzo. But he also writes the *Discourses*, with their apparently Republican coloration. The praises he directs toward the Medici are more or less mixed with reservations and critiques. He befriends a few young men, some of whom will hatch an anti-Medici plot in 1522. Our man is hard to follow.

The private Machiavelli is even harder to follow. His private letters and a few rare accounts reveal him to be: a cheerful companion who likes making fun of people; a libertine story-teller; a sullen, self-pitying type; a defiant spirit, an advocate of extreme solutions, a lover of paradoxes; a man as likely to find you a preacher as Pachierotto [who doesn't like the fair sex] is likely to "find a fair gallant lady for a friend" (F. Guicciardini to Machiavelli, 17 May 1521). What place did family members occupy in his life? He married advantageously, Marietta gave him six children. He seems never to have enjoyed family life. He seems to have enjoyed courtesans. Toward the end of his life, he fell in love with la Barbera, a singer of light morals, who seems to have made a fool of him. The few family letters that have come down to us, however, reveal a solicitous father and a very affectionate uncle for one of his nephews. As far as friendships go, things are once again uncertain. He had a few "faithful" friends, fellow sowers of wild oats. Episodically he entertained political friendships with more important men than he, the soft Vettori and the hard Guicciardini. Were these friendships or pseudo-friendships? We know little about the nature of Machiavelli's heartbeat.

II.

From the literary viewpoint, the most impressive and the richest corpus of works is that of Erasmus. With Petrarch he appears to be the greatest Latin prose stylist since the end of the Roman empire (Jacques Chomarat). He navigates with ease from one genre to the other: dialogues, orations, treatises, commentaries, paraphrases, translations, letters. Erasmus has learned from Cicero and Quintilian all the resources of rhetoric, and he knows them so well that he uses them with great ease. The man who wrote the *Praise of Folly*, the *Adages*, the *Colloquia* is a writer full of wit. The translator of the *New Testament* marches forward bearing the armor of a weighty discourse on method. The author of the discourse on *Peace* has a resounding eloquence. The composer of the *Preparation for Death* speaks with fervor. Erasmus writes easily, and fast; whenever he can he corrects himself while reading proofs; often he enriches his text from one edition to another.

What says this literary corpus? Provided one takes it in its entirety, its general lines are without mystery. It centers about three focal points, or perhaps two and a half: first the *Humanae litterae*, the ancient languages and literatures, eloquence and rhetoric; then the *Sacrae litterae*, the New Testament, the "philosophy of Christ," and the piety that derives from it; finally the Christian peace, and the Christian art of governing. Erasmus is a reformer, the man of a "Renaissance." The times before were times of darkness; the present time is a time of crisis (that of the Church, that of Christian Europe). A renewal is possible. It must pass by way of a reform of studies in favor of a literary culture that is disciplined by rhetoric. It presupposes a religious reform based on a return to evangelical sources and to an interior piety devoid of formalism or superstition. It signifies a political reform, finally, that repudiates war and its horrors, as well as the practices of tyranny. Erasmus conceives of this political reform in traditional terms: the essential thing is that those who govern should behave as good men. The key to everything is human behavior. Three reforming enterprises, just one success, the one that made Erasmus deserving of the title "preceptor of Europe" (Marc Fumaroli, Jean-Claude Margolin). The "humanities" replaced medieval logic: they were to be for several centuries the heart of European education. But the rest did not follow: war between Christian princes remained a very living practice, and Erasmus's hopes for an interior reform of the Church were dashed with the Reformation. He had prepared the way for Luther, and Luther had outflanked him.

If we look at Erasmus more closely, however, his image grows hazy. His enemies compared him to an "eel" (Luther), a chameleon, a Proteus. Some underlined the hardiness of his ideas, his boldness, his nonconforming views; others stressed his moderation, his smugness, his pettiness of spirit. Whether deliberately or not Erasmus leaves us hanging. He never gives the last word; he alters terms, tones, postures. Does his thinking lack firmness? Does he want to confuse the issues? He is pious, yet a mocker; he acknowledges the authority of the Church, yet he mordantly criticizes the Church of his time; he preaches the "philosophy of Christ," yet he "sanctifies" Socrates and "baptizes" Epicurus. Theologians frown at him. What, ultimately, is Erasmus's Christianity? He differs radically from that of his time, whether Roman or Reformed, by his denunciation, a thousand times repeated, of the abuse of compulsion in matters of religion (except for cases he judges extreme, like the Anabaptists), and by his untiring appeals for peace and concord. But for the rest, where does Erasmus situate himself? He reads the pagan authors from a Christian point of view: what does his Christianity owe these readings? He mocks the theologians and their pretensions: what does he leave for dogmatic theology? He wittily criticizes the exterior forms of piety: how far does his criticism go? He preaches an amiable Christianity and Christian folly: how can they be reconciled?

While the range of More's writings is not as extensive as Erasmus's, it is rich none the less: epigrams, a play, dialogues, orations, a Utopian narrative, commentaries. . . . His tone can be pleasing or eloquent, ironic or serious, he can be violent and even coarse. Posterity remembers More as a Latin writer, but he is also a major English writer (C.S. Lewis). His style is neither as brilliant nor as flexible as Erasmus's, but he has striking turns of phrase. From a literary viewpoint, *Utopia* towers above the rest by its rich inventiveness and by the genius of its dialogue.

More's work belongs in part to the humanistic vein; in part it follows its own lines. First come the strictly literary writings—or literary and philosophical: the Latin epigrams of his youth, the *History of Richard III* (1514) in both languages, and the *Utopia* in Latin. The epigrams have a dominantly satirical tone, the *Richard III*, which later inspired Shakespeare, has a serious and noble tone. Both plays contain an incisive criticism of tyranny. After these works comes the massive corpus of English works of controversy against his Reformed compatriots (1528–1533), wherein More is as unsparing as can be. These works are not without literary qualities, but they are often spoiled by vehemence of tone, by repetitions and by invectives. Finally there are the spiritual writings of the final months, written by the prisoner of the Tower of London. The most famous is the *Dialogue of Comfort against Tribulations*, written in English (1534), a work of consolation in the face of suffering and death, written seriously but good naturedly and humorously. These final texts have touched many hearts, bearing witness, as did his life and his death, to Thomas More's deep piety. As to the polemical texts, they bear witness to his passionate hostility to the Reformation. They seem in apparent contradiction to the *Utopia*, where religious freedom seems to be the rule. Is there more than one Thomas More? More the tolerant humanist of *Utopia* and More the scourge of heretics?

Machiavelli is also an artist with the pen. He attempted different genres—poetry, political treatises, theater, history—and was master at several tones—didactic, sarcastic, noble, bawdy. . . . From the literary viewpoint, his masterpiece is undoubtedly the *Prince*, whose scathing language hardly ever leaves its reader time to breathe. The writing of the *Discourses* is less tense, more labored, but with striking turns of phrase where the author's hand is visible. His theater and his letters give an idea of the extent of his literary gifts. The one exception everyone seems to agree upon is the following: he is not a great poet.

Machiavelli's work is varied in its form, less so in its content. With few exceptions, politics is never far away. The corpus of his work can be divided thus: first, poems written at different moments of his life. While in office, the Secretary wrote the *Decennali* (1504–1509), a verse chronicle wherein, beginning in 1494, he tells the sufferings of Italy, the blindness of Princes, the weaknesses and capitulations of Florence and, preceding that, the long oppression of the Medici. When out of office Machiavelli writes sonnets to the Medici, an epigram against Soderini, that "poor half-wit," love poems to la Barbera, and the *Golden Ass*, a farcical and allegorical, bitter and obscure poem wherein political allusions appear so mixed that interpretation is impossible. Secondly, political treatises: next to the *Prince* stand the *Discourses on the First Decade of Livy*, written at an unknown date, finished around 1519. This long text claims to be a commentary on the first ten books of Livy, but the author takes some liberties and the reader finds it hard to follow. One powerful analysis follows another, strangely ordered, and often discordant. The central theme seems to be praise for the Roman Republic, its political and social institutions, but the author can change viewpoints and take off in other directions. It has been said that in the *Discourses* one finds everything and its contrary (Francesco Bausi). If the key to the *Prince* is in the *Discourses*, it is certainly well concealed.

Let us omit the *Art of War* (1521). In third place come the comedies, the *Mandragola* (1518?) and the *Clizia* (performed in 1525). The first play, the most brilliant, tells how an old husband is persuaded to accept that his wife cuckold him, how his young, beautiful, virtuous wife is persuaded to cuckold him, and how ultimately everyone is satisfied. Trickery triumphs, and with it adultery. A monk rids the wife of her scruples, everything ends in church. It is reported that Leo X, the first Medici pope, applauded. Perhaps he was especially applauding the political allusions. Even these, it seems, have a double meaning.

Machiavelli's final work, *Florentine Histories* (1524), was commissioned by Cardinal Giulio de Medici and dedicated to the same Medici now become "our very Holy and Saintly Father and Lord Clement VII." Machiavelli adopted an original point of view: in the heart of this history, the divisions of the city. He was obliged to adapt his discourse to his dedicatee, but if the writing of this work makes concessions to the courtier's language, it also contains veiled critiques of the Medici.

We see that Machiavelli writes in various modes, but in a sense he writes most of the time in the same mode: equivocation. Not a single work of his, or almost, fails to raise questions. If one stays with apparent meanings, these texts are often self-contradictory, especially the *Prince* and the *Discourses*. Is Machiavelli incoherent, or changing, or opportunistic? Has he a hidden coherence and a global agenda? Is this some sort of vast hidden enterprise? He seems to say so in Chapter XV of the *Prince* and at the beginning of the *Discourses*, where he introduces himself apparently as a founder and a discoverer. What is this "effective truth of the thing" that he boasts about? What are these "uncharted lands" he intends to explore? But perhaps even this is a trick, or a piece of eloquent bravado.

III.

The strategic context of the writing possibly has a role to play. That context is not identical from one writer to the other, but it does have two general traits: the institutionalization of ecclesiastical censure, and the development of the printing press.

In the world inhabited by Erasmus, More, and Machiavelli, there are limits on the freedom to write. Beyond a certain threshold, the sanctions can be terrible. In the years after 1520, the struggle against the Reformation kindles the bonfires. Up until then, it isn't easy to estimate the risks of persecution. The margin of what is tolerable is a floating one. It is not the same in Basel, London, or Florence, varying according to the moment. From time to time a wind of repression blows, calling writers to order; definitions and condemnations rain down, and the storm blows over (Lucien Febvre). The election of Pope Leo X in 1513 opens a slack period. Judging by the daring ideas of our authors, however, this margin of toleration was not negligible. But wherever it stopped, did it lead Erasmus, More, and Machiavelli to restrain their pens or borrow indirect paths? In the case of Erasmus, the most obvious of the three, and the most exposed, a few things appear established: in part, at least, he is forced to navigate by compass, while guarding more or less successfully against official censors and relying on protectors. The Paris and Louvain theologians condemn some of his writings; other detractors attempt to block them. Erasmus replies, he corrects himself to give his adversaries less room to pin him down. Concomitantly he tries to gain the protection of Leo X, then of Clement VII, and he spares the sovereigns. In any case he is forced to write with reserve or subtlety. How far can he go?

Meanwhile the "printing revolution" changes many things. The written word acquires a new status; the text is protected from scribal errors; the number of copies multiplies; writers aim for a larger public. A triumphant humanism is inseparable from the printing press. Erasmus owes his renown to it and succeeds in living from his pen. He follows the printing of his books closely and does not think it beneath him to live in the shop and correct his proofs.

But the press also complicates matters. If circulation increases, must the divulging of ideas follow? More generally, how can the writer adapt his discourse to his readers when his readers are such a motley public? Raised on rhetoric, Erasmus knows these questions intimately. He will know them even better when the weapon of the humanists becomes that of the Reformers. In his advanced age, Erasmus will chide Luther for making subjects of public controversy questions that should remain hidden. How to get around this problem? By limiting one's public through language? This may work for *Utopia*, but will it work for the *Praise of Folly*, a work Erasmus is happy to see translated, in principle if not in fact? By the art of being advisedly silent, or writing with a double meaning? If such is the case, the craft of the writer as practiced by Erasmus seems almost impossible. So many readers, each calling for an appropriate language! On one side the censors, the protectors; on the other, different types of ordinary readers, forewarned or not.

In Machiavelli's case, the problem is posed in different terms. With one exception, none of his works was printed during his lifetime. We don't know the reason why. The exception is his military treatise, *The Art of War*, published in 1521, with its less biting, more measured tone than in his other works. Did Machiavelli let himself be guided by prudence? Or did he wish to compress the readership of his major works? Perhaps there were other circumstances? . . .

Let us now look at specific traits of each of our writers' situations. In Erasmus's case, it was his monetary needs. For ages he went begging for money: did the beggar have concessions to make? The most visible concessions, which were not of great consequence, were the dedications of his works, whose high-flown compliments attracted ducats and florins in return. The dedicatee could disappoint the author, like Henri de Berghes, whose funeral oration Erasmus made in these terms: "I celebrated the bishop of Cambria with three epitaphs in Latin and one in Greek. I received a mere six florins, which means that even in death he is equal to himself" (A.W. Hermansz, 27 November 1503). On the other hand, to what extent did Erasmus seek the glory that would assure his independence? If he sought it, how much did his writing owe to his desire for glory?

Thomas More did not have the same monetary needs, and his dedications are addressed to his friends. But the author of *Utopia* is within immediate range of a somewhat untrustworthy Prince, even if for the time being this Prince is a devout Catholic, faithful to the Pope, and on the side of the humanists' cause. In any case More's career depends on the good graces of Henry VIII and of his Chancellor, Cardinal Wolsey. When More takes aim at the social injustices in England (in Part I of *Utopia*), he wraps his criticisms inside a literary fiction written in Latin and is careful to place them in a more ancient period. Does his prudence go further than this?

The constraints and pressures that weigh on the author of the *Prince* are to all appearances the heaviest. He is a disgraced civil servant, he can only return to public affairs by the favor of his new masters. He has served he Republic; he must please those who have done it violence. At first sight, the *Prince* moves tentatively in this direction. Initially, Machiavelli had thought of addressing it to Giuliano de Medici. Finally, for unsure reasons, he chose to dedicate it to his nephew Lorenzo, at a date which seems situated somewhere between September 1515 and October 1516 (Roberto Ridolfi). If Machiavelli solicits and pays court, however, he also says many things that are out of place. For what reason should he make of Giuliano or Lorenzo a Prince, when the Medici tradition was to maintain Republican forms? Why so many deliberately shocking proposals which the Medici could hardly pride themselves in having addressed to them? How could the indolent, refined Giuliano be flattered by this image of a new Prince with such brutal manners? Why make of Cesare Borgia the model par excellence, when this foreigner, lost in reputation, hated in Tuscany, having died as a mercenary soldier, had much to make him unpleasant to the Medici? How explain the absence, among so many other examples, of the most illustrious member of the family, Lorenzo the Magnificent?

Section 3.
The Authors, The Historical Contexts

So our authors are not the type to live isolated in an ivory tower. What weight, then, must be given to the general history of the period? To what extent does it shed light on the authors' intentions, or perhaps on the unintended meanings of their works? The question has two faces: on the one hand this history is one of the objects of their reflection; on the other it can be the framework in which their thinking introduces itself. In the first case, the situation is the following: Erasmus, More, and Machiavelli are considering the political and religious questions of their time, and an awareness of that is necessary if we are to try to understand the significance of what they are saying. The difficulty for us is to see this history as they were seeing it. Much depends on their angles of vision, which are not identical in each of the three cases and differ from those we are inclined to take for this simple reason: we know what followed.

In the second case the difficulties increase: our authors' manners of thinking can be more or less dependent on history, whether it be the intellectual and moral climate, the questions and conventions of the times, the categories of thought. In certain respects they appear to be men of their time. Does this mean they are its prisoners? Historicism is firm: one never thinks outside the limited horizon of one's time. Historical conditions give the orders, thinking follows. But that is to prejudge the answer and to disregard many difficulties. The first is that the history in question is full of holes and obscure turns and that it is hazardous to interpret enigmatic texts in the flickering light of an uncertain history (even if abstraction can work miracles). Supposing that pitfall has been avoided, it is foolhardy to deduce what is thought from what is supposed to be thinkable according to the norms of the times. Plato and Cicero may be considered authorities at the time of the Renaissance; it is not sure they can be linked to the historical conditions of the XVth and XVIth centuries. Historicism would say they are "off the subject"; we must see what the people of the times were thinking. Erasmus may know the Epicurean Horace by heart; he may twice edit the Stoic Seneca; he may translate the iconoclastic Lucian and the wise Plutarch; he may be at home with Plato, Cicero, Homer, Aristophanes, Euripides, Vergil, Ovid, Juvenal, Terence and so many others; he may live at the same time in the company of the New Testament, translate it, annotate it, paraphrase it, comment on it; he may have a thorough knowledge of the Church Fathers, and edit a great number of them, Greek (Origen, Chrysostom, Basil) as well as Latin (Ambrose, Jerome, Augustine); he may have also read those who are not of his province, such as Aristotle and Thomas Aquinas; in short, pagan writers who think in many directions, and Christian writers who are in greater or lesser harmony with ancient wisdom: more than ten centuries of Western thought, can one imagine a broader horizon? Not worth the trouble, replies historicism, his thought is captive. Machiavelli may in his early years have recopied the *De Natura rerum* of Lucretius, heard the sermons of Savonarola, brandished the example of the Romans, and written hundreds of pages commenting on Livy; he may have read Thucydides, Xenophon, Sallust, Tacitus, Vergil, Plutarch, Ovid, Cicero, Juvenal, Herodian, very probably Aristotle, Polybius, Justin, and then Dante, Petrarch, Boccaccio; the Bible also, at least in part, enough to broaden one's outlook. "Pure illusion," replies historicism, no one can come out of the cave of his time, except perhaps the one who is speaking. Surely philosophers can err when they disdain history, but historians who are strangers to philosophy can stray when they fail to recognize the autonomous work of human thought. Reality is indifferent to the compartmentalization of disciplines. However that may be, let us bravely attempt to draw out the most significant historical data.

What, then, is this history which our three writers witness and breathe? As far as we can know it is the same and not the same. First of all, all three belong to the same world, that of Latin Europe united, until the Reformation, by Roman Christianity, where the life of the mind is without borders, where politics has something of the family quarrel. Secondly, Erasmus and More on one side, Machiavelli on the other, live in two distinct quarters of this same world. Italy stands apart, looking with disdain at the "barbarians" of the North, tearful to see them sweeping down on her in mutual confrontation. Italy's history has its own rhythms.

I.

This common history is, first of all, a politico-religious history dominated by two massive phenomena: the crisis within the Church, and incessant war, to which one might add the Turkish threat. The Church is corrupt, and not in any mediocre fashion. Its excesses date back a long way, the middle of the XIVth century, but they assume resounding forms, one might say, with a remarkable line of unworthy popes, among them Alexander VI Borgia (1492–1503) and Jules II (1503–1513). The former's reputation for hedonism, for deviousness and simony need not be reestablished even if legend and literature have charged him with more crimes than he really committed. That he had family spirit cannot be denied: in the hands of the Borgias, the Papacy resembled a land given over to pillage (Marcel Brion). In 1504 Machiavelli, tongue-in-cheek, wrote in his *First Decennale* the following funeral oration in honor of Alexander VI:

> Among the blessed was carried off
> The soul of glorious Alexander.
> The blessed trace of his steps was followed
> By three of his dear and familiar servants,
> Lust, Simony and Cruelty.

As for Jules II, besides the usual vices (subtracting nepotism, adding drunkenness), he was above all a warlike pope. A fearsome tactician and warlord, he extended the temporal power of the Holy See. In 1517, the famous *Julius exclusus e coelis*, a brochure generally attributed to Erasmus, shows the Pope arriving at the gates of paradise, wearing the tiara, covered with precious jewels. He rages, wants to force his way in, boasts of all he has brought the Church: gold, palaces, magnificent power. Saint Peter objects: what about the ardor of faith? Purity of heart? Contempt for worldly things? The door remains closed. Jules, outraged, promises to return with a powerful army.

Italians or Italianized, these popes are princes. Their state is vaster than the duchy of Milan or the republic of Florence. They are plunged to their necks in the intrigues of Italian politics and of European politics in Italy. Once in a while their power is reinforced by spiritual weapons, such as excommunication. The mixture of genres brings confusion to their politics, and the popes suffer loss of authority.

After the corruption of the head comes that of the members. Venality and misconduct are rife among the high Church dignitaries. As the saying has it, "Romae, omnia esse venalia," in Rome everything can be bought. As to the vast cohorts of secular clergy and religious orders, they do not escape this decadence. How far do they go? In a contrary sense, there is no lack of charitable works and pious examples. But in any case, the evidence points to the evil reputation of secular priests, canons, and especially the mendicant orders. The humanists are unsparing of them, Erasmus the first among them, calling for a reform of the Church. But this reform, so often talked about, will never be seen. What will come is the Reformation, which is not a reform but a break, and which, from 1520 onward, brings an irremediable division into the Latin Christian world.

The other overwhelming fact is the succession of wars. All their lives, save for brief periods, Erasmus, More, and Machiavelli watched their sovereigns wage war on one another. Machiavelli was, one might say, ideally placed. He writes to Guicciardini in 1526: "So long as I can remember, people have either made war or talked about it" (3 January).

These wars have two characteristics, difficult to sort out. There are wars in the old style, private quarrels between princes, matters of rights and inheritances; there are also new wars, wars between states, with European hegemony at stake. Europe at this time is a mosaic of political configurations: the Empire, national monarchies, the city-states of Italy, the ecclesiastical principalities in Germany. . . . The great powers fight for preponderance, the lesser powers seek equilibrium and change camps constantly. . . . All are locked in battle, periods of peace are mere truces, defiance reigns, violence is unleashed everywhere. In this early XVIth century, along with a progression of morals there is also what one might call a brutalization of the world.

Europe's battleground is Italy first of all. The Italian wars, in the strict sense, stretch from 1494 to 1516. There follows, beginning in 1521, the interminable war waged between the House of France and the House of Austria. The kings of France have set things in motion. In 1494, Charles VIII reclaims his rights to Naples and crosses the Alps. In one year, he has "conquered everything and re-lost everything" (Augustin Renaudet). His successor, Louis XII, also claims rights to Milan. From 1499 on, he alternates between successes and failures; by 1512 he has, in turn, lost everything. In 1515, Francis I takes over; the victory of Marignan gives him the Milan territory, which he then loses in 1525 at Pavia. The French, Imperial, Spanish, and Swiss armies clash on Italian soil, in variable configurations. The heads of princes are filled with ideas of domination and conquest. Charles VIII enters Naples in his role as King of France, Sicily, and Jerusalem; Henry VIII assumes the title of King of France; Chancellor Wolsey wants to be Pope; Francis I is a candidate for the Empire; Charles V of Spain, who has more than seventy titles, holds fast to his rights to Burgundy, which he holds from Charles the Bold. . . . While the great powers compete for Italy, Florence dreams of reconquering Pisa; while the world is falling apart, the Medici popes think first of their family interests; while the Ottomans advance in the East, Venice thinks only of its trading posts, and the other powers are occupied elsewhere. As for the Crusade to halt the advances of the Turks, it is always talked about, never done.

Looking at these events from a distance one might say this: in the course of these years one world is dying a slow death, that of medieval Christendom; a new Europe is progressively emerging and a new political form called national monarchy is asserting itself (even if for a time the old phantom of Empire comes back to life with Charles V). Seen by contemporaries things were evidently different. What did they see? With princes, and especially with popes, what apparently dominated was an extraordinary blindness. But such was not the case, it seems, with the authors we are considering, and a few others. So far as we can judge, they were acutely conscious of what appears like the nub of the period: the deep crisis of Roman Christianity. Each of our three writers observe this: the present Church is no longer able to bring order to the world; worse still, it is introducing disorder. Christianity is not regulating the life of prelates; the temporal ambitions of popes is bringing confusion to the affairs of the world; politics and religion are not in accord or disaccord as they should be. In short, the Church is on trial. The most critical of our writers is Machiavelli, who is perhaps crossing a threshold.

As far as war is concerned, it is equally quite present in their writings, but from all appearances they do not see it with the same eye. For More and Erasmus, war is a scandal; Christian princes do worse than the pagans. For Machiavelli, read literally, it is both a natural thing and a personal drama: Italy is being ruined, soiled, ravaged by foreign armies. Erasmus clings to the conditions of peace, Machiavelli pleads loudly and clearly for a remedy to Italy's ills.

II.

All of this explains why the Alps mark a dividing line. To the North and to the South, the great historical break does not occur at the same date.

For Erasmus and More, the rupture occurs around 1520–1525. During the preceding period, the hope of a renewal carries them forward. The years around 1510 witness the culmination of the "Northern Renaissance." Spirits are in ferment, the humanists gain ground. If there are subsisting scandals, the wind is blowing in the right direction. But the tempest that follows destroys all these hopes. Christian Europe tears itself apart and religious passions are unleashed. In 1524, the terrible "Peasants' War" explodes in Germany. At the same time, the two great Catholic sovereigns, Charles V and Francis I, are locked in ceaseless conflict. In 1527, Rome is sacked, burned, pillaged by the Imperial cohorts. Around 1533, the English schism is consummated. In the East, the Turkish armies pursue their advance, like a rising tide: Suleiman the Magnificent takes Belgrade (1520) and Rhodes (1521). He invades Hungary (1526), lays siege to Vienna (1529). A leaden sky descends over Europe; the vivacity and mirth of the *Praise of Folly* belongs to the preceding period; it is no longer time to laugh (Pierre de Nolhac).

South of the Alps, the great break has come much earlier, dating back to 1494. Italy, so proud of itself, so sure of its superiority, discovers that it is an easy prey. The golden century spoken of by Marsilio

Ficino is followed by the century of iron. Italy remains radiant, no doubt, especially in the artistic domain, but it is humiliated and mistreated. The French and Spanish powers fight over it like rag-pickers.

The Italy of the previous century, the *Quattrocento,* was not only the most prosperous country, it was the place where the Renaissance had taken flight before the rest of Europe followed suit. Florence was the new Athens to this new Greece. Scholars flocked from behind the Alps to study there, as they flocked to Rome, Venice, Padua. . . . Among the northern humanists of the early XVIth century, many had sojourned in Italy, among them Erasmus, Lefevre d'Etaples and John Colet. The Italian language had a status of its own. The learned men of the Peninsula have a passion for Greek; they cultivate Latin for the sheer prestige of it ; but they do not disdain to write in their own language, to which Dante and Petrarch have given their letters of nobility. Machiavelli, who writes in Italian, has great ancestors.

Italy's great weakness, however, was its political state: its fragmentation, its instability, its jealousies, its quarrels, its base political methods. States proliferate (kingdoms, duchies, cities, republics); allegiances are local (one is Florentine, Pisan, Milanese, Venetian, Neapolitan, or whatever); alliances do not last, conspiracies abound, the Condottieri maintain disorder, warlords create dynasties. Only Venice, rapacious Venice, escapes its disturbances and sets up a powerful State. Prestigious Florence lives in a political fever and institutional complications. Florence thinks of itself as the land of freedom, but the Medici bankers assume a dominant position by cheating with the rules. The civilization of XVth-century Italy is radiant with a thousand fires, but not in politics. And Italian politics does not change natures in the following century. Are Machiavelli's politics simply the politics of his time?

It is this magnificent, fragmented, and corrupt Italy that the French invasion of 1494 and its consequences will shake from top to bottom. There opens the time of "calamities," as Guicciardini calls them, a time that coincides with all of Machiavelli's adult life. A number of texts seem to testify to the fact that he felt the sorrows of Italy deeply. But the same Machiavelli, who ended the *Prince* with a vibrant appeal to Lorenzo de Medici to "take Italy and liberate her from the barbarians," uses an entirely different tone in a letter to Vettori from the same period: "As for Italians uniting against them [the French, the Swiss], you make me laugh" (10 August 1513).

III.

What does the history of ideas tell us? The question defeats us, tempting us to be selective, to write the history of the winners, to make clear what is merely confusing. The present writer's most reasonable temptation might be to throw in the towel. Failing that, let us try to pose a few markers.

Vocabulary can be misleading. The word *Renaissance* suggests a factitious unity. We are using it here for the sake of convenience but with these reservations: "Renaissance" does not say everything about the period; it can assume different forms. The central fact seems to be the following: there exists at this time a conquering spirit which intends to break with the Middle Ages (Scholasticism, the Gothic style, the monastic model), and advocates a return to sources or follows new pathways ; but the times are nonetheless confused. They are not of just one piece. One of its characteristics is the mosaic of ideas. Here are a few examples: The men of the Renaissance advocate a new science, but the old scholasticism which they mock and vituperate remains nonetheless powerful in the North. It keeps its hold on the universities; it keeps an eye on Erasmus. It is decadent no doubt, but it is not just decadent: Cajetan publishes a great commentary on Saint Thomas in 1522, Vittoria works at a renewal of Natural Law. The humanists, basing themselves on ancient wisdom, give nature and practical reason a clean scrubbing; but Luther blackens both, which have been soiled entirely by original sin. Erasmus and his friends enable the critical spirit to progress, but works of magic and astrology enrich the book dealers. Machiavelli himself seems to grant to astrology a certain credibility; his discourse on the fortune and the quality of the times, notably in Chapter 25 of the *Prince,* has an astrological background (A. Parel). The Renaissance is also a time when eschatological visions are in vogue. The thundering prophecies of Savonarola belong to this period, as does the aged Michelangelo's terrifying *Last Judgment* and Dürer's monumental plates of the *Apocalypse.* For many, including

Christopher Columbus, the end of days is near. The signs foretelling things to come are watched for. In Chapter 26 of the *Prince*, Machiavelli invokes "extraordinary facts [. . .] directed by God" which call upon Lorenzo de Medici to take charge of the "redemption" of Italy. But these signs are taken from *Exodus* (the sea has parted, manna has rained from heaven . . .). One wonders where the author saw them, and he presents them as if they are without precedent. Is Machiavelli joking?

Here are a few more examples. At this same time, Copernicus develops a new astronomy, Leonardo observes, invents, and calculates in a thousand ways, Paracelsus experiments and speculates in all directions; but Erasmus, More, and their literary friends remain cold in the face of nature's secrets. Leonardo, Raphael, Michelangelo cover walls or adorn edifices with masterpieces; but Erasmus in his travels or Machiavelli at home show not a single sign of interest. At the very moment when Niccolò is writing the *Prince*, Castiglione is working on his *Libro del Cortegiano*, sketching the model of the refined, amiable gentleman, civilized to the tips of his fingers. Cesare Borgia is disposed otherwise. In Padua, Pietro Pomponazzi, reinterpreting Aristotle, is teaching the mortality of the soul; from one city to the other, Ignatius of Loyola writes a first draft of what will become the *Spiritual Exercises*. Aretino launches his career as a toadying, bribing, obscene, and edifying writer; in 1534 he publishes his *Cortegiana*. The next year, Teresa of Avila enters the convent, the year after that Calvin publishes his *Institutes of the Christian Religion*.

All these historical actors belong to the same time and do not belong to the same world. They do, admittedly, have a common characteristic: they are powerful personalities. Such personalities were not missing in the Middle Ages, but these are usually outside institutional boundaries. In this sense, individualism makes a stride forward. Luther works in this direction with his doctrine of the universal priesthood: every member of the faithful is a priest, the dialogue with God can do without intermediaries. A new general orientation stands out: the mental space controlled by religious authority tends to lose its all-enfolding character, to the benefit of profane knowledge or, in the case of the Reformers, of individual conscience. The theologians lose ground, to the gain of the literary, the artists (soon the men of science), and individuals. If they all thought according to the same model, that individualism with which the Renaissance is credited would be nothing but an illusion.

In the strict sense, the Renaissance, when seen more closely, is not exactly the same beyond the Alps and on the Italian side. The humanism of the North is a Christian humanism; Italian humanism is more tainted with paganism. Erasmus and More belong unequivocally to the humanist movement; Erasmus is its head, and the years 1510–1520 can be qualified as the "Erasmian moment." The qualifier "humanist" attributed to Machiavelli is uncertain or problematical. Whether or not there was a "Machiavellian moment" within a conceptualized time (J.G.A. Pocock), such a moment is invisible within history itself.

What about Florence? As in Italy itself, but perhaps in more pronounced a manner, things in Florence are contrasted and mixed. A profound religious tradition coexists with a "worldly" system of values ("honor and utility," that is to say reputation and self-interest). Art is a curious assemblage of Christianity and paganism; of superstition and the prosaic nature of merchants. . . . The Florentine city, boisterous and feasting under the Medici, takes on the appearance of a monastery in Savonarola's time, reverts to a new period of laxness, then with a return to the Republic in 1527 reverts again to asceticism. The same men can be both refined and brutal, speak like skeptics and die a pious death. One has the feeling that Florentines of the Renaissance live what amounts to a double or a triple life. But how can one really know?

On the level of political representations, what makes Florence stand out is the theme of *florentina libertas*, which the XVth-century humanists have draped in Roman garb (Augustin Renaudet). One celebrates the Florentine city, daughter of the Roman Republic, motherland of freedom par excellence, motherland of all Italians, the ideal land of all men (E. Garin). What kind of freedom is meant? It has a double meaning and is subject to ambiguities: the freedom of the citizens (freedom of speech and civic participation) and that of the city.

In practice, however, it does not measure up to its ideal. The status of the Florentine citizen is never more than the privilege of a minority, and the principle of the freedom of cities adapts itself quite well to the subjection of neighboring cities, like the unfortunate Pisa since 1406. What, then, is the worth of these eloquent paeans of praise to the glory of Florence? Hans Baron has raised them to the rank of an important current of thought, which he called "civic humanism." In his wake, J.G. Pocock and Q. Skinner made of Machiavelli the most illustrious of Florence's "civic humanists." Their works impress by their erudition and their ingeniousness, but many pitfalls remain, the first of which is to bring these two propositions in agreement: 1) Machiavelli writes straight; 2) The *Prince* is written from a humanistic and Republican political point of view. Any failure to consider the art of writing condemns us to perform great feats in the art of reading.

SECTION 4.
The Texts, The Writing

Finally, before considering the unpublished texts, we must examine the key texts, the *Prince, Utopia,* and the *Praise of Folly.* As we have seen, what distinguishes these works is not so much that they are equivocal because they are difficult, uncertain, inexhaustible—so many great works are—it is that they are all of this to such an extent that their commentators have read opposite works. At the heart of the disagreement is the central inspiration which governs all the rest, and which has been interpreted in all sorts of ways.

I.

The *Praise of Folly* (1511), the *Prince* (1513), and *Utopia* (1516) are three short, dense, and dazzling works. All three sparkle with daring and literary talent. From the start, there is in each case something resembling a stroke of genius. Erasmus's is to make of Folly both the author and the subject of his praise. More's is to give life, as it were, to a new society extracted from his imagination. Machiavelli's is to adopt a traditional genre, the *Mirror of Princes,* and to break with tradition. Erasmus renews the old literary genre of paradoxical praise; More invents, or reinvents, a literary genre which will take the name of his book; Machiavelli takes up a genre dedicated to the edification of princes to say quite different things and to write a unique work.

Great works, said Orwell, are written by people who are not afraid. These three works are of that type. Erasmus and More take risks in borrowing an innovative and reckless literary form. They also take risks with the positions they hold, even if these are protected under the cover of fiction. Machiavelli holds daring positions in his own name; he is less adventurous as to form, but he is also less guarded. Erasmus's style dazzles with virtuosity; Machiavelli's is striking and impressive in its dryness and rapidity; More's has less sparkle, but his imagination compensates, with his art of giving things imagined the appearance of reality. If we add to this an extraordinary density of ideas, we see that, to all appearances, we are dealing with masters in the art of writing. But there is a price to pay. The attentive reader has a hard time. He stumbles against complicated turns of phrase or ambiguous words; he trips on formulations that appear obscure, unsure, or illogical; he desperately cocks an ear; he often has a hard time grasping the tone of voice. Erasmus and Machiavelli proceed very fast; More makes detours. At first sight Erasmus seems ill-assorted, More seems to lack equilibrium. Machiavelli seems more orderly, but as we advance in the work, we find some difficulty following the train of thought. Is there perhaps, in each case, a hidden order? The well-intentioned reader may be tempted to give up, and the translator to give notice. How to translate these difficulties from one language to another? One is tempted to skirt over them or around them: translation adapts, corrects, interprets; it is in great danger of being unfaithful. But how can one not be? The traps are legion, as we shall see later.

What the authors say of the writing of their works is equally disconcerting. Erasmus claims to have meditated his work between Italy and England and to have written it at More's home in seven days. More allegedly wrote his in rare moments stolen from sleep after exceedingly busy days , Machiavelli at the end of his nightly conversations with the books of the Ancients, after days of dissipation.[3] One can only marvel at such ease of writing: works hastily written, in short, and yet such brilliance of execution, and so many headaches for the applied reader! Perhaps other things should be taken into account— play, vanity, secrecy . . . who knows?

II.

The *Praise of Folly* appears, then, in 1511, or thereabouts, under the Graeco-Latin title of *Moriae Encomium*. The work is filled with Greek quotations and learned references—mere entertainment, says the author, but an entertainment strewn with erudition.

The book is dedicated to Thomas More, whose name (Morus), as

---

[3]   See the dedicatory letter from Erasmus to More and his *Letter to Dorp*, X, 1515; the introductory letter to *Utopia* addressed to Pierre Gilles; Machiavelli's letter to Vettori of 10 December 1513.

the dedicatory letter says, is as close to that of folly (*moria*) as his person is far from it. The tone of the book is playful and entertaining from the outset. But Erasmus immediately adds that trivial things can be in the service of serious ones. "I believe," he says, "I have praised folly in a manner that is not entirely foolish."

The text makes use of literary forms borrowed from the Greek and Roman writers: declamation, paradoxical praise, prosopopea.[4] But Erasmus takes risks; he raises the stakes. On the one hand he adopts literary conventions which could easily discourage the most seasoned of writers: Folly speaks alone, she must speak foolishly, she speaks of folly. On the other hand, he allows himself a great freedom: Folly can say many things that the author can hardly say in his own name; she is not constrained by logic; she is less constrained by conventions and by prudence. The enterprise was a bold one; it produced a masterpiece because the author was able to respect to the very end the conventions initially adopted, while exploiting the liberties he had allowed himself—that is to say, while developing a plethora of brilliant, piquant, eloquent variations on the theme of folly. A great piece of work, says today's reader, like yesterday's—even if today's reader might be tempted to cry mercy: this was more than he asked for.

The flip side of the coin is that these fireworks blind us rather than light our way. Erasmus is playing: when does he stop? Dame Folly plays foolish; she is gay, flighty, impertinent, illogical; yet at the same time, or on the side, she seems to say things that are far from inconsequential. Should we take them seriously? The text cannot possibly be summarized, but a juxtaposition of different comments on different

4   Declamation is a rhetorical exercise wherein the author defends a fictitious cause. In the case of paradoxical praise, the cause in question is ridiculous, inappropriate, or detestable, in short unworthy of praise. Prosopopea is a discourse by a conventional orator, whether it be a historical character, an animal, or a personified idea. At the start of his book, Erasmus appeals to this rhetorical tradition (Lucian's praise of the fly, of baldness, of quartan fever . . .). His share of formal originality is this: this seems to be the first time that the entire discourse is that of a personified abstraction (Jacques Chomarat). Sleep speaks in Homer, and Necessity in Horace, but for a time only.

themes might provide some idea of its content:

> Here I am, by chance, says the swaggering Dame Folly. I govern the world, I bring joy to gods and men. Everything that men do is mere Folly. To me is due the cuckold's illusion, the brute's madness, the stupid man's satisfaction, war with its miseries, pleasure with its honey. What would life be if mortals saw her as she really is? Prudence is on my side, wisdom on occasion, and those fables that allow us to lead that rough beast called the people. Besides, wise men are killjoys, stumps, closed to natural feelings, fools. My reign extends to filthy monks who bellow their psalms, to theologians so proud of their inane subtleties, to Pontiffs benumbed in their luxury, in short to all those who ruin true piety. I am not forgetting princes who, thanks to me, spend their time hunting, scheming, ransoming, waging war. Christianity itself is a type of folly bearing pious men toward some form of delirium. So, then, applaud, prosper and drink, you illustrious inductees of folly!

We see that Dame Folly undergoes transformations; it is not at all certain that she is the same from one end to the other, nor even from one passage to the other. The result is that on many occasions, we are not quite sure who is speaking: is it Folly, Erasmian irony that is, expressing itself by antiphrasis? Or is it Erasmus himself who dialogues with himself under the mask or says things he holds dear? Two things, it seems, are beyond doubt: first, that the *Praise of Folly* is an intellectual game, more or less; second, that it allows the author to practice his satirical form against his favorite targets (monks, theologians, warmongers, impious Popes). . . . But beyond that?

III.

Published five years later, *Utopia* is related to Erasmus's *Moria* in more ways than one. More follows the same path, borrowing from the rhetorical tradition of Antiquity (the dialogue, the imaginary travel narrative); he does not speak in his own name but makes a fictional character speak; he mixes the pleasing and the serious and, of course, he writes in the language of the humanists. On the title page of the *Moria* [*Praise of Folly*] one could read: *Libellus nec minus eruditis et salutaris quam festivus* (a book no less learned and profitable than entertaining). On his title page, More writes: *Libellus vere aureus nec minus salutaris quam festivus* (a truly golden book, no less . . .).

Utopia is nevertheless another bold stroke. More goes further than Plato or Lucian, making his imaginary society visible while in action. Book II, which is the main body of the work, is a long discourse by the philosopher-traveler Hythlodeus (or teller of nothings), describing with fulsome details and fulsome praise the Isle of Utopia (or of Nowhere), where the problem of men's life in common has been resolved. Literary convention requires a great power of creation; on the other hand, to create a world, what freedom for a writer! The first part, twice shorter than the second and added later, is less original in form. It is a dialogue in three voices: More, his friend Pierre Gilles, and the discoverer of Utopia. The tone is lively, the critique very vivid, the order dispersed.

The book's literary fortune is proof of More's success. But as was the case for the *Moria* we are not sure how to interpret it. Who speaks for the author? With the exception of Pierre Gilles, who plays a secondary role, there are three orators: the narrator More, who sets the scene, reports what was said, and, at the end, makes a few cautionary remarks; the character More, who questions and raises a few objections; and finally, and especially, Raphael Hythlodeus, an upright man, well versed in the Humanities, but also rigid, intransigent, oversensitive. Does More have a spokesman? Who is it? The central question is the same as in the case of Erasmus's *Folly*: the author is playing, no doubt, but when does he cease playing? The exercise is a pretense; irony plays a role as well as trickery and buffoonery. The main river that flows through Utopia is called *Anydra*, or without water; it bathes the capital, *Amaurote*, the obscure city, where rules *Ademus*, the head without a people. . . . And yet More's tone is not as offhanded or as frivolous as Erasmus's. In Book I, the fictional form does not obscure a criticism of warmongers, of monks, of the idle, of hoarders, and more particularly of the policy of enclosures in England. In spite of its fantasies, Book II conveys a feeling of seriousness. But are

Hythlodeus's comments always coherent? Does the author deliberately confuse the issues? Does More's work rank, ultimately, with Rabelais's *Quart Livre* or with Swift's *Gulliver*? Or should it be placed on the same shelf as Plato's *Republic* (which it presumes to imitate), or next to Cabet, Fourier, and others of the same ilk? In any case, here are the main traits of this utopian society, allowing for our inability to do justice to the astounding richness of the text:

> The first principle of the Utopians' constitution, says Hythlodeus, so wise, so morally irreproachable, is that nothing is private. No one possesses anything, but all are rich, since necessities and a life free from worry are assured. In Utopia one meets neither nobles parading their arrogance, nor the wealthy conspiring for even more wealth, nor the indigent reduced to begging. With equality, the lust for gain has disappeared, people are gay, lovable, benevolent. All live happy and free under the eyes of all and of a discipline freely consented: sleep at fixed hours, meals taken in common, identical clothes, regulated distractions, homes acquired by drawing lots every ten years, their doors always open. . . . The Island forms in this way one sole happy family.
>
> See what follows. In this excellent people, each cultivates pleasure and virtue, love of peace and, by obligation, military training, work in the fields and the activities of the mind; as well as this spirit of humanity which reserves slavery for the great criminals and authorizes, under certain conditions, euthanasia and divorce. In religious matters, each is free to believe what he wills, or almost. The sects live in peace; the holy priests are the same for all. In short, the best of Republics, the most in keeping with nature. The simple reason of the Utopians has worked wonders. Christians should take their inspiration from these pagans.

IV.

The literary form of the *Prince* is entirely different. This is not a fiction; it has no imaginary character. What we have here is a treatise wherein the author speaks in his own name. At first glance, he speaks without hesitations or circumlocutions. The voice which Machiavelli assumes here is recognizable among thousands, with its tone of authority, buttressed by examples, which creates such a strong impression, and these scathing, biting formulations which have shocked so many readers. And yet, this work is the most mysterious of the three.

The *Prince* presents itself as an orderly and demonstrative treatise. Doctor Machiavelli strings the chapters along, the propositions, the examples, with "a quick and decisive step" (Patrick Boucheron). No flowery language, but direct and trenchant, lapidary maxims, a choppy syntax. No philosophical preliminaries, but an immediate analysis of practices, with a shower of examples, anecdotes, portraits (from Moses to Cesare Borgia, from Darius's empire to the war against Pisa).

The introduction is abrupt and announces what is to follow with a series of distinctions: principalities and republics, hereditary and new principalities, entirely new or added principalities, principalities acquired with the arms of others or with one's own, through fortune or through talent (I). Republics being set aside, the question is to know how principalities "can be governed and preserved" (II). The reader understands that the work is being governed with a firm hand.

Upon closer look, however, what follows is surprising. The outline is much looser than had been announced. Machiavelli begins by following it, more or less; then he switches to something else. Beneath the appearance there reigns "a strange disorder" (Claude Lefort) Chapters I to XI take up the initial distinctions, but it is to discuss the art of extending one's states through conquest, and the art of acquiring power or of founding a State. The author's attention is drawn to *New Princes*. New categories also appear: civil principalities (an obscure or ambiguous formula), ecclesiastical principalities (in fact the Papal State). The following chapters stray from the original outline and go off in different directions: the question of arms (XII-XIV), the book's ambition (XV), the necessary qualities of the Prince (XVI-XXIII), the misfortunes of Italy (XXIV), fortune and virtue (XXV), a call for the liberation of Italy (XXVI). In chapter XV Machiavelli contrasts "the effective truth of the thing" to the republics and principalities that have been imagined. But what are these imaginary republics or principalities? Plato's *Republic?* The Kingdom of heaven? Something else? What is the import of this rupture? Why say it so late? The final chapter, probably an afterthought, is strange. The author changes his tone to urge the Medici to liberate Italy, adopting a pompous, lyrical, prophetic language that differs sharply from what came before.

The general tone of the *Prince* is also expressed in steely formulations which have given Machiavelli his black reputation: that a conquering Prince must extinguish the lineage of the former Prince (III); that there is a good use to be made of cruelty (VIII); that it is better to be feared than loved (XVII); that the Prince must act with the fox's cunning and the lion's strength (XVIII), etc. The initial shock of reading the book (Pierre Manent) is cushioned today by the status of the text—a "classic"—and by the *a priori* representations of Machiavelli. Understandably, he may have been violent; but things become complicated with a rereading. The author may be astoundingly brutal, yet he also invites the Prince to "satisfy his people and make them happy" (XIX), to encourage his fellow citizens to exercise their activities peacefully (XXI). . . . When he advises the Prince to use evil, he never does so except within the limits of necessity. One must look at things as they are, politics has its laws and its constraints. Machiavelli also says bad things about evil, as in Chapter VIII, when he speaks of villains who have become princes through villainy. It is true that this chapter is unclear, since the cruel and inhuman Agathocles is said to be both virtuous and lacking in virtue. Here as elsewhere, the author plunges the attentive reader, or the reader trying to be attentive, into depths of perplexity. This perplexity increases when he notices something else: Machiavelli says astonishingly bold things loudly, and at the same time he seems to write as if he were thinking under a veil. What does he have to hide? In the game being played between author and reader, the reader without *a priori* positions can easily be excused if he feels that "this author is too strong for me." We beg to be excused, then, if the *Prince* appears too complicated or too subtle for us to attempt an overall view of the work by paraphrasing it. The documents cited later will provide extracts of the book with commentaries by Erasmus.

These documents will also provide material to enrich the thinking of distinguished specialists in the art of reading these extraordinary works, and in the art of governing ordinary men. That, at least, is our wish.

BOOK I
MORALITY AND NECESSITY
(July 1517–March 1518)

CHAPTER 1
The Tender Commerce of Friendship

Essentially this first book groups together the first part of the corre-spondence between Erasmus and More on the one hand, Erasmus and Machiavelli on the other. To these are added a few letters exchanged between Erasmus and More and a letter from Machiavelli to Vettori. Here Erasmus and Machiavelli grapple with each other, in other words morality grapples with necessity.

In this chapter, the first texts will be found in chronological order, that is, two letters exchanged between Erasmus and More and a satirical text received by More at a proximate date. The tone and the content of the correspondence are in harmony with the letters al-ready known. The immediate context is as follows: for both friends, these years are years of grace. The respite of 1515 or 1516 continues.

Erasmus speaks on several occasions of a golden age that is coming. The new Pope, Leo X, is less scandalous to the Church than his predecessors. He is a Medici "to the marrow" (Ludwig von Pastor), looking after the good fortune of his family. He loves luxury, and his good nature conceals much trickery; but he is a friend of literature and the arts, and he appears peace-loving even if, in fact, he is not devoid of the temporal ambitions of his predecessors. The young sovereigns, Henry VIII, Francis I, Charles of Castille (the future Emperor Charles V) are young and full of promise. In August 1516, the Valois Francis and the Hapsbourg Charles sign the peace of Noyon. The specter of war seems to recede. At the same time, the party of the humanists gains the upper hand. Erasmus travels constantly, works himself to the bone, publishes abundantly. His Praise of Folly *is reprinted several times in revised and enriched versions. In 1516–1517, two of his chief political works appear, the* Institutio principis christiani *(The Education of the Christian Prince), dedicated to Charles of Castille, and the* Querela Pacis *(or Complaint of Peace). Also, and especially, appears his great work as philologist, translator and interpreter of Scripture, the* Novum Testamentum, *which provides a new edition of the Greek text, accompanied with long annotations and a new Latin translation. Erasmus's greatest challenge is his revision of the Vulgate, that is, Saint Jerome's translation, which was the unquestioned authority, a work which raised great turmoil and brought Erasmus an increased notoriety and much animosity. At the end of this year 1516, Thomas More gained acceptance as a man of letters with his* Utopia. *Editions followed in succession: Louvain, Paris, Basel, with Erasmus lending a hand.*

During these happy years, the two friends were very close. Erasmus crossed the Channel every year between 1514 and 1517. When they were separated, they wrote often. But then their paths drew farther apart. More entered active politics. Erasmus was careful to keep his distances He keeps looking for a fixed dwelling place: Francis I invites him to Paris through the intermediary of Guillaume Budé; Cardinal Ximenes de Cisneros (Montherlant's "Cardinal of Spain") invites him to Toledo; but faced with these offers, Erasmus dithers and finally settles nowhere.

I.
ERASMUS TO MORE
Louvain, 12 July 1517

Erasmus of Rotterdam to his dear Thomas More, hail!

[1] Since I have nothing from you, my dear More, I understand that you no longer belong to yourself. You have been drawn to the Court and the Court has you swirling. O that you might love your King the way friends of great literature should love amiable princes, I mean from a distance! What a misfortune to tie oneself down with them and their affairs when one knows how inclined they are to bowl you over, weigh you down and reward you with ingratitude! I have been entrusted in the Emperor's name [Emperor Maximilian] with a certain business, but I shall cross the Styx and the Acheron before I allow myself to get caught. Small intruders are all I need. When they intrude too much on me, I report sick. I fear the great Intruders, be they the most esteemed of kings like the most illustrious Henry of England. Heaven grant that he not turn you against Letters and that he allow you some leisure for the tender commerce of friendship.

I know, gentle More, that I am telling you nothing that you do not know already. But do not forget this word of advice from the most faithful of your friends: take care to care for yourself.

I can write you frankly, the carrier is reliable. I recommend this young man, but I don't wish to force you in any way. If you happen to need a secretary, however, you should know that he writes Greek and Latin with few mistakes and with a fairly readable hand.

I arrived in Louvain with all my belongings, and here I caught a nasty head cold. I am not complaining; I was expecting worse of our modern [scholastic] theologians. But how could I ever settle here? There are too many scoundrels waiting in ambush, and the Chancellor [of the University] is paying me a pittance. Where can I go? In Germany there are too many highway robbers, and too many inns where the stench is unbearable; in Paris, too many of these Sorbonne gentlemen; in Rome, too many pagans, whores, and empty promises; in England, too many dashed hopes, as you know. And everywhere this plague of monks! My dear More, if you have any ideas, let me know.

Here, in turn, is the good news: the conquerors are resting and the only conquest worth its while, that of minds, is going rather well. I speak of your Republic, of course [the *Utopia*], and of ours, that of the Literati. We are commanding the admiration of princes, we are holding our enemies at bay, and the new Pontiff [Leo X] is on our side. Who knows, perhaps Aristotle and Averroes are about to lose their status of Fathers of the Church? Perhaps the study of the three languages [Latin, Greek, Hebrew] will become the rule? And perhaps I'll find someday that blessed place where whoever devotes himself to Letters might receive a few ducats for the needs of the body and freedom for those of the soul? Another Isle of Utopia? Who knows?

[2] All our friends are happy in Utopia. They are breathing a new air which fills them with joy and the spirit of meditation. There is a magistrate from Antwerp, I'm told, who knows your book by heart. That's why it is wise to hasten the new editions as much as a carefully prepared printing will allow. As I told you, I sent my best boy to Basel with your corrected copy. I wrote to my partner Froben to get things moving, and so that things might be well done. You know that the Paris edition is in press. I haven't any of my own people there, and I fear the carelessness of the correctors. Scrupulous printers are as numerous as uninflated writers or poxless popes. Fortunately my friend Froben will succeed in doing fine work if he is well whipped and aided.[1]

[3] I tell myself every day that the edition of the *Novum Testamentum* was far too hasty. I took up the translation again and I'm ex-

---

[1]   Erasmus spared no effort to ensure the success of the *Utopia*. As the first edition, that of Louvain (December 1516), was soon out of print, he was soon thinking of new revised and corrected editions. This led to Paris (end 1517), but the printing was sloppy; then came especially Basel in March 1518, and again in November 1518. The Basel editions, which were of better quality and accompanied with engravings by Ambrosius and Hans Holbein, were the work of the printer Jean Froben. Froben was a friend of Erasmus, who was the godfather of one of his sons (that is why Erasmus calls him "partner"), and who was soon to become his official editor. The November 1518 edition, the fourth edition of *Utopia*, is the definitive edition.

pecting new manuscripts. If you see things that need changing, tell me immediately. I've heard from several quarters that the book is doing well. But I hear the muffled grumbling of our scholastic savants who are raging in the shadows and chomping on their complaints. How impertinent, this Erasmus, who not only mocks our glorious science in his *Moria*. He also pretends to come back to the Greek of the Gospel! What an idea! What pretense! What folly! Is he trying to foist the purity of the sacred text on us, who did not need to know Greek to construct the most learned theology there is, all fuzzy and contentious as it should be? In fact, our Doctors are so imbued with their all too human science that divine Letters are presumed to give them the right of way. Jerome's translation is enough for us, they say. As if Jerome were a prophet or an apostle! You know how much I admire him, but there are times when even Jerome nods.[2] And the scribes can be wrong. And passages have been added. They would have us believe that it is good scholarship to swallow the mistakes and mistranslations so long as they have been repeated a thousand times. And they call me a "grammarian!" I'm willing to accept that critique. Grammar deals with little things, but these little things govern big ones.

You know all this, gentle More, as well as the great art which is that of reading as one should. May some opportunity allow you to hop over to see me. That would give me new life. Farewell.

II.
MORE TO ERASMUS
London, 2 August 1517

Thomas More to Master Erasmus, hail!

I am confiding this letter, and a few others, to our friend from Flanders [?]. He is entirely devoted to you, as you know, but he is always in a mood to postpone his departure. I hope he will reach you before the end of days draws near.

---

[2]   Echo of a famous saying of Horace: "Even Homer nods."

I'm certainly in agreement with you when you refuse to let yourself get bogged down in the small affairs of the Great. And that you should wish to extricate me from them is proof of your affection. I know from a reliable source that these are people made to burden you with emphatic and vain trifles. You have no idea, I think, to what extent I am with them reluctantly. But how can one escape a Prince's call for service when he is so close? Or the benevolence of his Chancellor [Cardinal Wolsey] when he rewards you with such handsome promises?

Your *Novum Testamentum* is being appreciated as it should be by all those qualified to do so. At a meeting filled with high dignitaries, the bishop of Winchester said, to the concurrence of all, that your translation was to him worth ten commentaries. And our friend Latimer [an Oxford Hellenist] has the highest regard for your work.

Now I must tell you, my very dear Erasmus, that there are those here who read you from another viewpoint. They dissect your writings in search of any occasion to pick a quarrel with you. The highest placed among them is this Franciscan theologian whom you know [?]. Who can be more niggling than these mendicants who forget to beg [the Franciscan order is a mendicant order]! And so I beg you, be careful, do not rush to publish what you are currently working on. Review the whole text so as to not lay yourself open to intrigue or calumny.

We have been visited by a bachelor of arts just graduated from the Sorbonne who would not be disowned by Dame Folly herself. He knew Aristotle better than Aristotle himself, without knowing a word of Greek, naturally. "The works of Aristotle," he told us," are all approximation. We have ordered and systematized his logic and all the suppositions, ampliations, restrictions, and appellations that are needed." The syllogisms flowed from his mouth like milk from a woman's breast. But, thank heavens, not everybody in Paris is cut from that cloth. I have received from that quarter a joke which I'll show you when I can.

I am happy to learn that so any eminent men approve of our *Utopia*. What do our friends from Brussels think? I am eager to find out.

But your support is enough for me, my gentle Erasmus. Farewell.

I am sending you a small sheaf of letters from the Venetian

ambassador, from his secretary, and also from the Bishop of Rochester [John Fisher].

My wife sends you a thousand greetings. She thanks you for your note wherein you wished her a long life. To hear her, she herself wishes it, so as to be able to persecute me longer.

III.
THE FOUR CAUSES OF ARISTOTLE
AS TAUGHT TO B. PINAEUS

The following text was found in More's papers. It is probably the one he alludes to in the preceding letter. We know that it comes from the Sorbonne, but we don't know by what channel. This sort of hoax by students (or by their masters) was current practice at that time. Most of the time, it took the form of a pastiche of scholastic debate, with a predilection for subjects such as: "On the fidelity of whores toward their lovers." Somewhat later, a champion of mockery in this vein will be Rabelais.

We don't know what More thought of it beyond what he says in his letter to Erasmus. More wasn't prudish, but to our knowledge he never sent it to Erasmus.

Here follows an account by Beaficus Pineus, bachelor of arts of the University of Paris, on the way he understood as one should the four causes of Aristotle, and other subtleties by the same Philosopher.

On the tenth day in December of that year, I resolved to go and see my master, the most subtle and most learned Doctor Vitenbernus, so that he might help me disentangle the sayings of the Philosopher concerning causes, about which I couldn't see any more clearly than a navigator in foggy weather.

Lady Vitenbernus received me graciously and told me that unfortunately her husband had been debating for the past two days with a Scotist on the existential status of the mosquito. She noticed my disappointment and immediately showed me her good will: "Don't let that bother you. I can very easily explain to you Aristotle's four causes. I've hardly made use of them of late, and there is nothing better than an object lesson." She made me sit beside her.

"For the sake of the argument," she continued, "I shall leave being and take up change. As you know, things change. That's what makes the world go round. Now to make things change is nothing other than to make them go from potency to act. That is what my dear old husband understands less and less. At your age you will soon grasp what I am saying, and all the causes in question.

"*Ergo*, for whatever changes in the things of nature, the word *cause* can be used in different meanings. Firstly, *cause* can mean that with which things are made and which is the material cause. A statue is made with marble; what I'm thinking of is made of flesh and blood. But this matter never exists save by the form. I skip over the secondary subtleties in order to arrive at the crucial point: the piece of marble has a form, the statue has another. You follow me, the matter we are interested in here, you carry it on you, and well hung I think, composed of a form which, while waiting for other causes, is philosophically of little interest. But change will occur in keeping with what the Philosopher says: 'Matter desires form as the female desires the male.' By this we mean this form which firms up matter and gives it felicitous properties."

I looked at her quite flabbergasted because of her discourse on causes, and because of her nipples: hers were pink, round, lively and ready to pop out. She continued: "What you are insistently staring at, my young friend, is the efficient cause, or rather my most efficient part. It is that by which things change. Come closer, feel the cause and you will see the effect." I touched and saw right away that the reason was a good one. "I see that you have a good understanding of philosophy, and how a first body acts, insofar as it is in act, on a second body insofar as it is in potency. The sculptor uses his chisel to sculpt a statue. An honest lady with a bit of science acts and sculpts by herself.

"In a third sense, I have already said a word on this point, the cause can be formal, that is, that by virtue of which the thing changes. It is the idea of the statue that quickens the hand of the sculptor. Here, need I say, it is the thrust of nature which makes the blood boil and determines the *quiddity* of the thing. Matter is passive and indeterminate; form is active and determining, especially that form which corresponds perfectly to the intention and the appetite of matter."

I felt that philosophy was beginning to warm her up. "Come," she said in a lower tone, "we must end with the final cause, the one that counts, that fills, that justifies. That is the be-all and end—all of the change in things, the beauty of the statue, or, preferably, the satisfaction of our concupiscible nature." Moved as I was, I saw there the risk of modernism and the danger of spoiling her waistline. "But isn't the final cause the act of generation?" I objected. "It's the Doctors who say that, they don't understand a thing, and they don't know what experienced women know. Come quickly, but don't swing into action too fast. The final cause needs a subsisting form for a certain time." I followed her lesson, and though I somewhat missed the succession of causes, she wasn't angry with me. We parted very satisfied with each other and with philosophy.

CHAPTER 2
Institutio Tyranni

At this same period, Machiavelli is still undergoing what he calls in his dedication of the Prince *"a great and continuous malignity of fortune." Relieved of his duties by the new masters, he has retired to his family home of Sant'Andrea in Percussina, a little town seven miles from Florence.*

What does he do? How does he live? What we know of him is based on what he says in the letters written to Francesco Vettori between Spring 1513 and January 1515. One of these letters (10 December 1513) has, as it were, engraved in history the figure of Machiavelli in disgrace, with his miseries but also his noble hours. His day, he writes, goes like this: I rise with the sun and make my way into a wood that I am having cut down; I spend some time with the lumberjacks who are always having some falling out to settle; then I watch and catch a few birds while rereading Dante, Petrarch or Ovid. On the road to the inn, I talk with the passers-by and take note of the various moods and fantasies of men. After having eaten I return to the inn and idle around while playing tric-trac in the company of a butcher, a miller, and a couple of oven stokers. Then:

> *Mixed up with these lice, I scrape the mould off my brain and drink the malignancy of my Fate to the dregs, content to have her trample me thus, if only to see whether she is not ashamed to do so. But when night falls, I return home and enter into my study. I shed my muddy everyday garments and leave them on the threshold; I dress as if to appear in the courts and in the presence of kings. Dressed in proper attire, I enter into the antique courts of the men of Antiquity; they receive me as friends; with them I nourish myself with the food which is mine par excellence and for which I was born. Quite openly I dare converse with them and inquire into the causes of their actions; and they answer me humanely. And for four hours' time I do not feel boredom, I forget all my misery, I no longer fear poverty; death no longer terrifies me.*

Machiavelli then proceeds to announce that he is writing the Prince, *then follows with practical questions and arguments* pro domo: *should he or should he not dedicate the book to Giuliano? When will the Medici decide to hire him? Who can doubt his loyalty, which is so well attested to by his poverty? It is a beautiful text; but should the author be taken at his word, as his biographers do? If we consider this correspondence as a whole, we notice this: Vettori is, at the time, the Florentine ambassador to the Medici pope; these letters are, it seems, first of all an opportunity for Machiavelli to press him to intercede in his favor: "If our masters think it good not to leave me on the ground, I shall be happy" (18 March 1513); "It is impossible for me to remain for long in my present condition, for I am using myself up" (10 June 1514), etc. Vettori shows himself cordial; he sympathizes with Machiavelli and shows good will, but no actions follow, and he draws or accompanies his interlocutor into other terrains. Which ones? Those of great things and those of vain things, as Machiavelli says. The great things are the affairs disrupting Europe; the vain things are their indiscretions, or those of their friends, which they recount with a fickle tone. Neither of them is averse to using crude turns of phrase or blunt terms. Must we conclude, then, that these two men are speaking openly and without reservations? This seems doubtful. Machiavelli is asking for favors; he must stick to certain forms. Vettori puts him off with fine words; he too must adopt certain forms. The tone which they adopt to exchange their risqué anecdotes—isn't this, more or less, conventional? In the letter of 10 December 1513 for example, there is no doubt a more or less great dose of theatricality and the need to overstress the contrasts. Literary conventions also come into play: the image of the man of letters dialoguing with the Ancients was at the time a literary commonplace, illustrated notably by Petrarch, Boccaccio, and Alberti (Christian Bec). To a certain extent, difficult to determine, each of the two interlocutors is playing a role. Vettori is evasive, Machiavelli hardly opens up, or not at all.*

With Vettori, as with his other correspondents, Machiavelli is not forthcoming on one capital point: the meaning or the inspiration of his political works. During this period, he is writing or finishing his two major works. Of the Discourses *he says nothing, and of the* Prince

*he says little, says nothing to clarify it and speaks of it to have access
to the Medici. Machiavelli the political writer is a secretive man.*

*In 1517, as we have seen, Machiavelli is an unknown figure out-
side the little Florentine circles. It is therefore not surprising that he
should be the one to initiate the correspondence with the most famous
of the humanists. Unfortunately, the letter accompanying his dispatch-
ing of the* Prince *[to Erasmus] has not been found. This chapter opens,
then, with the letter wherein Erasmus tells More about the manuscript
he has received from Florence, and his reactions. We then provide the
annotations he has written in the margins of the* Prince. *There follows
a long letter wherein Erasmus informs Machiavelli of his reservations,
his grievances, and much more.*

I.
ERASMUS TO MORE
Louvain, 10 August 1517

Erasmus to his dear More, hail!

I am as ever without news from you, dear, gentle More. Has one
of your letters fallen into the water? Have you forgotten the art of
writing anything other than notes or dispatches?

Here is some news from Italy. I received from there a short time
ago a manuscript which left me speechless. I'm sending it on to you,
having had a copy made. I'm not sure whether this piece of writing
calls for the laughter of Democritus or the tears of Heraclitus. One
excuse is that he is a Florentine. His name is Niccolò Machiavelli, and
he had it brought to me with an abundance of compliments. Is he making fun of us? Has he lost his mind? Has he just come out of hell? He
urges the Prince on to war and tyranny. In your *Utopia* you warned
against bad counselors, I did the same in my *Institutio principis christiani*. Here is the bad counselor par excellence, and who takes pride
in being so, at least if I restrict myself to the surface and to what I have
understood. I'm not quite sure what lies behind this. Apparently the
only work of mine he knows is the *Moria*, and he gets it wrong, or
pretends to get it wrong. If I read him correctly, he compliments me
hintingly for my impiety.

The height of his deceitfulness is that this Florentine writes in Italian! I have called upon this friend of mine from Siena, but in spite of his help I have a hard time understanding at times, particularly the tone. This man can write, and he is devious. He has sharp formulations and rounded opinions, he can be dry and murky at the same time. Sometimes I have the impression that he is playing, but not in our manner. I'm not quite sure he isn't saying more than he thinks: perhaps to force the ear of the young Medici to whom the book is dedicated? To shock deliberately and make a reputation for himself? Perhaps the unhappy fate of Italy has made him ill? Or, on the contrary, is he saying less than he thinks? I suspect a terrible irony here. In short my feeling is that this Machiavelli has dipped his pen in poison, and that his soul is as pure as the public latrines.

I should add that our man boasts of having a long experience in political matters as Secretary of the second Chancery at the time of the Republic. Don't ask me whether this post had the slightest importance, I have no idea. I could have met this Machiavelli at work when I went through Florence in November 1506, but heaven spared me. I saw virtually no one. I have hardly any memories of that visit: the *David* by Master Michel Angelo, who had rather the size of Goliath; a murky, muddled government, with families or clans behind it, no doubt. The only thing I caught on to is that politics in Florence is like good taste in England or disputations in the Sorbonne: whoever is not of the country must give up trying to understand. To come back to our character, he fell with the Republic, the Medici threw him out. And here he is trying to recover his job with the new masters and knocking shamelessly at their door, bearing gifts of incense and poison.

Would you please ask the secretary of the Venetian embassy to make a translation and to send me a copy? If you have the time, tell me what you think. You are now a man of experience, make it profitable to your friends! You will find annotations which I have written in the margins, tell me also what you think. Now I must answer him, and I hesitate as to the manner. I am thinking, finally, of sending him a little lecture on the plagues of Egypt, which he has no trouble finding good or necessary, I mean tyranny and war.

What a burden, this undeserved reputation which makes me

receive epistles from everywhere, and even darkness from below. Every day I agree more and more with Epicurus's motto: "Live in obscurity." Excellent More, do not forget me. And you, be well.

II.
ERASMUS'S ANNOTATIONS
IN THE MARGINS OF THE PRINCE

The manuscript of the Prince annotated by Erasmus is unfortunately in bad condition. A number of annotations contain so many illegible passages, or almost illegible, that we thought it wise to give up trying to reproduce them here. We have also omitted the short marginal notes wherein Erasmus generally expresses his indignation or his perplexity. Here are a few examples:

– *Ch. V.*   *On the art of keeping a conquered republic:* What a labyrinth! Where is he leading us?

– *Ch. VII.*   *On Cesare Borgia.* It is madness to praise this ignominious man!

– *Ch. XIX.* *On the Roman emperors:* I can't make heads or tails of this. This madman makes your head spin.

The annotations which have been kept are preceded by the text commented by Erasmus. It is sometimes difficult to know where the commented passage begins and where it ends. We have done our best.

[1] *THE PRINCE,* III, [On the art of keeping or holding a new conquest. In the following passage, Machiavelli takes the case of conquered States which are of the same "province" and of the same tongue as the conquering state]:

[In this case] it is very easy to hold them, especially when they are not accustomed to live free; and to possess them securely, it suffices to have snuffed out the lineage of the prince who reigned previously. For since, for the rest, the former conditions are maintained, and since there is no difference in the customs, people live in peace. This was the case, as it may be seen, with Burgundy, Brittany, Gascogne and Normandy, which remained so long with France. And although there may be some disparity of language, nevertheless their customs are similar and they can easily bear with one another. And those who make such conquests, if they want to hold them, must take care of two things: the first, that the blood of their ancient prince be extinguished; the other, to alter neither their laws nor their taxes. And so, within a very short time, they form one and the same body with their ancient principality.

ERASMUS'S ANNOTATION: What a bandit! Is he speaking in general? Is he baiting the hook for the Medici? Italy offers a thousand possible victims. And keeping them is an easy thing provided you first apply this so simple rule: bleed the entire lineage of the Prince. This Machiavelli is so proud of his maxim that he repeats it, and on a quiet tone. Tell me, you bloodthirsty creature, why you don't look at this more closely. How far must the killing go? The sons, the grandsons surely, the brothers, the nephews and grandnephews no doubt, all the other relatives, I suppose? Take heed not to stop too soon, for fear that an avenger might rise from the ashes [Vergil]! And what must be the manner? Discreetly, no doubt, with the dagger, the rope, poison, what else? What great political tactics: crimes long meditated, and systematically executed! But your criminal Prince will sow hatred among all the faithful followers of the former Prince (must they all be killed?) and he will open the way to criminal ambitions; he who assassinates through ambition will raise up other ambitious people who assassinate in turn. Tyrants, say you, have a short vision and a short existence. What have the kings of France to do with this point? I don't know that they have ever applied this maxim. Who are you trying to fool? The kings of France choose their wives for political reasons. I'm thinking of the daughters of Brittany,[3] they haven't reached the point of killing all the offspring.

---

3   Anne of Brittany was first married to Charles VIII, then to Louis XII; her daughter Claude was married to Charles of Angoulême, the future Francis I. We might add that the maxim commented with indignation by Erasmus is among those which contributed most to Machiavelli's sinister reputation and to the idea of "Machiavellianism."

[2] *THE PRINCE*, III [On the desire for conquest in general]:

It is a truly very natural and ordinary thing to want to acquire; and always, when men do it who can, they will be praised, or they will not be blamed; but when they cannot and want to do it anyway, here lay the error and the blame.

ERASMUS'S ANNOTATION: Conquest is natural! Why don't you just say that men are made to devour and reduce one another to slavery! Any conquest is good provided one has the means for it! Why don't you write an encomium on the Vandals, the Huns or the Turks? And do you think that everything can be forecasted? Mars is an insensate and extravagant god, only a fool relies on him. He is also a furious, barbarous, destructive god. But then what does the suffering of peoples mean to you?

[3] *THE PRINCE*, XII [On good laws and good weapons]:

The principal foundations that every State must have, the old like the new and the mixed, are good laws and good arms; and since there can be no good laws where there are not good arms, and where there are good arms it must follow that there are good laws, I shall leave aside any discourse on laws and I shall speak of arms.

ANNOTATION: He is joking, I think, or he is railing. Good arms make good laws indeed! The most cruel tyrant, armed as he should be, can boast of having good laws. Nero no doubt was a great legislator, or Agathocles or Septimus Severus! Where does all this twaddle lead to [Horace]? Arms are never more than evil means, which must be used with restraint and only when necessity wills it. Good laws in fact allow one to reduce the portion of necessity.

[4] *THE PRINCE*, XV [On the scope of the work]:

It now remains to see what must be the Prince's modes of government toward his subjects or his friends. And because I know that many have written on this subject, I fear, in writing myself, I shall be held presumptuous, all the more so as I am departing, in disputing this matter, from the orders of the others. But since my intention is to write something useful for whoever understands it, it has seemed to me more convenient to go directly to the effectual truth of the thing than to the imagination of it. And many have imagined republics and principalities which were never known or seen to exist in truth as such. For there is such a distance between the way we live and the way we should live that whoever leaves what we do for what we should do learns his ruin rather than his preservation. For a man who wants to profess to be a good man in all regards must necessarily go to ruin, being among so many others who are not good. Thus it is necessary for a prince, if he wants to uphold himself, to learn to be able not to be good, and to use this and not use it, according to necessity.

ANNOTATION: If I understand correctly, this discourse is addressed to those who can understand it. What is there to understand that might be said in a whisper? The author says horrendous things in a loud voice; what is he saying in a whisper? What sort of game is he playing?

Does he want to throw overboard all the Ancients and Moderns [Christians] who have reflected on political matters? Have they never said anything about "the effective truth of the thing"? Was there nothing worthwhile before Doctor Machiavelli? Does he want to unmake and remake everything according to his idea? Why does he skim over everything without ever quoting anybody? What is he aiming for exactly? No doubt he is thinking of the wise Plato and his Republic of wise men. And that entire wise lineage of thinkers who have urged the Prince to be wise. Mere fantasies! To the dustbin! As if a model were without value because it remains a model. As if Princes were to be pushed down their incline rather than pulled upwards; as if what should be were foreign to what is. What should be is to speak in a spirit of truth; do you ignore that, O teller of effective truths!

[5] *THE PRINCE*, XVII [On men in general]

For one can say this in general about men: they are ungrateful, fickle, pretenders and dissemblers, cowards in the face of perils, greedy for gain. So long as you do them good, they are all yours [. . .] but when need befalls you, they revolt.

ANNOTATION: This beast has learned from Circe the art of changing men into swine. And he is teaching the Prince of swine the art of holding them. Now there's a claim to fame! Men are crooked, you say, and elsewhere you say they are gullible. How do you resolve this contradiction? If men are gullible, it's because they naturally trust their own kind. What becomes of this characteristic if all men are evil, simulating and dissimulating?

[6] *THE PRINCE*, XVIII [On the art of governing and on making good use of the beast]

Thus, you must know that there are two ways of fighting: one through laws, the other by force. The first is particular to men, the second to beasts. But since, often, the first does not suffice, one must resort to the second. Therefore it is necessary for a prince to know how to make good use of the beast and of the man. This point was taught covertly to princes by the ancient authors, who wrote how Achilles and many other ancient princes were given over to be educated by the Centaur Chiron, in order to become his disciples. Having a teacher who is half-man, half-beast, then, means nothing other than that a prince must know how to make use of both natures; and one without the other cannot endure. Since, therefore, a prince must of necessity know how to make use of the beast, he must choose the fox and the lion, for the lion cannot defend himself from snares and the fox cannot defend himself against wolves. One must therefore be a fox to recognize snares, and a lion to frighten the wolves. Those who stay simply with the lion do not understand this.

ANNOTATION: If the Prince is both lion and fox, what becomes of his subjects? Asses held by the collar? Oxen destined to the slaughter? Christ expressed his preference for animals who represent the contrary of cunning and brutality. Doesn't he call himself the *lamb of God,* doesn't he call the *lambs* to himself?

This Machiavelli will stop at nothing. As to the Chiron of the fable, he is telling tales. What an idea the poets would have had to choose the most benevolent of Centaurs, the most just (said Homer) to teach one to play the beast!

I see also that laws are here opposed to force whereas a while ago they were being confused with weapons. And I see that the chapter's title says one thing ["How princes must keep their faith"] and the content of the chapter says the opposite. Has Sir Fox lost his compass or is he still using cunning?

[7] *THE PRINCE*, XXI [On inside matters]:

A prince must also show himself to be a lover of the virtues by giving recognition to virtuous men and by honoring those who excel in an art. And then he must convince his citizens that they can peacefully exercise their trade, in commerce, in agriculture, in every other pursuit of men; so that one person does not fear to adorn his property for fear of confiscation, and another to open up a trade for fear of taxation. But he must prepare rewards for whoever wishes to do such things and for whoever thinks, in whatever manner, of giving more grandeur to his city or to his State.

ANNOTATION: Now you're singing out of tune, Machiavelli, here's a passage that makes sense. But what is supposed to be the Prince's first concern, which is to watch over inside matters for the prosperity of the people, comes very late and isn't consistent with the rest. A few drops of wisdom in an ocean of follies, are you trying to pull the wool over our eyes?

III.
ERASMUS TO MACHIAVELLI
Louvain, 19 August 1517

Erasmus of Rotterdam to Sir Nicholas Machiavelli, hail!

[1] I did receive, Signor Machiavelli, your praise of the folly of Princes. I would willingly congratulate you if I were sure it should be taken the right way, that is, as the precise opposite of what you say explicitly. But I have some difficulty in grasping your tone. Why didn't you write in Latin? Try as I may to summon up what I know of Italian and to seek the help of friends better equipped than I, I am unable to follow you in all your labyrinthine paths. Are you a sage who plays the fool in order to denounce the tyrants, or a fool who prides himself in being wise in order to cheer them on in their work?

Shall I confess this? I'm afraid the polluted air of Italy has gone to your head. In any case, whatever your intentions may be, if I judge by the results, it is the lions, the foxes, and all the birds of prey on earth and in heaven who have reason to applaud.

I'll skip over a thousand things wherein you show a brilliant talent for muddying the waters: your self-confidence in uttering abominations, and your assurance in reversing your opinions; your way of talking or double-talking about Scripture; this taste for sophistry which leaves one wondering whether you're joking or not; and this firmness in conducting tortuous demonstrations which lose your reader completely. What are you aiming at? Intimidating the half-wits? Getting the Prince's ear? Saying more between the lines, or saying more than you know? I must admit I admire the care you take in retracting your statements and in twisting words. This Prince of yours who must both make the people fear him and lean on its friendship—some magician! This Machiavelli who teaches the Prince to be suspicious of everything and then asks for his confidence—what an artist! And how am I to interpret this *virtù* which sometimes walks straight and more often drags itself in the mud? And this *fortuna* of such diverse fortunes? Are you trying to get the better of us, Signor Machiavelli, or are you getting the better of yourself, with your doctoral airs so full of authority? Or might it be that under the mask you want to play games? I have nothing against this, provided it be for good reasons. I fail to see any, and frankly I see nothing gay or pleasant in your treatise. Are you perhaps having a hard time putting your ideas in order?

Enough of this. I haven't time to go further. Let me simply concentrate on what is apparently at the heart of your most scholarly treatise: the judicious advice given by the perverse counselor par excellence.

[2] Surely you are aware, Signor Florentine, that princes who forget their princely duties are among the world's calamities. What do we not owe them? They pile misfortune after misfortune upon the human condition. Corrupt princes corrupt their people, warring princes take glory in the carnages they inflict, grasping princes rob their subjects. What are these little fleecings, these crimes that occur

in the ordinary course of things, compared to the highway robberies perpetuated by so many States and—height of misfortune—by so many Christian states?

Princes are men, as you and I are, Signor Courtesan, only their condition is not ours. They live in luxury, with flatterers at their feet, entirely free to do as they please. They live surrounded with pitfalls, with contrary passions, in an avalanche of dangers; finally, they live exposed to the gaze of all while setting the tone. It is a well-known fact that princely vices spread as quickly as the Neapolitan curse [syphilis]. So many temptations, so many risks! Princes must ceaselessly be on guard, first of all against themselves, and their advisers must ever be watchful. And you, what do you do, Signor Adviser? You encourage them where you should hold them, restrain them, disarm their passions, strengthen their conscience. If I have understood correctly, this whole very shrewd treatise is an exhortation to the Prince to behave as a tyrant. And these few precautions you take don't make a difference. It seems the word *tyrant* never flows from your pen. In a writer as clever as you that cannot be unintentional. You glorify the methods of tyranny without calling them by name. As far as you are concerned these are merely the necessary and ultimately ordinary tools of the art of governing states. Whoever opposes the King to the Tyrant falls no doubt into these fantasies which according to you lead a Prince to ruin. It follows that in the course of the centuries great thinkers have been very blind. This whole procession of philosophers, led by the illustrious Plato, who call on those who govern to conduct themselves as good men, to be wary of themselves, to serve the public interest and not particular interests, all these highly renowned figures, we used to take them for wise men. What madness! These are dreamers, makers of illusions, fantasizers. Thanks be to Thee, divine Machiavelli, you have awakened us from our slumber; you have given us back our sight. For behold! Now the truth has been revealed: the Prince who behaves as he should works only for his own power; and to do this he uses all the means imposed by Necessity. What a magnificent discovery! You find lead and you see gold. All the tyrants of yesterday and today will be beholden to you. You bring them honor, what a pity if it doesn't get you some position or other!

While waiting, allow me to remind you of a few of these old things that you dismiss with a stroke of the pen. What, in truth, does it mean to win or extend power for oneself? It means to conduct oneself as a pillager, not as a Prince. Or, to speak your language, it is to behave as a beast, with the arms of the lion and those of the fox. Your Prince has no other concern for his people, I mean the sheep, than those needed to avoid their becoming enraged. How glorious it must be to give orders to sheep, or asses, or oxen! And what even greater glory it must be to massacre the surrounding cattle or to pen them in. But it is the grandeur of kings to rule over free men; it is worthy of a tyrant to bind and deceive within, and to enslave without. To keep the peace, to establish concord with justice, that is worthy of a true King. In short your Prince is not only the enemy of other peoples, he is the enemy of his very own. That is a good definition of the tyrant. I am surprised that it has escaped your sagacious wisdom.

I am aware, Signor Florentine, that I am not doing justice to this ingenious science of political things which you have applied yourself to so persistently. Oh, you aren't advocating a vulgar tyranny; no, your good counsel is addressed to a Prince worthy of becoming a tyrant of great merit. It sounds just about like this: never go half way in doing evil; lie like a devil, hardily, constantly; rely on no one but yourself, on your arms, your creatures; think constantly of war and its massacres as the most natural thing in the world; be liberal with the goods of those who cannot harm you; take the vulgar man for what he is, inclined to let himself be intimidated and tricked provided his own goods are spared; in short, never forget that to make a good use of the beast, what counts are the claws, flair, and cunning. Here lies the effective truth of power.

These are fine and good recipes for infamy. Perhaps I've forgotten some on the way, don't hold it against me. And you will excuse me for not arguing with you on this terrain. My poor science couldn't possibly compete with yours. "Power," as Plutarch said, "gives wings to the vices." You have added a method; let me compliment you.

[3] Your way of making use of ancient and modern history is surely in keeping with your method. You have everything ass backwards, or al-

most. Of course you do things with the virtuosity of Master Fox: there are so many examples, and they tumble down so fast and look so much like a scholastic theorem that your reader is outflanked, ready to capitulate and to believe what you are saying. But if I would rather not discuss detail, I do know enough about history to see that you treat her the way you recommend fortune should be treated.

What do the ancient and modern annals say, if one knows how to read them? They say that good Princes are rare, or extremely rare. Oh, to be sure there is no lack of heroes enshrined by the approval of the centuries. And the magnificent titles bequeathed by history are legion: so many *divine emperors, invincible conquerors, illustrious kings, most serene princes,* and even among all these Superb Ones, a *Catholic king.*[4] And yet how many are there who deserve to escape the defaming epithet flung by Achilles to the face of Agamemnon: "king devourer of people!" [*Iliad* I, 231]. But what do you care, Signor Machiavelli, you find good examples in abundance and you have little trouble finding them. These are generally furious rascals of the type you enjoy, and you color them in your own manner. What delightful company! These tyrants of Greece and Sicily about whom you find ways of saying likeable things; all these Roman emperors whose cruelties don't make you shudder; your Italians of today, cloak and dagger adventurers who slit one another's throats well or badly according to whether they strike first or too late. I am not forgetting those you present as the models par excellence, those you call the *new princes.* I'm not quite sure what you mean by that, or whether the New Prince is a founder or a usurper or a conqueror or merely bestial to your taste. But no matter, these grand examples speak for themselves: Cesare Borgia, expert in vile things; Ferdinand of Aragon, the most crooked of the crooked; Septimus Severus, who knew how to play the beast so well. If we judge the grandeur of men by the ills which they inflicted on their fellow humans, your "great men" have well deserved the esteem in which you hold them.

[4] An allusion to Ferdinand of Aragon, *Catholic king,* whom Machiavelli presents as one of the models of the *new prince,* and whose lies and betrayals appear to Erasmus as uncatholic as possible.

Let me pause for a moment on this Cesare Borgia to whom you give so much of your attention. Of course there is much in him for your taste (didn't he kill his brother, pervert his word of honor, steep Romagna in bloodshed?). But his duplicity was not such that Fame should fail to include it as part of his record. I was in Italy shortly after his demise, and I know the reputation he left behind. I fear that all of your talent combined might not be enough to travesty this villain into a hero. And how did he finish if not miserably? Everything he constructed with iron, poison, and deceit collapsed like a house of cards at the death of his father Alexander [Pope Alexander VI Borgia]. You know all these things intimately. Why choose such an example, which does not do justice to your method? And what should we say of Alexander, whose art of deception you praise so highly? How much time was needed for this unworthy Pontiff to be recognized as such? The word of liars devalues like bad money. You should remember that; if you are so enamored of princes who have no word of honor, what is yours worth?

[4] Let me revert to a point on which you outdo yourself in the role of Prince's fool . . . I mean war. The art of governing, you say, is first of all the art of waging war. The primary virtue of the Prince is the science of weapons, and his primary concern must be putting it into practice. What is more natural than the desire for conquest? See Achilles, Alexander, Caesar, and the rest. Quickly, to horse, put on your helmet, wield your sword, be ready to lead a mass of men to the crippling, maiming, beheading, crushing of the nameless enemy facing you! Ah, Signor, you promoter of crime, in what filthy swamp have you gone to draw your water rather than drinking it at the living source? I can see only one possible excuse, . . . you don't know what you're saying.

War is gentle to those who do not know, to the ignorant, the blind, the sleep-walkers, those who don't want to know. In which category do you place yourself? Your subtle treatise is a call to arms and—have I read correctly?—I've not read a single paragraph, a single line, a single word on the *effective truth* of war. What the life of men becomes when this plague begins to spread—is that unworthy of your interest?

Is it because its victims are preferentially the poor folk, the humble, the silent, in short, those who don't clutter up the historians' pages? We know what tender necks they offer the knife of the cutthroats. Are you unaware that these are beings of flesh and blood like you and me? Or are your eyes hopelessly dry?

For myself, I have never ceased, nor will I cease, to plead for peace and concord, among Christians and beyond. Do me the favor of rereading the *Praise of Folly* or of reading *Dulce bellum inexpertis*, which you will find in the book of *Adages*, or the *Querela pacis*, which I wrote for the use of King Francis I and of my prince Charles of Burgundy.[5] In these works subtlety seemed to me quite pointless: I collected all my energies in order to show the afflictions without number which war brings. Our princes easily avert their eyes from this, especially when they become heated, and they heat up pretty quickly, especially when they are badly advised. Shall I admit this? Often, while writing these pages, my heart failed me and I had to whip myself to describe so many horrors. Not merely the horrors of battle, but all those companion horrors: crops destroyed, cities laid waste, virgins and mothers thrown to wild beasts, so many sufferings, dirges, miseries. And in their wake moral confusion, famine, banditry, impiousness, and that spirit of revenge which sows anew the germs of death. Hell and its Furies could not do better. War lets loose the beast. Is that why you love it so much, Signor Machiavelli? But I'm saying too little: man at war is worse than the beast.

What better and more shameful example can I give than that provided by our time! Was ever war fought by the pagans with as much constancy and more cruelty than what the Christians do? What tempests have wars not unleashed in recent years? How many treaties torn up after hardly being signed? What a succession of ravages? My God, when will it end? Today I see a tentative and timid peace bringing a haughty and repulsive war to heel. What man of honor would not be at her side? Oh may this abominable age come to an end: we have

---

[5] "War is gentle to those who have not waged it," 1515; "The Complaint of Peace," 1517 (a little work often reprinted, which remains one of Erasmus's most celebrated works). Charles of Burgundy is the future Charles V.

been constantly at war, nation against nation, city against city, Prince against Prince, people against people; and also—something even pagans consider impious—ally against ally, parent against parent, brother against brother. And how lightly and ferociously they do it! Has there ever been worse than this banditry we call soldiers? And what country has been more ravaged than yours, Signor Machiavelli? I see that you have been lamenting the present state of Italy. But I also see that you kindle the warlike madness of the princes. In short, you deplore some of the effects and you continue to cherish the causes.

These causes you transform cosmetically into good reasons. Let me first revert to this one, which I find extravagant: that the desire for conquest is something very natural and very ordinary. What a fine reason! An ordinary bloke takes someone else's goods by force, he's a crook; a Prince raises an army to take other people's cities, the thing is natural. That proud pirate had it right, whom Augustine speaks of: when Alexander the Great asked him: "What right have you to infest the seas?" he answered, "as much as you have to infest the universe. But because I do it with a measly ship, they call me brigand; you do it with a big fleet, they call you Emperor."[6] Why don't you call things by their name, and this thirst for conquest a low passion? Fable and history, and you in their wake, incense the great conquerors. But the prestige of the name is deceptive, and all these illustrious conquerors, Achilles, Xerxes, Cyrus, Alexander, were nothing but madmen, if you believe Seneca. Must I remind you of some of their acts of madness? The divine Achilles draws his sword against his king, and the great Alexander against his best friends; the illustrious Xerxes orders the sea to be whipped with rods; Alexander the Great has himself saluted as a son of Zeus and complains that this world is too small for his victories. One wishes that, rather than stir themselves up and rave, they had concentrated on administering their cities properly! They would not have tormented foreign territories with their arms, they would not have died so soon, and they would have earned a more solid glory. So, Signor Adviser, might I suggest you take your cue from Cineas, the wise counselor of that fool Pyrrhus? Seeing the latter wholly fixated

---

[6]   The anecdote is recorded in *The City of God*, IV, 4.

on his conquests and ready to set foot in Italy, he said to him: "the Romans are great men of war; if the gods allow us to win, what good will this victory do us?—The answer is obvious, Cineas, we'll take Italy immediately.—And once we've conquered Italy, what shall we do?—Sicily will be ours.—Will that be the end?—Not at all. We'll cross into Africa.—And then?—Then all of Greece will be in our hands.—But in the end, Sire, what shall we do?—You make me laugh, Cineas, we'll take it easy and we'll live happily." Then Cineas replied: "And what prevents us, Sire, from resting right now and eating well? Ultimately we'll gain nothing by suffering and making others suffer so many ills and travails?"[7]

Our modern conquerors—are they any wiser? Look at the kings of France: every Spring, or every Autumn, they cross the Alps to wage war in Italy. They win, they lose, they go back, they come back. And the blood flows, dangers threaten, expenses pile up. The kingdom of France is the most flourishing on earth, and would be even more so if it had not given in to the irrational passion of conquest. You spend much of your time focusing on the mistakes of Louis XII, but you say nothing about the first mistake of all, from which all the others flow. If only Louis, twelfth of that name, and before him Charles VIII and after him Francis I, had left Italy to the Italians! On this subject, and on many others, see what my friend Thomas More says in his wise and foolish *Utopia*. There you will hear foolish Cineases, or perhaps foolish Machiavellis advise the king of France to follow the path of Pyrrhus. Lend an ear, here is a great and beautiful undertaking: first take Milan and take back Naples, then annex all of Italy, then subjugate Flanders, then take Brabant, Burgundy soon afterwards and whatever must follow. What do you think of that Signor Machiavelli? Do you approve of these natural desires, as you might call them, or might you by some miracle be attentive to what the narrator says *in fine*: the good counsel would be to take in the sails and sail back to port.[8]

---

[7] Erasmus is here summarizing in his own way the famous dialogue reported or invented by Plutarch (*Life of Pyrrhus*, XXX). Plutarch adds: "These last words offended Pyrrhus rather than make him change his mind."

[8] Erasmus is quoting freely from a passage of Book I of *Utopia*.

I come now to this other reason which runs through your entire treatise, concerning war and the rest: I mean necessity. Princes are of the opinion, and they complain about it freely, that they are drawn into war in spite of themselves. But, except for certain cases which I set aside, I see in this mere posturing. Or, if you prefer, the exercise of this art which you know so well, the art of deceiving others and of deceiving oneself. Behind this, ordinary passions are at work, not to mention incredible rubbish. There is of necessity the passion of satisfying one's ambitions, one's self-interest, one's anger. And if real necessities are produced by the course of war, what necessity was there in entering into these necessities?

Signor Machiavelli, let go the biases that blur your vision and consider the wars of these recent years. What do you see? Irascible old men [King Louis XII, Pope Julius II], who first enter into an alliance, then wage a relentless war against each other, one having provoked the fury of the other by calling him a drunkard (something no one was unaware of in Rome). The next phase brings a trio of inexperienced young men [Francis I, Henry VIII, Charles of Burgundy] who, fired up by bad examples, hurl themselves against each other, more out of boldness than ill-will; meanwhile an experienced prince [Ferdinand of Aragon] wraps himself in piety and justice to betray everybody; and the Vicar of the Kingdom of Heaven [Jules II] takes up his arms relentlessly for the sake of earthly principalities. Each of them, no doubt, has rights to put forward: dust-ridden titles, treatises violated a thousand times, bogus offenses. How insubstantial these august foreheads, wearing their crown or their tiara! How can one fail to be astonished? Or fail to be astonished in seeing people so little astonished? Or fail to be astonished that you aren't astonished, Signor the great politico? What extraordinary blindness!

Don't get me wrong, I'm not saying that we must avoid taking up arms always and everywhere, I'm saying that necessity is, most of the time, one of the masks assumed by human madness. I'm setting aside the cases where, unfortunately, one must allow for real necessity: cases where the failure of all attempts to save peacefully what must be saved makes war inevitable. I'm speaking of cases where the invading barbarian leaves you no other choice but to defend yourself, cases where

our brothers are at the mercy of a cruel enemy or are disgracefully enslaved. But even then it is with reluctance that a good prince sends his
armies into battle, and not with a wicked smile, Signor warmonger.

[5] Let me provide another reason, ultimately the most important,
for rejecting yours. It surpasses all the others: war is a scandal in a
Christian country: it offends, it defiles, it profanes everything that
Christ has taught us. Do the Gospels leave you with a deaf ear, Signor
Machiavelli? I see you prostrate before the idol of power, hardly a position to incline you to listen to the sacred Word. In your works, Christ
never appears. I understand that: he is the Prince of peace and concord;
everything he said, everything he did condemns your writings. Shake
the Gospel every which way, you will make nothing come out that
does not breathe peace, has not the sound of friendship, has not the
taste of charity. Understand what Christ left to his friends on the eve
of his death. He left them neither horses nor guards nor the right to
command. What did he leave them? He left them peace. And what did
the Apostles teach after him if not peace, gentleness, love—always!

You will tell me no doubt that it suffices to look at the present
world to convince oneself that Christ is betrayed every day by his own.
On that point I've already granted you much, and will grant you even
more: that our Christian world is an affront to Christianity; that
monks, theologians, bishops are very much involved; that Pontiffs conduct themselves in an impious fashion; that there was even one [Jules
II] who took himself for Caesar. That one, a man fit for your taste, I
saw him march in as a conqueror in Bologna in 1506, proud as a
Roman emperor, whereas his brow should have been covered with
shame. But, in the face of so many betrayals, what must we do? What
must we do if not rise up against it, and with our whole soul? And
what are you doing, learned Machiavelli? You are determined to make
a virtue of treason. The ills of our times are due to our princes not
conducting themselves as Christians. What are you proposing? Inciting
them to do worse.

I suspect that you consider Christian maxims as illusions. Only
weapons count; the rest is smoke. I take up the strange chapter where
you speak of the founders [VI]. I'll skip over your way of mixing fable,

history, and Scripture, in order to come to one of those definitive propositions where one sees the master's hand. This admirable proposition, let me retranscribe it so as not to get it wrong: "It follows from this that all armed prophets were victorious and all unarmed ones were ruined." Are you taking us for fools, Signor Machiavelli? What do you make of the prophet who overcame the world? How did the Apostles spread his word? How did his disciples conquer an Empire which had until then resisted all the weapons of kings? With iron and fire? With a sword in their hands? Or was it by a wholly spiritual fire about which you seem to know nothing? Revise your judgment; it is the martyr who defeated the soldier. And yet, against this humble and gentle word, the world had reacted with all the weapons you can dream of: tribunals, legions, governors, confiscations, proscriptions, exiles, dungeons, racks, rods, axes, crosses, stakes, wild beasts, executions. I haven't even mentioned the philosophers, the sophists, the orators, the magi. What defenses! They crumbled in the face of the unarmed truth of the Gospel. Who today offers sacrifice to the gods of the pagans? Who knows Zoroaster? Who bothers with Pythagoras's riddles? This metamorphosis of the world, with what weapons was it wrought, O most profound Machiavelli?

Of course, as I've said, the primitive Church puts the present one to shame. The salt has lost its savor, the tares have grown, profane things have regained the upper hand. All the more reason to take up the fight again, I mean the fight of the unarmed, which converts men's hearts. And who knows? Perhaps even yours, my senseless Signor.

[6] Among the first in need of conversion, naturally, are the princes. And princes are troublesome people; you must know how to take them in order to take them back. Nathan made use of a trick to lead David to repentance; Aristotle advised his dear Callisthenes to weigh his words in Alexander's presence. See also the *Utopia*, where Thomas More suggests following an oblique way [*ductus obliquus*] so as not to clash with the sovereign.[9] For myself, I keep my distances, I

---

[9]   The famous episode where Nathan speaks in parable form to make David become conscious of his fault and repent is recounted in II Samuel XII,

abstain from favors which are just so many hindrances; and I do not flatter, but I sing praises to a good end. You see the difference, Signor Courtesan, it's a matter of offering the Prince in the guise of praise the model of the good King. There are compliments which stroke the beast; there are others that bridle her.

I shall not speak here of the Prince's education in hereditary monarchies: because this letter is already too long; because it would be more reasonable to choose them rather than rely on the vagaries of birth; because princely heirs never have more than one preceptor who is really doing his job, I mean the horse who throws the Prince as well as the plebeian head over arse; finally because I've dealt with this question in my *Institutio principis christiani*, which I include with this letter as a matter of scruple. You will find there not much science for your taste, but good principles. Here are a few to whet your appetite.

History is not a good school for the Prince; it is often badly established, badly understood, badly taught. So many historians are nothing but fools who glorify other fools who serve as foolish examples to foolish readers!

The true glory of the Prince lies within his State, in these business dealings which sad counselors never mention, or almost never, and the purpose of which is the well-being of the people. How many sad princes lose their fortune waging sad wars, blind to the profits that would accrue from investing in their State.

The Prince can never lie with impunity. Cheating works for a time only, yesterday's cheated learn fast to cheat in return. Lying engenders lying, suspicion engenders suspicion The vile Prince, like his vile counselor, ends up seeing nothing around him but rascals. Outside his State, he cannot make peace when no one believes in his word. What a great life: no sure minister, no real friend, no firm ally! What a life worthy of envy, so solitary, so filled with fear!

[7] But I'm singing for a deaf man. How could you possibly

1–5. The King had sent Uriah the Hittite to his death because he lusted after his wife Bathsheba. The passage of *Utopia* Erasmus speaks of is in Book I.

understand when you are walking so haughtily in the opposite direction? If I've understood correctly, you are writing not only as a courtesan of the Medici, you take glory in what you are saying. What
glory? Laurels in hell? I remain dumbfounded by so much art, so much
care taken to add to the misfortunes of men. Do you know where
you're going? What do you have in mind? You're playing the beast, I
think. What are you hiding beneath your mask? I don't know, and I'm
sorry for it. I cannot do your work the justice which you deserve. I
shall therefore take my leave of you, but first I want to leave you a
few remarks which will tell you of the pains I have taken in my search
for your claims to glory.

Let me consider once more the content of your teaching. Tell me,
what are you professing so learnedly, if not something every tyrant
has practiced in the course of history without the aid of your treatise?
Princes know only too well how to behave badly; they have but to
look at one another or consider the immediate result only. It follows
that your wise counsels are largely superfluous. Even if I suppose that
those men thirsting for power are in search of good readings, a bad
reading of Aristotle in his chapters on tyranny could suffice [*Politics*,
V, 10–11]. You know the *Politics*, Signor Machiavelli, and you are not
unaware of the rest. So what are you offering? Are you saying anything new? I suspect that your objective is not so much to teach a
method as to give the justification. What are you doing? You adopt a
tone of authority and sinuous ways to say infamous things which are
by no means new; but their very infamousness prevents them from
being admitted, except covertly. Your great art consists in donning the
doctor's bonnet in order to abandon all shame and liberate all scruples.
The Princes are tempted, you give them learned reasons to give in.
Their conscience gets in the way; you weigh in with all your science
to silence it. The big argument goes like this: necessity reigns, and in
the name of necessity it is good to do evil. Am I right, Signor Quibbler?
Is the whole object of your discourse to say merely this: in politics one
owes it to oneself to be evil, and therefore evil is innocent? Is that the
meaning of your enterprise, the reason for your pride: to give evil men
a clear conscience? Think of this. Let me suppose that, to your glory,
new princes begin to proliferate, that a new Prince appears every day.

What a free-for-all of ambitions! What bloody confusion! The whole universe upside down, the rule of the strongest and the most deceitful, war without end. Is that what you want?

Next I consider your manner of writing or teaching. I certainly cannot untangle all its strands, but what I see is that it deals very loosely with history, with texts, with the rules of exposition, with the rules of disputation. I've already spoken of this in passing; let me add a few words on this subject. I am, most eminent Machiavelli, a mere grammarian, bound to his in-folios like a galley-slave to his oar. I exhaust my little strength chasing after manuscripts from place to place. I edit them with a maniacal care, . . . I mean the care of a philologist; I translate some of them with a great application; I try to interpret them with all the discernment I am capable of. Perhaps you are aware that I edited, a short time ago, the text of the *New Testament* (I ruined my eyes establishing the text), accompanied with notations and a revised translation. You also know, perhaps, that this edition had the honor of pleasing our Sovereign Pontiff Leo X, who comes from an illustrious house, as you are not unaware. I can therefore suggest this reading to you for the love of the Medici and for the good of your soul. In short those are my Herculean labors: to sort out, to scrub, to clean, so that everybody might have access to the pure sources. I hope you will understand, then, that among the many trials that your work put me through, there is your way of treating texts and writers. What an offhand manner you have behind that grave bearing of yours! First of all, toward Sacred Scripture. You treat Moses on a par with Theseus, David on a par with Borgia (are you serious?), you attribute their victories to their weapons alone. Do you mean to be blasphemous? Do you believe that he Old Testament is nothing but a repository of stories that you can arrange as you see fit? And how flippant you are toward the ancient philosophers! You don't even condescend to quote them, except Xenophon in passing, and you relegate them to darkness with a stroke of the pen. Any debate on this matter would be pointless no doubt, so let's just drop it. If I understand correctly, any reasonings contrary to yours must be circumvented. Is that one of your war strategies? However, I can clearly see much flippancy and much maneuvering in a doctor who prides himself in telling the "effective truth of the thing." Is that your claim to fame?

I cannot go further. But what I can assure you of, without hesitating one second, is that tyrants deserve the fate to which Seneca consigns them: let them be hanged with the robbers and the pirates! And let's hang with them the perfidious counselors who assist them and flatter them! Don't clutch at your throat, *carissimo* Machiavelli, I'm only half serious. But I feel obliged to warn you to be careful. If your little book brings you the favor of a Prince to your taste, you'll be in trouble. Do you think that a tyrant's creatures are immune from his blows? Be careful, lions who are foxes or foxes who are lions are not a company to relax with, even for serpents. I would advise you for your own good to throw your manuscript to the dogs and to make better use of your talents.

Take care of yourself as best you can.

Chapter 3
Liber Necessitatis

This chapter contains four letters. The first is addressed in September 1517 by an apparently bitter and disenchanted Machiavelli to Francesco Vettori, who has become Florentine ambassador to France.. At the court of Francis I, Francesco Vettori took part in the negotiations concerning Lorenzo de Medici's marriage with a princess of France. These negotiations were laborious. They led, to the great joy of the Medici, to Lorenzo's union with Madeleine de la Tour d'Auvergne, who was related to the House of France (May 1518). In the meantime, Lorenzo had been made Gonfalonier of the armies of the Church, then Duke of Urbino, following the conquest of that duchy shamelessly plotted by the Pope. It is because Lorenzo was made Duke in October 1516 that Roberto Ridolfi could affirm that the dedication of the Prince *was anterior to this date (otherwise Machiavelli would have addressed the young Medici with his new title). The letter is crafted in much the same style as the other familiar letters addressed to Vettori: Machiavelli uses a great freedom of language, even to the point of obscenity. He complains of his fate, but he does not provide the key or keys to his writings.*

We should add that on April 13, 1519, Madeleine de la Tour d'Auvergne gave birth to a girl, Catherine, who was to become Queen of France, but who will, first, soon become an orphan. Her mother died as a result of her delivery of Catherine a fortnight later: illness claimed her father a week later. After Giuliano's death in 1516, fortune once again struck the Medici. In Florence, where Lorenzo's princely manner and authoritarian inclinations were a source of alarm, there was a general sigh of relief. What Machiavelli's feelings were is not known.

The other letters do not call for a lengthy presentation. First comes Machiavelli's rejoinder to Erasmus's indictment. It is written in the language of the Prince, *which differs greatly from that of the familiar correspondence. The themes of the* Prince *can be found here, but also a number of ideas developed in the* Discorsi. *It should be noticed that this letter contains fewer ambiguities or artifices than are found in the great texts. Could this be because Machiavelli is writing to a single*

*addressee? He treats this addressee as an adversary and strives to re-
duce him to silence. It is doubtful that he betrays what he really thinks.*

*Machiavelli's rejoinder is followed by a familiar letter of Erasmus
to More where, among other things, he abandons the "Machiavelli affair" to his keeping. More's response promises a sequel to the* Utopia
specially intended for the author of the Prince.

I.

MACHIAVELLI TO VETTORI
Florence, 12 September 1517

Magnifico oratori florentino Francesco Vettori [To the magnificent
Florentine orator Francesco Vettori]

Magnificent ambassador, dear partner, I hope this letter will reach
you in your new dignities. I haven't received anything from you in
ages. I find myself as on a deserted island here, for people know absolutely nothing. I hear nothing but the malicious gossip of the public
square: will the flood come? Will the Turk cross the sea? Should we
think of a crusade in our time?

I bless this wise fortune which brings you the luck you deserve. I
spew out this unsavoury fortune, which insists on playing me every
possible dirty trick, so much so that I'm at the point of being good for
nothing, either for myself or for others. And I see that in the midst of
so many affairs in which my experience might prove useful, I'm alone
in this fleabag like a bloody prick [*cazzo*].

Perhaps God knows, but surely I don't nor even you, what must
be done to make the Medici decide to hire me, even were they to start
by making me roll a stone. And yet my little work [*The Prince*], if only
it were read, would make them see that in the fifteen years I dedicated
to the affairs of the State, I never gave nor gambled them away. But I
have trained myself not to desire the slightest thing with intensity. May
their will be done.

I sent my treatise to the most illustrious Erasmus of Rotterdam. I
thought him a hardy old man, but he answered me with a deluge of

indignations and pieties. The way this guy looks down his nose at me without even knowing what he's talking about, I'm going to knock his teeth in.

In Florence, on rare days when I go there, the Riccia woman always tells me that I take things the wrong way. From that viewpoint or the other, I hope your stay in the land of France is well furnished with women. You've said it yourself, there is nothing more delectable to think or do than fucking a woman [*il fottere*]. The pleasure taken today will not have to be taken tomorrow. I shall always believe, with all due respect to the Batavian monk [Erasmus], that Boccaccio is right when he says: "*It's* better to do and repent than not to do and repent." Be happy.

II.
MACHIAVELLI TO ERASMUS
Florence, 5 October 1517

To the most illustrious and learned scholar Erasmus of Amsterdam

I send you a million thanks, most illustrious Erasmus, for your magnificent sermon on political matters. For never has one seen peace and gentleness defended with such violence and hot air. And I thank you for your sage nuggets of advice, which are equal to those you give to princes. I bet that sovereigns will put to good use the counsels made for them, as I shall make good use of the counsels meant for me.

Now, you should know that I put into my treatise a long experience of modern things and a sustained reading of ancient ones. And you tell me from the height of those pious readings which you have made a habit of: *non licet* [that is forbidden]. I can only answer that a blind man knows more about colors than glorious Erasmus about public affairs.

[1] For you know nothing about necessity, and what must be done so as not to be a loser. Since this is the point that matters above all

else, I shall say enough as to be understood even by someone deaf. Thus you hold against me what I have to say about one's own arms, and you use your entire eloquence to disarm people. And all will agree that it would be a good and noble thing if everyone followed you; but whoever knows the way of the world, even slightly, will also agree that the rogues will not follow. Therefore whoever listens to you will lay himself open, fully naked, to enemy arms. And the rogues who will not listen to you will have good reason to tell you how grateful they are. Cultivate your great wisdom, Master Erasmus, but know this: in the things that interest us, it is foolish to be wise by oneself.

As to your great opus [*Institutio principis christiani*], I would say the same. I am sure it would be a good thing if you had seen things clearly. But these are fairytales for children. For your way of conceiving the education of the Prince is that it is necessary and sufficient for a good Prince to be a moral Prince. I would agree with you in a nonexistent world, or in a world produced by our imaginations. Whoever is only good and good by himself is headed for ruin. And if your Prince, Charles of Burgundy, listened to you, you could have reason to be worried. But let me reassure you. From what we know of him already, I have no doubt that after having complimented you, he would proceed to serious matters that leave you out of the picture entirely.

Now considering things that are true, I should say that the Prince, and especially the new Prince, or one who is worthy of becoming one, is exposed to constant danger. And if he wants to succeed and defend himself and increase his power, he must use the means that I have said. If facts accuse him, results will excuse him. For one must deceive or risk being deceived, depend on one's own arms or be at the mercy of others, strike first or risk being struck, attack or lay oneself open to peril, conquer or be conquered. Piero Soderini, Gonfalonier of Florence, no doubt governed the way you prefer: for he thought he could extinguish envy and evil with time, kindness and good fortune. And he did so wonderfully that he lost power and honor, as well as his country. The poor half-wit didn't know that time doesn't wait, that fortune changes, and that malice is appeased by no other means than the death of the malicious. Wherever Necessity requires it, audacity becomes wisdom. And whoever fails to recognize this necessity is doomed. If you find this offensive, go back to your pious books.

As to examples, I could give you many others besides those found in my treatise. But I should like it to suffice, to make you see how blind you are, to provide these two general rules, which suffer few exceptions.

The first is that the Prince who wants to assure his security must in no way depend on anyone else. Men's feelings either depend on the Prince or on themselves. And I say that wisdom consists of relying on the feelings that depend on you. Then the most pious Erasmus comes along screaming to high heaven and endangering those who listen to him. For to bank on friendship is to expose oneself; to trust is to make oneself vulnerable. And since you [Erasmus] seem to be ignorant of everything on this matter, allow me to say a few words.

First, it is preferable for a Prince to be feared rather than loved because men love to their liking and fear to the Prince's liking. He who wants to be loved puts himself under the control of the other, while he who has the means to make himself feared bases himself on what is his. For one can never be sure of men's friendship, and one is usually mistaken as to their affection. But you can be sure they fear you when they know you are ready for wisely dispensed cruelties. For men are never foolish whenever their life or their possessions are involved.

I affirm, moreover, that it is better to be on guard than show trust. If I show trust in the other, and he betrays me, I lose. You say that one must show trust, because mistrust engenders mistrust. I say we must be wary because good faith delivers itself into the hands of bad faith. And whoever delivers himself once risks delivering himself entirely. That is why the truth about human actions is that suspicion is wisdom and confidence is foolishness. I should add that your virtue is not worthy of praise, for it is a sin to deceive people as you do. And if you think that granting favors will guarantee you against infidelities, I say that you are still wrong, as an infinity of examples show. I shan't pursue this, so as not to overwhelm you.

Concerning the second general rule I want it to deal once again with the good use of one's own arms. So, the Prince must endeavor to keep his subjects in such a state that that they neither think of harming him nor can. And the remedies are not the same in both cases. The first, as I have said, is to avoid the things that would make you hated or despised by the people, and to act in such a way as to be feared and respected. And to win fear and respect, there is nothing like an extraordinary and memorable action which takes hold of men's spirit and leaves them in awe. That is why, with all due respect to you, I shall never hesitate to cite the actions full of virtue and ferocity of the Duke of Valentinois [Cesare Borgia]. And I shall always cite the example of the time when, after endowing Messer Remiro d'Orca [a cruel and expeditious man] with full power to force Romagna into union and obedience (which was done in a short time), he then, one morning, on the Piazza at Cesena, had him cut in two, with a wooden block and a bloody knife beside him. He thereby purged the spirit of the people and brought the upheavals of Romagna completely to an end. And I say that the peace you love so much was bought at that price. But you want the effect, and you curse the cause.

Consider also how wise it is to proceed hardily, at one stroke, rather than to be in the necessity of ever holding the knife in your hand. When one lets too much time go by, however, the memory of the punishments fades and men embolden themselves to try new things and to speak ill of their Prince. It is therefore necessary to remedy this by renewing terror and fear in men's minds. And as the example of Rome sufficiently shows, this is no less true of republics than of principalities. In so conducting himself the Prince will be dispensing more pity than those who through an excess of pity allow chaos to continue, giving rise to confusion and plunder. I conclude from this that whoever thinks like Erasmus and chooses weakness avoids being reputed cruel but shows the way to cruelties without number.

Now for those who are thinking, or may be thinking in future, of harming the Prince, I do not think it useful to prolong any discussion of this, for it is an entirely necessary thing to put them to death. I can already hear you protesting, Reverend Erasmus, but if the Prince listens to you, or those who head a free government [a Republic], then the time they spend delaying will mean their downfall. This is primarily true during a change of government. Whoever establishes a principate and does not kill Brutus and whoever establishes a free government and does not kill Brutus's sons condemns himself to ruin.[10] For to maintain the State one must be secure against one's enemies. For the same reason, a new Prince will never be assured of his principate so long as those who have been stripped of it still live. I know, gentle Erasmus, that you find this sort of medicine repulsive, and that you want to say good things about goodness at all costs, and bad things about badness. But to ignore necessities is to think badly, and thinking badly is not a way of acting well.

[2] At present I want to consider the things that make you so war-like, which are those of war. I will tell you what I know about war, having spent fifteen years serving my country [Florence] in the midst of foreign inundations. I have reflected ceaselessly on these things in past and present times: all of this with much fatigue, which is something you have taken pains to avoid.

To begin with, you should learn that in this world two contrary humors are to be found: the desire to conquer and the desire to not be conquered. From this arise the two reasons to wage war and to expand, one to extend one's domination, the other to avoid the domination of others. If a city doesn't threaten the others, she is the one who will be threatened, and being threatened she will feel the need and the necessity of conquering. This is all the more true because human affairs being in motion, they must either go up or come down. It follows that necessity is stronger than all your good reasons, and that a city can maintain itself only if it expands, and it can maintain itself by expanding only if it is properly equipped for conquest.

As an example I shall cite the highest and the most glorious of

[10] Lucius Junius Brutus (not to be confused with Marcus Junius Brutus, Caesar's adopted son), was the nephew of King Tarquin the Proud. He was the principal author of the plot which put an end to royalty in Rome, and became the first Consul of the Republic in 509 B.C. This same Brutus had his sons killed for having conspired for the return of the Tarquins and for the fall of the Republic. The expression "to kill the children of Brutus" signifies the extreme severity of necessary measures to preserve a budding Republic in the face of conspirators.

them all, which you take great pains to avoid, that of Rome after the kings had been expelled. This grandeur can be explained in two ways. The first is that this Republic was well equipped for conquest. (I shall tell you how this was so some other time.) The second is that the Romans knew what no wise Prince is unaware of: that you cannot preserve your domain unless you enlarge it at the expense of those who wish you ill; that you must act without delay, lest by putting too much faith in time the cure might arrive too late; that you cannot avoid a war, but do nothing except defer it to the advantage of the other.

I am not saying that exceptions to these rules cannot be found. This island of Utopia, which you love so much and which I don't have the honor of knowing, is worthy of your praise if it is so lost at the end of the ocean that people can live there sheltered from all conquest. Ask the Magnificent Thomas More to bring you there. Or if by misfortune peace is not established there, find a deserted island where you might make peace with yourself. But please allow the good Prince to hold these fantasies for what they are worth, and never to deter his thinking from war. Let him wage it, let him prepare for it, let him train for it. I don't mean to say that Erasmus's principles cannot have happy effects, but only provided they are put into practice by the enemies.

Let me now look at the state of Italy and consider the reasons for its misfortunes. I say that these misfortunes are due to the sloth and laggardness of the princes of my country, resulting in the loss of the art of war. Indeed, before having felt the blows of the transalpine soldiers, the Italian princes thought it was sufficient to know how to write and indulge in subtle arguments. These naive fools thought that times don't change and that, the weather being calm, they were forever sheltered from storms. But fortune avenges itself on fools who let their sins turn them into victims. That is why 1494 brought sudden terrors, precipitous escapes and colossal defeats. That is why Italy was overrun by Charles, plundered by Louis, soiled by Ferdinand, robbed by Francis and dishonored by the Swiss. It is a known fact that a Prince's weakness attracts the assailant and cannot contain him. All these misfortunes distress you, good man that you are, but the only remedy you can offer is pious sermons. To hear you talk, it is only a matter of changing men's hearts and begging the conquerors to give up their conquests. Never has medicine done a better job of killing a patient. For while waiting for this miraculous thing, arms succumbing to prayers, the conquered will sink into the mud and the conquerors will swallow up everything. If I drop these stupid notions, I can only say that in view of these evil times, what the Italian states really need is a true Redeemer with good troops and a well-sharpened virtue. For if fortune does not capitulate to prayers, men must not capitulate to fortune. They must know how to enter into necessity to save themselves.

[3]I know, most gentle Erasmus, that this liquor will appear very strong to your delicate gullet and that you prefer only words that taste of milk and honey. But these mellifluous words can only have two effects, one of which is to weaken men, the other to hand the world over to scoundrels. It follows that the effective truth of your discourse is to cause a harm that you do not want, and to fail to do the good that you do want. Intentions being good and the effects evil, one can see that you yourself provide a superb example of these dire fantasies which you tell me reproachfully that I am straying from.

I say, in turn, that you always sin in the same way, which is to fail to understand necessity. For when you cling to the idea that, if the cause is good, the effect must be good also, you fail to see the chain of causes and effects. The reason is that you are unable to see men as they are. To complete your education, allow me to clarify this point.

Of men in general, one can say chiefly two things. The first is that they are ungrateful, greedy, envious, fickle, malingering and secretive. The reason for this is that nature has made them insatiable, first of all about wealth and honors. The desire of acquiring wealth is never satisfied, nor is the envy of some and the ambition of others ever extinguished. Nor is the fear of losing ever forgotten. Those who own much want to protect themselves by owning more and by instilling fear in others; those who have nothing want to possess in turn and inflate their envy with the desire for vengeance. Men are always either insecure or unhappy, suspicious or greedy, and therefore disposed to betray, quarrel, oppress, steal. If there is something to take, they immediately abandon the promises they have sworn and the memory of good deeds done: if there is something lost, they mourn over it more than they would a father slain. The real truth is that men are never good except by necessity.

The other thing I mean to say on this subject is that these same men are hostile to dangers, blind in the face of changing times, devoid of virtue. If they are evil, they cannot be so with grandeur; either because they are not in keeping with their times, letting themselves be buffeted by the winds of fortune, or because, when the opportunity to perform an evil action having something grand or generous presents itself, they do not dare. In 1505, Gianpaolo Baglioni of Perugia recoiled, in spite of all his past villainies, at the magnificent opportunity which offered itself of killing Pope Julius II. Yet such an act, whose wickedness would have been surpassed by its grandeur, would have brought him immortal glory and, without a doubt, Erasmus's secret satisfaction; for he would have been the first to show these prelates the esteem which they deserve and which you have every good reason to give them.

From all this, namely that men are evil but don't know how to be so honorably, it follows that, if things are left to themselves, the result is confusion and chaos, animosities and quarrels. What results, in short, is the ruin of the state. I say that it is necessary to break this fatal necessity. What is needed are great actions measured by their effects. Hence the necessity of those good weapons which are cunning and force, to place evil men in a novel necessity which is that of acting well. Hence again the necessity of having men of great virtue, new princes without fear or weakness, with a discerning eye for necessities and opportunities, faithful to the good if possible, ready for evil if necessary. For never, or rarely, has a principate or a Republic been seen which has been well ordained at its beginnings or well reformed from top to bottom other than by a single man. And when such a Prince performs a great action which is undoubtedly evil but good in its effect, no wise spirit should reproach him for it. To support what I'm saying, I only need to cite Romulus, Moses, Lycurgus, Solon and others like them. And if Erasmus grumbles, it is because he still doesn't know what the effective truth of the thing is.

[4] I come now to the quarrel you are picking with me over the great men I give as examples. I shall speak of Moses and David, those men of great virtue I speak highly of, while you reproach me for speaking evil of them. And I say that whoever reads the Bible in a sensible manner cannot deny what I say of them in my treatise; for he will see that Moses was forced to put to death an infinite number of people to enforce the observation of his laws. That sensible reader will also see that necessity having forced the Hebrews to find new lands, Moses led them into a foreign land where they killed the inhabitants, took their goods and created a new State. If you deny that Moses was an armed prophet and that he found his arms necessary, you do not believe the Old Testament.[11] Concerning David, I say that he was equally an excellent Prince and for the same reasons. For he knew how to make good use of his own arms, as he did to conquer Goliath and to defeat and conquer all his neighbors. He had so many qualities in the art of war that he bequeathed to his son Solomon a kingdom at peace. But Solomon's son, Jeroboam, having neither David's virtue nor Solomon's good fortune, inherited little more than the sixth part of the Kingdom. Anyone who knows how to read correctly knows that these princes were no different from the others in this respect: they needed to be well provided with virtue and armies to survive.

[5] I don't want to neglect a final point, which is the magnificent remedy you prescribe. For you preach a return to the sources of our religion in order to remedy the ills of the present. To subscribe to this, I shall first say that it is necessary for a sect to return when it must to its beginnings if it wishes to survive. This is what Saint Francis and

[11] On the killings ordered by Moses, see *Exodus* 22, which narrates the episode of the Golden Calf, when the "stiff-necked people" was struck down because of its rebellion against Yahweh; and *Numbers* 25, which tells of the execution of the Israelites who were guilty of having conspired with the god Baal in the land of Moab. In both cases, the sin attributed to the Israelites is that of idolatry, and Moses acts following the wrath of Yahweh. On the conquest of the land of Canaan, Machiavelli employs short-cuts, since the biblical narrative does not attribute it to Moses, who dies at the threshold of the Promised Land (*Deuteronomy*, 34).

Saint Dominic did, and without them our religion would have fizzled out. Through the practice of poverty and the imitation of Christ, they revived it in the spirit of men. And they did it so well that through confession and preaching they convinced people to obey, always and without a murmur, the prelates and heads of the Church who live in such dishonest fashion. Hence those who believe are inclined to be slothful and those who command are abandoned to the judgment of God. That is why the latter do all the evil they can without fearing this judgment, because they don't see it and don't believe it. One understands why the superb Erasmus should want to participate in this sort of renewal.

[6] I have said enough concerning you. Of all the things I have put forth in this letter, it must be concluded that between peace and war, the King and the tyrant, the contrasts don't have the starkness that you claim. As to the Republic, which does not escape the laws of necessity more than anything else, I leave you to reflect on it. That is why all the distinctions derived from written authorities, which you adopt as your own, are just so much hot air. For if fortune is changing and the opportunities are unequal, the quarrel is ever present, as well as the necessity that goes with it. And the reason, which must be understood easily, is that men having at all times the same desires and the same humors, it is necessary that the same effects follow. Such is the way of the world, my dear Erasmus, or, as you would say, its folly. I understand that it should be difficult for you to accept this. But God has made things thus, or let them be made thus. I would suggest, concerning your lamentations and your invectives, that you address yourself to Him.

I should like to give evidence of my interest in those things that awaken yours. Would you have the kindness to ask the Magnificent Thomas More to send me his *Utopia*? It's being talked about here, but no one can find it.

III.

ERASMUS TO MORE
Louvain, 5 February 1518

Erasmus to his very dear friend More, hail!

[1] To begin with, let me ask you to entrust my boy Jean, the bearer of this letter, with those of my letters or yours that you judge worthy of publication, after a few modifications. And please urge the young man to come back to me as fast as his legs will carry him.

Excellent More, take care to stay well and not to lose yourself in the business of the Court. For myself, I'm getting ready to leave for Basel, or perhaps Venice, led there by the *Novum Testamentum*.

I want the new edition to come out as soon as possible, protected by the approbation of Leo [Leo X], even if it takes the rest of my strength. I have already made many additions and many corrections, but the work is endless; and how can I hope to disarm all the Preachers [Dominicans]? And yet, around me, the recriminations have stopped. The theologians I rub shoulders with have become amiable. Shall I be obliged to review my categories? No doubt I hear the echo of a few yappings by little friars—I don't know which, in Cologne or Bruges. But that's far away and from the back of the hall, as it were.

For the road, I'll need a horse easy to mount and tireless. I'm inquiring everywhere. Try to help me if you can, gentle More.

At last I've seen the *Utopia* printed in Paris. As I feared, it's full of mistakes. But I have another piece of news which redeems the first: the Basel edition is in press. I had shaken these Basel people and told them to be more diligent. They excused themselves about Budé's delay in delivering his Preface. They now have the text and have gotten to work. I'll see to it that things go swimmingly, so that in the near future your Island might be loaded with Literati who have come there for fun and instruction.

[2] All princes, those of the Church and others, should do the same. In Rome, the Curia has lost all sense of modesty. What is more brazen

than these repetitive indulgences? And now comes this project of a war against the Turks which, if I am not mistaken, is nothing but a masquerade to allow the Medici to conquer more land. The Pontiff, as you know, has made of his nephew Lorenzo the head of the pontifical armies. Who would dare think that he is looking for something other than the good of Christendom? If we continue this way, we will sooner have degenerated like Turks rather than drawn the Turks to our side. The Pope and the kings, with the exception of yours, surely, treat the people like cattle. What a magnificent example for those infidels we are attempting to draw to the true faith!

This is enough to please the infamous Florentine, he of the square bonnet. I received a reply from him, which I append to this letter. As we might have suspected, this little master doesn't like disputation according to the rules. The critiques of the opposite party, the questions of his own non-sequiturs, he skips over. It's his method. He chooses his own playing field, clings to his positions, and from there he shoots his reasons like so many arrows. If the Devil is the most tireless of quibblers, that one is a first-class demon. He posits reason upon reason to give the Prince good reasons to act as a criminal. Ultimately it's always the same one: you can't do otherwise or you are destroying yourself. He keeps leaning exclusively against these laws of necessity which he keeps drumming into your ears, and which are merely ways of approving human folly. As to the "ruin" which worries or troubles him, it is surely not that of the soul. For examples, he provides them only when he feels like it. As you will see, this wretch claims to read sacred Scripture as one should and, there again, he twists the text violently. To put it quite simply: he takes God out of Sacred History. It's like reading a tragedy while leaving out the greatest of its heroes. As you might expect, he delights in the wars and devastations related by the Old Testament, where he finds material for his most bloody maxims. But that all these cruelties were allowed the Hebrews (or their leaders) out of consideration for the times and of the spirit that reigned (like the permission to divorce one's wife, for example); that the reader shouldn't be satisfied with the bark of the tree, but that the deeper meaning is under the letter; and that the Bible shouldn't be read the way one reads Herodotus or Livy—all this is apparently a million miles from his thinking. Not to mention his offhand manner, which allows him to call Moses the conqueror of Canaan. This guy gives me the creeps. I have the feeling that he always has some blasphemy on the tip of his tongue.

I won't go any further. I'll not honor this rascal with a sustained correspondence. The game isn't worth it. He doesn't want to debate, he wants to win a battle, and he sharpens his tongue accordingly. His only virtue is his obscurity; let him keep it. I have more than my share of troublesome people, and it is more than I can bear. Finally, I leave it to you to determine whether this argument should be pursued. He has asked that you send him your *Utopia*, I transmit the message.

I know that you are constantly in the King's presence. I have no doubt that you are short of free time, but you are also able to observe political matters from up close. Perhaps you'll be tempted to pursue this treacherous enemy on his own ground.

Be well, you, the most loyal of friends.

IV.

MORE TO ERASMUS

Thomas More to Lord Erasmus of Rotterdam, hail!

London, 12 March 1518

I am happy to learn that your new *New Testament* will soon be in press. It's equally good to know that ignorance and envy are lowering their voices.

Has our horse found its way to you? I believe him strong enough to carry you, with all your wisdom. I hope you will like him. You speak of your indebtedness to me—It is nothing compared to my indebtedness to you: Erasmus's friendship is worth all the horses in England and beyond. I'm not even counting all the pains you have taken to make my lucky island blessed by fortune. I await the Basel edition with the impatience of a schoolboy.

I've read the Florentine's work in a translation done by our friend B . . . [illegible]. You know how scrupulous he is, one can rely on him.

He had a difficult time, he told me, for this fox's style is—these are his words—"gripping and confusing." Like you I am dumbfounded by so much impudence, led astray by so many roundabout expressions. You have made your own critique; let me add mine: he makes an outline, but doesn't follow it; he places great examples on the same level as minuscule ones; he anticipates other examples, but doesn't provide them; he gives titles to his chapters, the content of which is elsewhere; he says one thing and further on he says the contrary. What game is he playing? I give up, as you have already done. But I have the same feeling as you: in the depths of this labyrinth, I'm sure there's a Minotaur lurking somewhere.

I hardly dare take up the pen after you. First of all, you have said all that counts, and you've said it in your usual way, which leaves me awed and intimidated. But since you are inviting me to pursue the animal in his lair, I'm going to do it by playing a game. I'm writing for his instruction a supplement to Raphael's voyages, and I must admit I am enjoying doing it. It's a distraction from all the problems which the King's affection and the Cardinal's [Wolsey] burden me with. The flatterer of the Medici doesn't know the pleasures of exile. I'll also be sure he receives the *Utopia*, since he has asked for it. If he chokes on it, it will be a sign of the Utopians' wisdom.

I envy Basel, after Louvain. They don't know how lucky they are. Dear, dear Erasmus, fare well.

Book II

Realism and Utopia

(April–December 1518)

Chapter 4
The Island of Prince Atecratos

In this Book II, the correspondence continues. More takes over. The debate shifts to the terrain of political realism. More counters the necessity invoked by Machiavelli with another necessity, the infernal necessity which drags the tyrant down. At the heart of their quarrel is the confrontation between the efficacy of cunning and that of legitimacy. The author of Utopia *is also brought around to an explication of his work.*

In this chapter is to be found a satire of Machiavellian politics addressed by More to Machiavelli, preceded by a letter of Introduction.

I
MORE TO MACHIAVELLI
London, 1 April 1518

Thomas More to Signor Niccolò Machiavelli of Florence, hail!

My eminent friend Erasmus has told me of your intention, Signor Machiavelli, of travelling to Utopia. I could not hope for a more illustrious visitor, and I am sure that Raphael Hythlodeus, the sailor-philosopher whose words I am merely transcribing, will smile with pleasure (he smiles so little). I must beg you to be patient, however: the Louvain copies are all gone and the Basel edition is in press. But it will be sent you as soon as it appears. In it you will find an engraving by Holbein, representing this philosophical island with a faultless fidelity. Above all, you will find this Republic of sages, which will flatter your taste for the truth of things.

While waiting, allow me to send you a few pages of a narrative written by my friend Raphael [Hythlodeus], which I had lost through absent-mindedness. You will learn that your glory has spread even to the New World, and that your teaching has been of great benefit to the Great Atecratos of Atecratia.[1] You can put an absolutely blind faith in this story, which deserves as much credibility as the pertinent examples which make for the authority of your treatise.

This narrative pays you the tribute you deserve. Myself, I haven't the leisure to do justice as I should to your knowledge of things. Please forgive me. You know how pressing public affairs can be, and how obscure your great work is. I dare not invoke necessity at my modest level, but since you make of necessity the natural condition of politics, I shall benefit from it.

Besides, Erasmus, that great scholar, has already told you all the good that is to be said of your treatise. If I am not mistaken, you took it badly. You say that Erasmus succumbs to pious fantasies, that real politics lies elsewhere, in a place where morality is subservient. You will be pleased to see that the non-philosophical sailor who has written the great story of Prince Atecratos places himself on the same ground as you.

I shan't say more. I leave you in good company. Be well.

I have changed my mind, in order to say a word about my little work [*Utopia*], since you don't yet have it in hand, and since my friend Raphael is unknown to you. You should know, then, that this sailor,

---

[1] That is, error in power. Até was in Greek mythology the personification of error.

well versed in things of the mind, became an associate of Amerigo Vespucci, an admirable man, like everything that comes from Florence. He stayed with him during the last three of his four voyages, except that on the last voyage he landed in these unknown lands. He then travelled through a number of regions and discovered a number of unknown peoples, among them the Polylerites [the many drivellers], and the Macarians [the blissful]. Especially he spent many years in the land of Utopia. I'll leave it to you to discover, as soon as you receive my work, what this philosophical city is like. It is even more beautiful than Plato's. I enclose the rest of the narrative.

II.
SUPPLEMENT TO RAPHAEL'S VOYAGES

So, Raphael had just finished his astonishing narrative on the Republic of the Utopians. I had countless questions on the tip of my tongue, but since he was visibly tired from having spoken so long and stirred up by his speech against pride, I paid him the compliments he expected and led him to the dining hall. But during the dinner I couldn't help questioning him further about his extraordinary voyages:

–   You have learned so many things, my dear Raphael, that we have something to chew on for ages; but, forgive our insatiable curiosity, did you see yet other peoples in these immense regions?

–   Now see who is being insatiable! Yet what I told you about the best of Republics, the wisest and the happiest, should be enough to satisfy you. You should know that I left this isle of the blessed only in order to make it known.

–   Yes, of course, we understand perfectly and we will do our best to assist you. But since we are about to take leave of each other, we wouldn't want to miss any of your unequaled experience in these new worlds.

–   I have told you all I have seen. But since you insist and since we still have time, I'll tell you another story. It's about a vanished island whose terrible story was told me. I got this story from a Utopian who recopied the narrative of a man from over there transmitted by a sailor from here who had come back in one go. The story is worthy of consideration, even if the narrator has nothing of the philosopher about him. You will see how this island had nothing Utopian about it. I have the paper in my baggage. I'll read it to you after dinner.

A moment later, Raphael read us the promised adventure. I give it from memory, as I did for the preceding narratives. But I've already admitted the pains I have taken to dispel any doubts by colouring my omissions. For my chief preoccupation is that there should be no fraud in this text, and that the effective truth of the thing should shine forth in its pure splendor.

Memoir on the life of the Magnificent Atecratos of Atecratia, the greatest and most virtuous Prince in the world, and on his immortal works accomplished in the light of the wise and profound method of Master Niccolò, by the most faithful and ingenuous Thalassopos [drinker of the sea], a native of the island and a sailor par profession.

This story I am about to tell can assuredly be considered true, truthful, and genuine. For everything that I say here I saw with my own eyes and heard with my own ears. Everyone knows that one was supposed to live with head down in Atecratia, but I still had the habit of looking around. I say also that all the things said, thought, or noted by the Prince, I have obtained from my childhood companion Onos Thynnocephalos [Tuna-headed Mule], the executor of his Master's sublime and dirty jobs, and who like his Master, trusted nobody. And if anyone has any doubt as to how I was able to find out everything I am recounting, I say he can't understand a blasted thing.

[1] Let me begin. The Isle of Atecratia, once called Cenotopia [empty place], was located southwest of the great island of Utopia. One reached it by following the morning sun, carried by currents which good sailors, of which I was one, knew how to master. This

island was as beautiful as Calypso's, which is reputed to be the most beautiful in the world. According to some traditions, confirmed by the Ancients, it was once a flourishing island before it was acquired by the Superb Atecratos. He became its Prince, gave it its name, and with his ungrateful people he did these glorious and memorable things I am about to tell.

But I must first recount how Atecratos took the helm of the State; and before that how he learned this science of political things, which never failed him, or very little. Atecratos was a native of a neighboring island, with the same language and the same customs. Hardly out of his diapers, he was abandoned by those who had made him and taken in by a fox and a she-lion. As we have said, that was a good beginning.

So one day came a ship governed by Captain Vespucci, of whom it is said that he discovered four worlds. A lieutenant from the crew engaged a conversation with Atecratos, who was still a young man. He spoke to him of an island named *Florence,* where everyone has a brush in hand and a mask over his face. He spoke to him of a paradise named *Italy,* where demons have chosen to live; he spoke to him also of the art of governing states as surely as Vespucci piloted caravels. And to do this, one had to take as a compass the discourse written by the man who calls himself Master Niccolò or the Philosopher. And the book that he had written is called *the Book.* Atecratos said later that he had learned more from this discourse than all the sailors of the world in their voyages. Immediately he had thought to himself: I know my course, I shall be the Cesare Borgia of the southern seas. Let the winds of fortune blow as they should and the world is in my pocket.

[2] I continue, therefore. A few years later, Atecratos came down to the island where I was. He set foot on land by himself, leaving on the vessel his arms, faithful soldier of the fine buccaneer sort. He was coming as a friend, he said, returning from an expedition among fierce pirates. He soothed the crowd a thousand times with his words, distributed gifts, and kept his soldiers on board with these instruments which serve to maintain discipline among crews: the whip, rum and sodomy.

The island was then governed in the following way: a Prince who was a wet blanket, a flaccid people accustomed to him and to his lineage, a touchy group of Grandees who were constantly quibbling in the Senate.

Atecratos said to himself: here will be my Romagna. And since he could play the fox admirably, he managed to win over everybody. One day he announced his departure and gave a feast. That night, he had his henchmen step off the boat, took the Prince and the Princess aside and plunged into Necessity with sword in hand. Immediately he occupied the Palace, sent for the Senators, put several of them to the sword, had himself elected by the others, threw these last into the depths of a dungeon. And he had it everywhere proclaimed that the former Prince had conspired against the people, that a new Prince was henceforth on the throne, and that he sought nothing except the friendship of his new people.

The wise Atecratos then endeavored to consolidate his positions. He consulted the Book. The first thing—Master Niccolò insists on this—is to bleed the descendants of the conquered Prince. Atecratos sent for the brothers and sisters, sons and daughters, nephews and nieces, brothers-and sisters-in-law, and others of the same ilk: and he did what had to be done. He was brought great-great cousins who were still nursing. The Prince calculated with moderation. At what point does one think himself satisfied? The divine Machiavelli does not stop at these details. But in taking up the Book again, he saw that Duke Cesare was worthy of praise for having almost reached his goal, which was "to wipe out the whole line of Lords whom he had ransacked." Enough parsimoniousness, he said, throw them into the grave with the others!

In the North, malicious men made trouble. The Prince wasted no time in petty disputations. He sent his most bloodthirsty captain with the order to perform good, lusty criminal deeds. Calm returned. So, he ordered the captain seized, had him tortured in the grand manner and cut in half at the right place. What is to be done now? He reread the Book at the seventh chapter where it is spoken of the Duke's grand actions:

Whoever judges it necessary in his new principality to

assure himself of his enemies, to win friends, to conquer by force or fraud; to make himself loved and feared by the people, and followed and revered by the soldiers; to crush those who can or might harm you; to renew the ancient orders with new methods; to be both severe and pleasant, magnanimous and liberal; to wipe out an unfaithful militia and create a new one; to maintain the friendship of kings and princes, so that they must willingly do you good or be hesitant to offend you—that prince cannot find fresher examples than the actions of this man.

Well, well, thought Atecratos, I've done some of what needs to be done. As to the rest, hell! I have to go about it with subtlety. I must change the rules, that I know, but in what direction? What would Cesare [Borgia] have thought up? One must be feared and loved by the people, no doubt, no doubt, but damn it! How do I go about it? I need a faithful militia, yeah! My boorish mercenaries aren't enough, but where can I recruit soldiers I can trust?

To be perfectly truthful I must say that the Great Atecratos had come up against the gustiest winds of fortune, blowing full blast. Ominous signs were appearing both in the sky and on land. The mercenaries wanted rewards. "Must I rob my subjects of their property?" the Prince asked himself. "Master Niccolò is not of this opinion." The captains were giving him strange looks. He saw fear in the eyes of some, greed in the eyes of others. Bad jokes were to be heard, told here and there by tasteless wags. There were even wall inscriptions: "Death to the Usurper!"

– What's wrong with them, Atecratos said? I've done nothing that Cesare would not have done. And I can't hold back this populace with my band of swordsmen. I have got to hold these scoundrels back. Let's see, let's see, I have to consult the Master.

So he took up the Book again and reread it line by line. He emerged from his reading in a slight state of confusion. He became self-absorbed, like a sailor on the point of mapping his route. Suddenly he had an idea: "I'm going to call a meeting of all the experts in the matter to sort things out. That's the solution, goddam it! A Council of Niccolologists! They will tell me how to apply the maxims of the divine Machiavelli. Of course, nobody must let the cat out of the bag. I know, I'll need a few good locks."

[3] So the subtle Atecratos called upon all the experts in the science in question. He did it secretly, with many requests and many reassurances. And they came with their expert knowledge and their academic gowns from all the faculties of Niccolology. Atecratos welcomed them warmly, quarantined them and stuffed them with compliments. After which, he opened the Council:

– Most eminent Doctors, most expert on the greatest expert of them all, he who enlightens wise princes, he who is worthy of advising Moses and Alexander in the northern countries and advising me in the south, I have brought you together so that we might have yet greater insights into his teaching. Here's the situation: I am a Prince, and a new Prince. I have acquired this principality with the force and the cunning you know about. Now, to do the great things that I am called upon to do, I would like to clarify a few points with you. The first question I would like to ask you is this: how can I keep the rabble in hand? Yes, what I mean is, how can I be sure of the people? Must I crush it? Win it over? Make myself feared and loved at the same time? Make it contented and stupid? Sort these things out for me. What exactly does the Philosopher say, as you so rightly call him? I have my own notions about this, but I would like to hear yours on this matter. After that, we'll talk about arms, ministers, and other related questions.

– To answer your question, Lord Atecratos, began Doctor Morosophos [the wise fool], one must respect the requisites of minor logic, otherwise known as formal logic, and know how to distinguish the antecedent clause from the consequent clause. On the above-mentioned question as to how to be sure of the people, the Philosopher's position is firm, provided you learn to understand it in all its rigor and in conformity with principles. If someone objects that there are different schools of Niccolology, let me answer that all the others are nothing but sophistry and paralogicity.

Therefore, to shed light on the matter, I shall treat it in five points, beginning with the nature of the people. To be assured of the people, we must know it well.

First, the fact that you are a new Prince is no cause for alarm, for, as it is stated at the start of Chapter III, "men willingly change their lords in the belief that they will fare better." Hence we conclude that you can count on this desire for new things.

Second, the people is easy to please, for as it is demonstrated in Chapter IX, all it asks for is not to be oppressed. This humor is far easier to adapt to than that of the Grandees, who would tend to oppress the people. *Item*, at the start of Chapter XIX, the Philosopher writes that "any time the great majority of men are deprived neither of honor nor of property, they live content." It follows, therefore, that the Prince, provided he endangers neither the possessions of his subjects nor his women, will easily win over the friendship of the people.

Third, this friendship gives your power solid foundations. For the people, when treated as it should be, remains faithful in the hour of adversity. This is what is meant in Chapter IX: "Let no man reject my opinion with this trite proverb: "He who builds on the people builds on mud [. . .]; if he who builds on the people is a Prince who knows how to command and a man full of heart, who does not get frightened in adversity, who has not failed to prepare his operations and who, by his courage and his orders, gives heart to his people, he will never find himself deceived by them, and he will see that he has laid good foundations."

Fourth, these foundations are necessary to you. For as the Philosopher has written in this same chapter, "with a hostile people, a Prince can never be secure, because there are too many of them." Furthermore: "For the Prince it is necessary to have the friendship of the people; otherwise he finds no remedy in adversity."

Fifth, and consequently, we conclude that to win the friendship of the people is possible, easy, solid and necessary. The Philosopher's immortal teaching is that you must enlist the people to your side in this way. For as the Book states in Chapter XIX: "well ordered states and wise princes have thought out with all diligence how not to make the Great desperate and how to satisfy the people and to keep them con-

tent, for there lies one of the most important concerns of the Prince."
Moreover, concerning the ways of winning the people over, these are
great in number. Magister *dixit* [The Master has spoken] in Chapter
IX, and these ways vary according to the cases. On this point, one
must follow the Philosopher and keep going.

– Not at all, not at all! Atecratos exclaimed. What sort of demonstration is that if you don't breathe a word about the means of
doing it? Tell me, tell me, how is it done?

– The practice must be deduced from the above-mentioned consid-
erations if adapted to the characteristics of the times. You will find
them easily, Lord Atecratos

– *Nego, nego* [I deny it, I deny it], interrupted Doctor Cholesophos
[the bilious wise man] with a flushed face. All of this is deceitful
and wild. Allow me, August Prince, to do justice to the Philosopher, to the people and to your grandeur. For the true doctrine is
totally other, and I shall prove it in five points.

First point, a new Prince must overcome his very newness. For, as
is explained by demonstrative reason in Chapter II, he hasn't going
for him the positive favor of the people which in hereditary principalities are provided by seniority and continuity of power. Moreover, he
has going against him "the incredulity of men who don't really believe
in new things unless they come to have a firm experience of them"
[VI]. Hence it follows that the friendship of the people is not assured.

Second point, the people is not easy to satisfy, for it is made up of
evil men. "Of men, in effect," states the wisdom of the Philosopher,
"one can generally say this: that they are ungrateful, fickle, pretenders
and dissemblers, cowards in the face of peril, greedy for gain" [XVII].
Item: "for men will always turn out bad for you unless necessity makes
them good" [XXIII].

A third and correlative point: the wise Prince should not attempt
to lay his foundations on the people's friendship. For as it is written
in the Book, Chapter XVII, "so long as you do good to the people,
they are all yours, offering you their blood, their property, their lives,
their children , as I said before, when the need for them is far away;

but when the need befalls you, they revolt." Moreover: "And men hesitate less to offend one who makes himself loved than one who makes himself feared." From this we must conclude that he who bases himself on the people bases himself on sand.

Fourth point: the friendship of the people is not a necessary one. The reason is that fear provides an adequate and surer compensation. For, as the Philosopher states in the same passage: "it is much safer to be feared than loved; [. . .] for love holds by a bond of obligation which, because men are wicked, is broken at every opportunity of private profit; but fear holds by the dread of punishment, which never leaves you" [XVIII].

Fifth point, and consequently: one must conclude that the love of the people is a difficult, fragile, and unnecessary thing, and that fear allows you to lay necessary and solid foundations. That is assuredly the Philosopher's teaching. As to the means, they are not hard to see if you follow the example of Cesare Borgia and the maxims of the Book on the good uses of cruelty.

– *Concedo et nego [I approve and I deny]* at the same time, replied Doctor Pachysophos [the thick wise man]. Dear and esteemed colleagues, you are both right and wrong. For, according to the divine Machiavelli, men are at the same time ungrateful and capable of gratitude, rebellious toward novelty and greedy for it, credulous and incredulous, fickle and constant. That is what makes Niccolology both profound and rich. That is why the Prince must play on both love and fear. All of this is as crystal clear as the rivers of Atecratia.

Prince Atecratos was frowning more and more over his bushy eyebrows.

– But how in the devil can I make myself both feared and loved? I can no doubt be cruel in small numbers so as to inspire fear in large ones, and yet not be hated. But if I am cruel, how can I be loved? And if I'm not cruel enough, how can I be feared?

– I cannot say more on the good faith of the immortal text, said Doctor Pachysophos. But when the practice is firm in its principles, the practico-practical follows without any difficulty.

– But look, replied the Prince, if the people are this and that at the same time, is there a point when it is only this? And then what does one base oneself on? Do you see something allowing me to seize the people, and depending on me?

– There is one and only one, said the Doctor Cholesophos, and that is fear.

– Now there's a good point, said Atecratos with such a brilliant smile that I saw the whole company nod in approval. I don't know why, but the Doctors stopped quibbling.

– Now let's go on to arms, to these good arms that Master Niccolò speaks of so often. How do you see this problem? Speak to the point, I beg you, consider this question closely. This is not a matter for speculation or endless cogitation. It is a serious question, I mean a question that deserves our full attention; the question, you see, which allows us to resolve all the others.

Doctor Morosophos began to speak again.

– The solution can easily be deduced from the propositions of the Philosopher. That solution is that the people must be armed. I shall prove it by two arguments. The first is that other types of arms are dangerous. By "other arms" I mean mercenary and auxiliary arms which are demonstrably "useless and dangerous," according to Chapters XII and XIII. The second argument is that it is said in Chapter XX: "It has therefore never happened that a new Prince ever disarmed his subjects; better, when he found them disarmed, he has always armed them, for, if they are armed, these arms become yours. Those you are suspicious of become faithful, those who were faithful remain so; and all, former subjects that they were, become your partisans." Hence we must conclude that a Prince's best arms are his subjects in arms.

– But, said the Prince, if I arm my subjects, they will no longer fear me. How can I control them? I shall be at their mercy.

– You see very well that you need the friendship of the people.

—   Allow me, allow me, objected Doctor Cholesophos, the real meaning is elsewhere. "Good arms" means your own arms, those which
are yours, those which permit you, as for Cesare Borgia, to depend
on yourself alone. This point is not subject to dispute in Niccolology. Now it is said of these one's own arms in Chapter XIII that
they are "those who are composed either of subjects, or of citizens,
or of your own creatures." Concerning citizens, I skip this point
since we are talking about a Principality and not of a Republic.
Considering the subjects, how do you go about making their arms
yours? By appealing to their friendship, as Doctor Morosophos
would have it? But it has been established that friendship makes
you dependent on others, and that fear alone is fully in your control. By the reality of fear? But facing an armed mob, the Prince is
disarmed and "the fact of being disarmed makes you despicable"
and places you in danger [XIV]. Hence we conclude that the only
remedy is for you to bank on your armed creatures and control
the people by this means.

—   My creatures, you're right, my creatures, that's the point. But tell
me, tell me quickly, how do you see them, these armed creatures?

—   Those are the men you will be sure of, because they depend entirely on you.

—   Of course, of course, but who are they exactly?

—   Exactly?

—   Exactly. Atecratos's tone of voice had changed. One felt a cold
shiver in the room. "I don't like these approximations which make
my head wobble. I shall help you, distinguished scholar. You see,
I already have my own band, people who are mine because they
know that their fortune is glued to mine. Although. . . . Well, there
are too few of them, I need troops, and sure troops. And, gosh!
Where can I find them? I've thought of mercenaries, but Master
Niccolò doesn't care for this remedy, and I cannot doubt his wisdom. But then, where can I find my 'own' arms? Counsel me
well."

The room fell silent. Then Doctor Pachysophos bravely continued to speak.

– Magnificent Lord, the Philosopher does not take up this matter exactly, and, surely, he cannot cover every subject. But the answer you are looking for can be found in the examples he provides in Chapter XIII, where he says that if you examine them, "the mode of ordering one's own arms will be easy to find." The examples given are the terrible Hiero of Syracuse, the young David in his combat against Goliath, King Charles VII of France, and the Superb Cesare Borgia, whose virtue you match. You must also consider the case of those Roman emperors who are spoken of in Chapter XIX, and who were expert in banking on their soldiers in order to harm the people. That was a necessary choice, soldiers being more capable than the people. We have no doubt that in meditating these examples you will find the answer you are looking for.

– By the devil's horns, I haven't called this assembly for you to dump your dirty work on me. I've read closely what concerns Cesare, I have seen the principles easily enough; but for the execution, we see that Master Niccolò—may his name be praised!—is nowhere on the playing field. The Duke "created a new militia," "turned to his own arms," all well and good; but my heavens! Where did he find these soldiers which are his and yet are not for sale? What think you, learned Masters?

– We say that we cannot say more than the Book says. May your Greatness learn to accept what makes the grandeur of Niccolology.

– Oh! Sure, what a grandeur! But at least tell me about fortresses. I don't know whether I'm supposed to build one or not. What does the Philosopher say, exactly?

– That question is easy, illustrious Atecratos, said Professor Pachysophos. To tell you what the Philosopher says exactly, we must consider several points. First, as it is written in Chapter X, the Prince who is always in need of another to defend himself must build a fortress that will permit him to defend himself without the help of others. Secondly, as the twentieth Chapter shows, the Prince who is more afraid of strangers than of the people must not build a fortress, whereas the Prince . . .

– That's enough, Atecratos broke in, I see what light your science can bring me. I had a few other questions, as I said, but we'll defer that to some other time.

Atecratos was silent for a moment, then he continued on a softer tone:

– Well, I don't want to close this session, which has brought so much to our understanding of the Book, without submitting to you, illustrious Doctors, a problem that I find bothersome at present. Now: I've already accomplished a memorable action worthy of what the great Cesare once accomplished in Romagna. But the people are still not sufficiently satisfied and stupid. What other dramatic action of the same vintage do you recommend?

– Kill your general, said one. —Or your ministers, said the other. — Put your advisers to the sword. —Have all the Grandees beheaded, or what remains of them.

– These, surely, are praiseworthy ideas. But I'm thinking of something else: I'm going to start by hanging all of you.

All of a sudden, the experts began to wave their arms like windmills in a hurricane.—But you had promised us your protection. — And benefits.—That would be treason.—A violation of your word.—An unimaginable cruelty.—Worst of all, an insult to science.— Don't make me laugh, fellow Niccolologists, haven't you read what Master Niccolò says about deceit, secretiveness, and the right way to be true to one's word?

– *Distinguo, distinguo*, my good Lord, the Philosopher speaks of the art of fooling men, not men of science.

– But aren't men of science men?

– Surely, no doubt, assuredly, but these men are exceptions and shouldn't be the object of a Book when they are its interpreters. *Amplius* [moreover], in the eyes of the vulgar mob we aren't important enough for this action to be memorable. Believe me, Magnificent Lord, reason is opposed to it, it would be wasteful.

—   On the latter point, I could follow you, eminent Doctor. But this is merely an hors-d'oeuvre. Besides, I have another reason, an entirely demonstrative one: I must liquidate you, for otherwise you're all going to betray me and divulge what we have said and must not be divulged.

—   No, no, please, you can trust us, most Serene Atecratos.

—   How can I be sure, most profound Doctor?

—   We assure it, we swear it, we promise it . . . , may the Philosopher be our witness.

—   But the Philosopher recommends mistrust so as not to depend on anyone.

—   Once again let us distinguish, sublime Atecratos. The maxim is true *in generalibus* [in general]; it is not so in this particular case.

—   And the reason?

—   The reason is that we are Doctors.

—   How can I be sure that Doctors cannot lie?

—   Because men of science necessarily tell the truth.

—   But Master Niccolò says that all men are liars.

—   Yes, but in saying that he also says that some men are not liars. When the Philosopher utters that generality about lying, he tells the truth, makes himself an exception to the rule, and us along with him. Science assumes a superior point of view.

—   I see, I see. If we follow you, there are two sorts of men: the ordinary rabble, who lie as they breathe, and the experts who always tell the truth.

– Right, right. You've caught on to the heart of the matter, and it relieves us of any guilt.

– But tell me, can't an ordinary liar play at being an expert? Or can't an expert betray science?

– I can't say, certainly not in our group.

– For what reason?

– I 'd know the liar, no doubt.

– And suppose you are the liar?

– No, no, in no way, especially in this case, *nego absolutive* [I deny this absolutely]. Maybe Doctor Colesophos, but not me, I swear it on the Book.

So they started accusing one another and exchanging cream-puff arguments rather than reasons. Atecratos calmed them down by ringing for the jailers.

– What a bunch of jerks you all are! You have understood nothing . Yes, there are two types of men: the new Princes, and suckers like you.

Atecratos thought: these Doctors are nothing but small fry, I need an exemplary punishment. So he summoned from the land of the Turks an expert in the art of torture. And he had them impaled on the main square. They took three or four days to expire, stretched out like sails in a windstorm, groaning like an old hull in a tempest. The spectacle made a big impression. Parents brought their children.

Atecratos rejoiced, but one could see him Niccolologizing without cease. And since my sources are sure, I can say how his thinking went:

– Being a Prince is decidedly a tough job. I am held back by all these rascals they call the people. Their number makes me powerful, all well and good, but their number also makes me weak. Why in the hell should I be their master and yet be obliged to them? Finally, whether it's a matter of making myself loved or making myself feared, I must always be looking after them. If the world were as it should be, the Prince should be able to do without the people. Hell, I'm caving in to the very fantasies that Niccolò condemns. Let's start all over again and see what the necessities are. The first is to settle right away this question of the Prince's own arms. Creatures, my creatures, there's the remedy. Unless, surely, the populace surrenders to me as it had surrendered to this wimp whom I dispossessed. Oh, fuck all! What did this slug, this coward, this loach, this no-dick have that I haven't got? I have the *virtù,* as the Philosopher calls it, that is needed, what am I missing? There is something wrong here.

[4] Atecratos reread the Book, reread it again, learned it by heart. His parrot, named Nicco, kept repeating: "My creatures, my creatures!" After a few sleepless nights, Atecratos had a word with Thynnocephalos:

– I have perfectly understood the necessities and the art of being a most ferocious lion and a most foxy fox. Here goes: the people, you've got to start by scaring the living daylights right out of them. For that I need well-armed creatures and well applied cruelties. For the cruelties, I won't have to look far. But the people, that rabble, it's also a question of not being hated, and if at all possible, to satisfy them. Here's the trick: I'll offer them a few torture sessions with the intention not merely of terrifying them but also of purging their passions and thereby making them feel good. I'll also give them what I don't take from them, for I will force my creatures to deprive themselves of armed robberies and virtuous women. The people, cured of its terror, will be relieved. Finally, I'll give them some good, humane-sounding speeches, about righteousness, mercy, religion, anything to fool these silly twits. What do you say? Isn't that a damned generous program, and faithful to the divine Master? Now, I have to settle the question of my own arms, those of my creatures, that is. They must be mine without any chicanery, and held very firmly. How, otherwise, if they are not sure and under orders, do you expect to prevent pillaging and what follows, this recreation of all gun-carrying people, which is everyone's custom everywhere? For this, I'll have to indulge in a few inhuman cruelties which will make me, like Septimus Severus, terrible and venerable. I'll also need something to reward them. If I'm unable to pressure the people, there's only one way, I'll need some booty. That's what these asses of Niccolologists were unable to tell me. All you need is to know how to read. Salvation, like glory, lies in conquest. That's how I'll have the wealth I need to satisfy my creatures without cleaning out the rabble I have to handle carefully. To do this I'm going to arm the most appropriate fraction of the people, taking the right precautions. It's in this sense that the Master's chapters on arms and on war must be read, filling in the holes. Blessed be Niccolò!

So Atecratos recruited, willingly or not, the most virtuous of the brigands of the island, the crooks, the kneecappers, the swindlers, the outlaws, the pirates, the lockpickers, the extortionists and others of their kind. He made them great promises of booty and great threats of cruelty. He placed among them some of his band as spies, and he chose some of the new recruits to spy on his band.

Thus he created a superb army that was just drooling with valor and greed. And he led them on to the conquest of the adjoining isles. He proved himself a great warlord, toppling his enemies over, conquering peoples, handing open cities over to his soldiers, who put them to good use. These conquests being made, he noticed that the people had taken maddening habits of freedom in his new states. So he did what needs to be done on such occasions: he dispersed the inhabitants, confiscated their wealth, put the men in shackles as soon as they said boo, beat them up if they complained. A thick and magnificent silence fell over these far-off lands. Nothing was to be heard except the warden's whip and the informer's whisper. But the crowd would applaud when Atecratos the Invincible went by in his Conqueror's chariot. People sang his praises, written by the great Flatterer.

Atecratos's glory in no way altered his wisdom. In interior matters he put his maxims into practice and found them satisfactory. In the art of purging the passions of the people he did wonders. The former Grandees that he kept in his dungeons he sacrificed by the handful every year at the great Feast. And when that supply went dry he took new Grandees, those on whom he had lavished great honors. That's a good system, he said, but whenever he honored someone, people saw him blanch. Every six months, he uncovered a plot and cut the plotters to pieces. The great Flatterer would put up posters on the clemency of the Prince who terrified the bad and satisfied the good. Atecratos's glory beamed like the noonday sun on a calm sea.

At this point I'd like to tell a little anecdote which is, I believe, welcome. Mighty Atecratos adored his daughter, named Nicoletta, who was the simplest of creatures. She was kept in the palace, but bit by bit she had learned what was going on outside. So, with the folly of her innocence, she became alarmed. —My Lord Father, she said one day, I have been told that one of your ministers has had his head cut off. May I . . . —A plague on whoever told you that! I'll have him hanged. —I've been told lots of other things. Why, Father, must you appear so terrible? —Necessity, my daughter, sheer necessity. —I don't quite understand, Father, be kind enough to explain. —That means one can't do otherwise. Master Niccolò has made that clear once and for all. —But then if the equitable gentleman Judges have been thrown into jail . . . —Necessity! —If the inhabitants of the island of Arcadia have been enslaved? —Necessity! —If the guards are everywhere? —Necessity I tell you! —But, forgive me Father, is this necessity so necessary if it costs so much? Can't you free yourself from it? —You are foolish. Do you want me to lose my power as well as my head? Come now, these are not matters for young girls, think of pleasing your father instead.

[5] I come now to those terrible times when fickle Fortune proved jealous and hostile to Atecratos's glory. Beyond his borders, the conquered peoples began to show bad will. They balked at having to work, dragged their feet, didn't feed the animals, stole tools, played dead as soon as the whip looked elsewhere. Worse still, some jailers were brutally stabbed. The great Atecratos punished, punished some more, but those surviving continued to show lack of good will. It became necessary to double the guards, the watchmen, the executioners, all this for a result that wasn't commensurate with all these measures. Atecratos was dejected. Inside the state, the people would proclaim its

gratitude on the appointed day; but it was pointed out to him that some undesirables were complaining, especially when the necessity of procuring the Prince's own arms made taxes go up. The Prince's prudence began to get shaken. —In that gang of people, he told Thynnocephalus, all I see is criminals. You know what Master Niccolò said, suspicion is always appropriate. So I want you to be on guard, keep watch, check, spy, do what has to be done. Think of it, how terrible! So much grandeur at the mercy of a mere knife!

That's when the great Affair exploded. The diary of Dame Conopos [Midge] was found. In it she had written: 1) clean the chamber pot; 2) set out a trap for the fox; 3) pierce the wine vat. The ultra-secret services were quick to discover the hidden meanings and to uncover the conspiracy: 1) get rid of those who govern; 2) organize a conspiracy against the Prince; 3) pierce him with a dagger. Moreover the Dame confessed everything after a couple of whippings.

The audacity of this plot led Atecratos to adopt new precautionary measures. Already he never went out without twelve legions at his side and three breastplates underneath his silk and gold garments. He did better. He changed beds three times each night, dug secret passageways everywhere, hired twelve doubles. And then he published the following decree:

> In the name of Atecratos the Superb, the great Benefactor of the people, let the following decree be observed:
>
> Article 1: Whoever is within fifteen steps of his Greatness the Prince must be fully undressed;
>
> Article 2: Whoever coughs or blows his nose or spits or clears his throat within ten steps of the Prince will be thrown to the lions;
>
> Article 3: Each of the Prince's dishes will be tasted twelve times by twelve different tasters. Among the tasters must be five ministers, chosen by lots every day.

And he placed soldiers everywhere.

But the wise Atecratos knew that he had to guard himself from the guardians. He thought: How can I be sure that my own arms don't fall into other hands? That they won't betray me? Who will give me loyal men? The wretches are everywhere. Suspicion, suspicion, that's the name of the game. So he doubled the supreme guard with a special guard charged with watching it. Then he created a magnificent guard to watch the second. Then followed the terrible guard and the dreadful guard. Every morning he would review them and look carefully at their eyes. —Fuck all! he told himself. Why must cunning be hidden in others as well as me?

Fortunately, Atecratos delighted with his courtesans in the pleasure of smelling incense, which is the reward of great men. His courtesans would tell of the Sovereign's magnificence, the people's gratitude, the world's admiration. But such was the Prince's wisdom that he didn't let himself be fooled by these words.—Those who grovel up to me are vicious crooks, envious, ambitious: at the first storm, they will jump off the boat. They are all deceitful, they all want my position. Yet I can't kill them all. And whenever a foreigner would pass by, he would give him an audience and ply him with questions: Tell me things as they are. Over here they're all liars.

And since I want to say, since I have said, the genuine truth, I will say that Atecratos then had a moment of weakness. And he wrote in his diary:

I am the Master and I am alone, more alone than the most wretched of my wretched subjects. I can speak freely with no one. They are all dangerous. How unfair! So many pains, so many efforts, so much virtue, so many dead bodies! And I must live surrounded with foxes and vultures. Not a single friend at my side, not a single loyal man to serve me. What have I done for fortune to take such revenge on me? If I have abused others so much, it was for myself, for my glory and the contentment that has to come with it. And, devil take me! I'm not happy. Could it be that I have been mistaken? That Master Niccolò has deceived me? Oh, fuck! Where have I gone wrong?

Suddenly he remembered this seditious little book which had made him angry for ages without letting up, a little book that spewed one insult after another:

> What is your claim to govern, you miserable fool? Force is a weak foundation, always in need of propping up, plugging gaps, reinforcement. You will never be our King, never will you have the legitimacy, which is needed for consensual obedience and authority in the State. You fool, such is the fate of tyrants, always in the breach, always on the tightrope. Watch out! Your enemies are everywhere!

But Atecratos pulled himself together very quickly. —What a lot of crap! He thought. My glory is beyond reach . —And he recovered his reason and his strength. To the very end he remained up to his old form, even more so.

[6] I now continue and finish this story where you will see the grand and tragic end of the Prince and the shipwreck that followed.

The wise Atecratos was now heeding nothing but his virtue. Finally, he published the following daring decree:

> I order the people to be free
>
> I command him to love me
>
> I order him to be happy
>
> Under pain of iron, fire, water
>
> Whip, rope and the rest

But the people were bristling with ingratitude. An infamous song was peddled around, which I don't want to include in this memoir. I will only recite the opening lines so that this disgraceful piece might be known to the whole world:

> Atecratos the pig
>
> Wants pettings in the brig (bis)
>
> Atecratos the toad
>
> Wants smooching on the road (bis)

So in one supreme effort, Atecratos resolved to make the most memorable of his memorable actions. He resolved to assault heaven and conquer God. But how? How reach him? Thynnocephalus advised him: challenge Him to a duel. The Prince ordered a big ceremony where he challenged God to come face him. His subjects were filled with fear and admiration. But God ignored him. So Atecratos the Great called Him a coward, a lily-livered wimp. The heavens, intimidated, grew dark, but God stayed hidden. Finally, the Prince said: — You see, God has abdicated; henceforth I am the Supreme Being. —People fell to their knees.

Nevertheless, impudent Death was approaching. A divine decree banished her from the Principality, but the Grim Lady still prowled around. They put a price on her head, guards were multiplied, traps were set, but the Tricky One was still on the loose. Never was Atecratos more magnificent than in this merciless combat against a disloyal enemy. His eyes hurled cannon fire, he frothed at the mouth, his smell spread throughout the State. At every minute he rallied his troops: —What are my goddam 'arms of my own' up to? Let them grab that bastard woman or I'll tear them limb from limb!

He died in this combat, sublime and enraged. Soon his death was known to all. All were stunned. A great silence fell. Time seemed frozen. Suddenly a great burst of rain fell, as if heaven itself had burst. But it wasn't rain; it was the tears of mothers, women ignorant of great political matters, that spurted into people's eyes, made rivulets in their faces, flowed like torrents. These women wept stupidly for their vanished men, their tortured sons, all these lives crushed to nothing. They wept so much, and with so much unreason that finally the island was swallowed up forever.

CHAPTER 5
Nowhere and Elsewhere

In this chapter, the disputation, or quarrel, begun in the preceding chapter, is continued. More and Machiavelli exchange barbed remarks and arguments on the foundations of politics, the laws of necessity . . . and on their respective works. More clarifies the meaning of Utopia. *Machiavelli refuses to do likewise for the* Prince.

I.

MACHIAVELLI TO MORE
Florence, 8 July 1518

To Sir Thomas More in London

I know, most glorious More, what high functions are yours, and I know that your time is frugally allotted to you. I thank you, therefore, for the pains you have taken to send me your famous opus, and to precede it with a supplement intended for me. You honor me greatly in treating me with such flattering attention.

So you are following in the footsteps of the eminent and candid Erasmus by appending a political lesson to his moral ones. Let me say that, in order to do so, you are telling me bedtime stories. I have skimmed over your speeches, Lord High Dignitary, and —let me tell you—I am somewhat alarmed as to the fate of your kingdom if King Henry and his Cardinal [Wolsey] happen to be listening to you. I cannot help advising you, please, to come and breathe some Italian air: you would be away from your affairs, your Latin would become less coarse, and, for the affairs of State, you could see them in broad daylight. The northern fogs don't seem to sharpen the vision.

[1] Considering first of all the smallest, or the least talkative, of your imaginary islands, I say you are taking the easy way out. It's easy, after all, to make fun of something with examples that are made up for the occasion. It's less easy to mull over and decipher ancient and

modern annals to understand the way the world functions. I say also that your way of joking is not entirely what we are used to here. We prefer it lighter, more subtle, aimed exclusively at the deserving. But I shouldn't be angry at the air you breathe.

As to your great man [Atecratos], you tailor him to your measurements in order to make me responsible for all the sins of heaven and earth. I say he's either simpleminded or tactless. He's a lion, no doubt, but he's also a stuffed fox. Of cunning allied to force he hasn't the slightest idea, or if he knows bits and pieces of that tactic, he uses it without wisdom or discernment, judging by the effects that you imagine. And since your character can't read correctly, I'm not the man to blame. It follows that your cunning is worth his when your intention is to ruin the credibility of Cesare Borgia, and Machiavelli's, with a vulgar forgery.

Master More, I have neither the leisure nor the taste to be your instructor after being that of your illustrious friend. However, I would like to enlighten you on two points on which you are totally blind, I mean the art of winning the people over, and the art of attaching men to you so as to make them your creatures.

On the first point, I say that the Prince must act in two ways, one which is to govern the opinions of the people well, the other which is to govern the people's fears and hopes. As to the first way, governing the opinions of the people, one should know—I have already said this and you don't seem to have understood—that men see only from up close. They judge by effects, and especially by those which touch them. For the rest, the vulgar mob is taken in by appearances. And in this world, amiable More, there is nothing but the vulgar mob. The result is that the wise Prince is the master of his reputation. He must follow these two rules, which brook no exception, or rarely: always strive to show in your actions grandeur, courage, gravitas, firmness; and in your words, good faith, honesty, humanity, religion. The Prince thereby provides an excellent opinion of himself, and, with this pretext, all the means he will make use of will be judged honorable. If your imaginary Prince is unable to act with this prudence, I can list many real examples to establish that. Allow me to cite just one Prince of the present time [Ferdinand of Aragon], who never preaches anything except good faith and peace; and he is an arch-enemy of both. Had he observed one or the other, he would have been deprived of his States more than once.

As to the second way of winning the people over, let me equally come to the point. (For the rest, distinguished More, consult my treatise.) I say, therefore, that when the Prince is weak, the people are demanding, easily discontented, always dissatisfied. But when the Prince is wisely cruel and is dreaded by the people, then they can be satisfied more easily. They are happy when they aren't frustrated in their possessions and their honor. For the kind deeds of the weak Prince are never enough to satisfy the needs of his subjects, whereas the absence of misdeeds in a strong Prince deeply relieves the fears of his. If, then, the Prince knows how to inspire fear and to act with prudence, he makes himself loved by the people, or at least makes himself not hated. For respect can be allied with fear. As an example, allow me to offer the one you dislike so much, I mean that of the Duke of Valentinois, who was so successful in winning over the friendship of Romagna. He was also able to do a million other things that your half-wit Atecratos would be unable to do. Fantasies are misleading, especially when one uses them as a shelter.

Coming now to the second point, I say that the Prince must fasten to him those who will become his creatures by renewing orders, as David did when he became king. For he filled the hungry with good things, and the rich he sent away empty.[2] Similarly, every wise Prince must see to it that in his city there should be no condition, no function, no amount of wealth whose holders should ever fail to recognize that they owe it to him. That way the Prince fastens certain men to his fortune and, provided he treats them with a strict benevolence, neither too near nor too distant, they will be loyal.

I conclude, then, that these ways of acting, and a few others you will find you know where, permit one to face real necessities and to avoid those you speak about, which defeat only those who have un-

---

[2] A hardly disguised but transposed quotation from Luke I: 53. These are words taken from the *Magnificat*, or song of thanksgiving sung by Mary at the time of her "visitation" to her cousin Elizabeth. Machiavelli uses the same device in his *Discorsi* (I, 26).

derstood nothing. I see clearly where you see the mistake which, in your opinion, governs all the others. You want to confuse me with that mistake, while making your readers laugh. But the well-advised who will laugh while reading you will be laughing at your expense. The indictment you bring against me is based on things that were imagined for the Prince, opposing legitimate and illegitimate power. I say that this distinction is a lot of hooey, or just about; I say that all power presumed legitimate is born illegitimate; that real founders dispense with all inheritance; that legitimacy is won by arms and dissimulation; that it is lost by flightiness, petty-mindedness, and irresolution. I understand, most honorable More, that you have a hard time seeing the fortunate power of cunning allied to force, and the unfortunate powerlessness of goodness. I would pay tribute to your honest naiveté if it were not so harmful to the State, and if it didn't lead you to satirize in the wrong way. The sad sack of your sad comedy [Atecratos] is the tyrant of your dreams: you love hating him and you celebrate his troubles. The new Prince is something quite different, and you are not up to understanding him.

[2] I come now to your little work which has made your well-deserved reputation, sustained by the good offices of your friends. Your travelling companions in this work, the subtle Erasmus, the refined Budé and others like them, deserve to be complimented for their friendship.[3] I can add nothing to your glory, so I must confess that I had some trouble taking interest in these folktales. But since you have been so kind as to a send them to me, let me say a few words.

So, in my treatise [the *Prince*] I put new wine in old bottles. You do just the opposite: a new bottle for a sour wine. With you it's always a matter of forsaking what is done for what should be done. And I say that your imaginary highroads are in fact beaten paths. On them we meet all those writers who instead of the effectual truth of the thing prefer the imagination of it; and what characterizes your genius is to lose your way even more.

---

[3]   In the Basel edition of March 1518, as in the November edition, the text of *Utopia* was preceded or followed by praise-filled letters by Erasmus, Guillaume Budé, and Jerome Busleiden.

About the form I'll say little. I see that you really strain to give imaginary names and to say funny things. I'm sure some people find you funny. But I say that this writing smacks of sweat, all-night vigils, and your far-off island. One tires of trying to follow you in all your tricks. I see a writer who takes the stage to dialogue with a sea-salt philosopher about an Island of Nowhere where reigns the greatest of all Republics, superior to the divine Plato's. I say that you give yourself a lot of trouble, and it's your reader who pays the bill.

I leave aside your allusions to present things, to get to the bottom of things. This marvelous city of Utopia, suppose we agree that it's more admirable still than Plato's illustrious Republic. For his imagination stopped at the government of the wise over the vulgar, whereas yours is more daring. In Utopia, as we see, all men have become wise. They are benevolent, courteous, generous, frank, courageous, loyal; and they form a just, prosperous, happy, brotherly society. It could seem that our religion has succeeded in achieving on this fortunate island what has been achieved nowhere else. But let's set ourselves straight: the Utopians are pagans who in many ways act as Christians should but don't. What I see in Utopia are the effects of a miracle, and I don't see the cause. Of course I've heard, through the mouth of your explorer, that this "miracle" has been produced by the common ownership of things; but I'm not quite sure, O devout More, that your piety is satisfied with this answer, and I fear that your fantasies may make you go over the top. Take men as they are, insatiable, envious, ungrateful; carry them over to your island where no one owns anything for himself; and they will become what no one has ever seen that they could be. It's true that your paper creatures have great virtue, which will make all tyrants sigh with envy, for they do everything you order them to do.

It would be mere repetition to enlarge upon what I have said before. I wish only to add that there is much disorder in what you say. The rules, the customs, and the institutions are made up of bits and pieces that seem hastily cobbled together. I have glanced at the institutions of the State, I saw endless complications in just a few lines, I yawned with boredom and went on. I did the same, and for the same reason, on morality and religion. On war, finally, a subject about which I have some ideas of my own, I lost your train of thought once more. I don't understand why the Utopians, who are so pleasant in town, are so vicious in war. Have they learned necessity? With reference particularly to these bestial men you call the Zapoletes, I note that the citizens of Utopia buy them on credit, expose them to the greatest dangers and watch them perish with the satisfaction of the debtor who sees the credit sizzle out with the creditor. I say that your dreamed-up Utopians are no longer what they should be. Yet you keep dreaming. Believe me, good Sir, closet politician that you are, mercenaries are men of war, grasping, suspicious, fierce in protecting themselves. Never would they allow themselves to be fooled that way. By the way, if I remember correctly, you don't talk about them in the first part of your book as twits. I've noticed, great logician, that you contradict yourself, here and in many places. If you think you've seen a number of contradictions in my treatise, I'll bet they are not of the same order.

I shall stop here, having, I'm sure, neglected many things. But wherever I go in Utopia, I always end up going nowhere.

[3] I conclude, therefore, dear Man of Letters, that the practice of letters which is yours or Erasmus's is not really worth all that much praise. Your writing corrupts energetic minds and weakens souls. So much so that you achieve one thing only, which is to create slavish men, as the soft virtues of the current religion would have it. Fortune desires something entirely different if you expect to make it your own. Fortune is a woman: she must be beaten and taken by force. I regret hurting your feelings, ingenuous Sire, but such is the way of the world. Few men understand it, and you are not one of them. Let me say one thing that you would find difficult to criticize: it is cunning and force which are the keys to the Kingdom. For the Kingdom suffers violence, and it is the violent who bear it away.[4] God chastises the simpletons and the weak, using the subtle and the powerful. Take care and fare well.

---

4   "The Kingdom suffereth violence, and the violent bear it away," Matt. XI: 12 Douay -Rheims version).

II.

MORE TO MACHIAVELLI

Thomas More to Signor Nicholas Machiavelli of Florence, hail!
London, 12 September 1518

I am touched, Signor Machiavelli, by the attention you have been willing to show my little book. I fear, however, that my innocent joke on the art of being a tyrant in the island of Atecratia has made your blood boil somewhat. Hot blood is a bad counselor when it comes to reading as one should.

In every piece of writing, as you know, the addressee is to be kept in mind. Your own glorious opus, if I have understood correctly, is addressed to the new Prince, to whom you make it a point to offer the worst possible pieces of advice. My little opus is more modest. I restrain myself from advising my illustrious King Henry to solicit the votes of Syphograntes, Tranibores, or their like; or to advise the Most Reverend Archbishop of Canterbury to take a wife. No, my imaginings must be taken *cum grano salis* [with a grain of salt]. They target only friends, and friends of friends, who love good literature and good humor, who have a penchant for Dame Folly and don't let themselves be trapped by human folly. I invite them to the island of Utopia to have fun with me. They know what it is to play, and to go a little beyond play. Those who aren't in on the game must drop out or try to grasp the rules of the game. Irony plays a role, to be sure, and irony can be a serious matter, as well as joking for joking's sake. Smile, Doctor Machiavelli, there are many facetious remarks in these pages. But perhaps smiling isn't in keeping with your dignity, or perhaps you have some trouble smiling in Latin. I recommend Lucian to you if, like Hythlodeus, your Greek is better than your Latin.

[1]Let's look at the rules. The first is not to bore, or better, to amuse. My God! This little opus would be so awkward and boring if one were to read it as the best regime in itself, or even the best possible regime. One would have to sort things out, and what a headache that would be! You tell me that I contradict myself and that I go off the

deep end. You're quite right. I deny what I've just said countless times more than you think. My book is chock-full of non sequiturs, they swarm in the company of nonsense and lots of other things. They bump into each other from one sentence to the next, sometimes within the same sentence. I offend logic with a logician's tact. By taking me seriously you are not taking me seriously. Maybe you're right.

Would you like a few topographical details concerning this Isle of the Blessed? Here's how our philosopher-seaman begins his discourse:

> The Island of the Utopians in its middle part (where it is widest) measures two hundred thousand yards. It is hardly narrower in the rest of its length, it narrows gradually on both sides up to its extremities. These extremities are, so to speak, traced with a compass, forming a circle of five hundred miles and giving the island the aspect of a renascent moon. The waters that penetrate between these horns, which are roughly eleven thousand yards apart, spread throughout an enormous vacuum [*ingens inane*], surrounded by circular tracts of land which block out the winds. . . .[5]

To put it differently: the island of Utopia in its widest part is hardly wider than the rest, which narrows in other parts. Its circumference is five hundred thousand yards, its diameter cannot be inferior to two hundred thousand (Utopian geometry is better than ours). I do not

---

[5]   More's Latin in his *Utopia* is frightfully complicated (the Latin he uses as a letter-writer is easier). The explanations given in this letter determine what the translator's policy should be. The translation should be as literal as possible without betraying the text. Of course, word-for-word translation can obscure the text, and denature the tone or the style. But the translator must at least see to it that the translation does not erase all the deliberately incoherent features of More's text. In view of this policy, it would seem that translators have until now been too serious. I must add, however, that the translations offered here have borrowed from those (the most literal and the least "touched up") of Edward Surtz in English and André Prévost in French. I might add that they could not have been done successfully without the benevolent help of eminent Latin scholars (see Appendices).

take into consideration that vast interior gulf, since it is perhaps reasonable to reduce to nothing that "immense vacuum" surrounded by the land "of nowhere." Look at the engraving which opens the book, drawn by a very dear friend.[6] The gulf or lake has disappeared, returned to its vacuum. The rest, this should not surprise you, is in keeping: the nearest cities are twenty-four miles away, while each having arable lands at least twenty miles in radius.[7] The cities are square without being so, the streets facilitate traffic and cut the wind, the river which runs alongside the capital runs right through its middle. . . .

These, of course, are only modest jokes, as are the puns on proper names. You have caught this. Let me go on to more serious matters, I mean the way the Utopians consider moral questions. —You will remember that that Hythlodeus speaks abundantly about these questions. Here is what can be retained from his discourse. With some pruning and tightening of the argument, here is what he says. I don't think I'm distorting his thinking:

In Utopia, moral philosophy and religion coincide and do not coincide. A philosophy which banks on reason alone needs the support of religion. Reason does not suffice. But this religion is founded on reason. Reason suffices. Reason supports virtue by directing its attention to that which is beyond nature, but virtue consists in following

6   Thomas More refers here to one of the two editions of 1518. The engraving is thought to be by one of the brothers Holbein. In the 1516 edition, the engraving gives a substantially different picture of the island. The gulf is visible but far narrower than Hythlodeus indicates. These lines of More's merely confirm what careful readers had seen. See in particular Alain F. Nagel, "Lies and Limitable Inane: Contradictions in More's *Utopia*," *Renaissance Quarterly*, 26: 2 (Summer 1973): 175–179. For a general discussion of the contradictions between the text and the images, see William A. McClung, "Designing Utopia," *Moreana* 118–119 (June 1994): 9–28.

7   This stretch of arable lands was twelve miles in the 1516 edition. In the 1518 it became twenty. The correction adds an incorrection. The translators (Marie Delcourt, André Prévost, Edward Surtz, Robert M. Adams) are not of this opinion. They use, as they should, the 1518 edition, but they re-establish the number of 1516.

nature. Religion is austere by nature, morality is ordained toward pleasure. They go together. The morality of happiness is that of pleasure [*voluptas*]. Pleasure is the rule and not the rule. Pleasure is agreeable, the harsh road of virtue is not. Pleasure concurs with virtue. It follows that some acts which are not pleasurable are pleasures. Correlatively, some acts which are pleasures are not pleasures. Those who feel them are wrong, they are not feeling them. Pleasures are pleasurable only if they bring legitimate pleasures.

Health is the foundation of all pleasures and a pleasure in itself. Eating and drinking are not pleasures in themselves but necessities, of the same sort as scratching when you have an itch. One should indulge these pleasures joyfully (evening meals, for example, have sweet delicacies in abundance). The pleasure of scratching oneself is of the same nature as the pleasure that permits generation or the pleasure that frees the intestines of their excrements.

Then comes the conclusion which hardly needs to be reduced to its logic, that is, to its contrary. Hythlodeus asks himself: have the Utopians chosen, or not chosen, the right way? Here is his answer. If you will allow me I shall cite the text:

> We haven't the time to discuss this, and it isn't necessary. We've endeavored to describe their institutions, not to plead in their favor. In any case, I am sure that, whatever you may think of these principles, there is not a more excellent people or a happier commonwealth anywhere in the whole world.

In short, I'll abstain from all praise, but this is the best.

I return for a moment to this state of health that so many of the citizens of Nowhere worry about. Here is a passage where our teller of nonsense strings reasons together in two equally irrefutable ways. I quote once again for your benefit:

> All Utopians, or almost all, agree about the fact that health is a pleasure par excellence. Since pain is to be found in sickness, which pain is the implacable enemy of pleasure, as sickness is the enemy of health, why, conversely, should there not be pleasure in the peaceful possession of health?

[. . .] In fact, if we affirm that health is not felt as such, they are saying that that is an opinion quite far from the truth. What man, when he is awake, can fail to feel that he is in good health, if it be not the one who isn't in good health? Is anyone reduced to such stupor and lethargy that he doesn't recognize that health is pleasant and delectable to him? As for delectation [*delectatio*], what is it if not pleasure [*voluptas*] under another name?

The first reasoning gives this: 1) health is a pleasure par excellence; 2) in fact illness engenders pain; 3) now pain is the enemy of pleasure; 4) as illness is the enemy of health; 5) therefore health is a pleasure. The Utopians could say equally well: 1)Life is par excellence a crime; 2) in fact death engenders innocence; 3) now innocence is the opposite of crime; 4) as death is the opposite of life; 5) therefore life is a crime.

As to the second way of demonstration, it can be broken down as follows:

1) He who is in good health is conscious of being in good health.
2) The proof of this is that a man in good health feels that he is in good health.
3) Unless he is not in good health.
4) Now any man in good health feels this good health as a pleasure.
5) Who in fact can be in such a state and not feel this good health as a pleasure?
6) Now that which is a pleasure is a pleasure.

What do you think of this, most sagacious Machiavelli? The logic of the Utopians resembles their geometry. Hythlodeus splits hairs endlessly, confuses the issues, throws a veil of seriousness over everything. But it suffices to give the strings a tug to see how they are tangled up, confused, mixed together. I took the trouble, you didn't derive any pleasure. Perhaps there's a moral to this story.

I don't want to leave this deep philosophy of the Utopians without having you share another of those imaginings of mine which you like so much. I'm imagining a congress of learned doctors where the spirit of seriousness fills all the minds, and where these modest pages of mine are the focus of their attention. The Utopians are a mixture of Epicureanism and Stoicism, says one. No, says the other, it's just the other way around. No way, says a third, the Peripatetics are the major takers here. You've understood nothing, says a fourth, this text is saturated with supernatural light. I am afraid they are about to come to blows. One participant then reminds them of this other sublime principle which the Utopians think dictated by nature: love yourself as you love your neighbor. The sequel worries me a little. In any case, I'm not certain if I should advise you to follow this great maxim. If you, Machiavelli, are to love yourself as you love your neighbor, you won't get out of this alive.

About government, on the other hand, Hythlodeus has very little to say. In the space of a few paragraphs he sweeps the whole problem away. He sweeps it away so well, in fact, that he would have a mother cat searching for her kitties, even a Florentine mother cat. You've tripped over the problem, I understand, I've done my best. Come now, let me recapitulate a few articles of this wise constitution. In every city, the people elect, by families, Syphograntes, henceforth called Phylarchs, among which are designated a few Tranibores, today called Protophylarchs. These are chosen among the Literati who are elected by the people, after being recommended by the priests, after the secret suffrages of the Syphogrants. The assembly of Syphogrants chooses the Prince among the candidates presented by the people, to be designated by the Senate, itself made up of Tranibores presided over by the Prince. (You follow me, I hope, Signor Machiavelli.) The Senate, which meets every three days or more, invites to its sessions two Syphogrants who change every day.[8] To avoid any conspiring between the Prince and the Tranibores, it is forbidden to discuss public affairs [*inire consilia*][9] outside the Senate (which, let me remind you, seats the Prince

8   The text reads *omni die*. The French translators have corrected this to "at every session."

9   The expression *inire consilia*, which is used in the *Utopia* and used here by More, has been subject to scholarly debate. It admits several translations, from "to discuss together, emit an opinion," to "hatch a plot."

and the Tranibores together) or outside the assemblies of the people (which remain to be defined). I shall stop there in my discussion of each city. For the whole island, I shall let you see the little there is to see. I wouldn't want to pour scorn on Hythlodeus's offhand manner of writing.

Must I continue? The rest is in keeping with what we have been saying. Concerning war: these paper citizens abhor it out of humane feeling, but they can wage it for futile reasons, and they wage it with an art of maliciousness that surpasses you, gentle Machiavelli. You have seen this when we discussed the Zapoletes, and you might see it in these benevolent rules that forbid pillaging so as better to extort money from the conquered country. After this holy war, here is religion: in Utopia, each is free to decide what he must believe, it being understood that all are held to believe in the immortality of the soul and the Providence of God. Whoever breaks with these is considered as the scum of the earth, but he is in no way punished. He is not even obliged to conceal anything provided he doesn't utter a word in public. Everything considered, diversity reigns: some adore a star of heaven, others think an admirable man divine, the greatest number believe in a highly philosophical God. Everything considered, unity reigns: all with an ardent soul participate in the same ceremonies in the same temples: there the holy priests, dressed in birds' plumes, lift to the moon, the sun, or the Supreme Being the same prayers, so well-crafted that they can be recited by all while applying to each in particular.

As you see, our hardy explorer does nothing but contradict himself. He interrupts, retracts, refutes himself constantly. The rule he sets either destroys itself or is destroyed by what follows (a contrary rule, exceptions, counter-examples). Such is the rule of the Hythlodean discourse. There are exceptions, surely, there are especially many other examples. I leave it to your acuity, which is great, to find them behind these exhibitions of seriousness. That's the game.

The game also allows the imagination to wander. Allow me this fine little pleasure of a roll call: the Utopians piss into gold receptacles, they change clothes once every two years and stay as clean as can be,

More's letter does not resolve the problem, but it does indicate indubitably in which direction the solution lies: in that of the greatest incoherence.

they have armor that allow them to swim effortlessly, they make admirable war machines that resemble toys, they present the fiancée to her fiancé in the simplest apparel, and vice-versa, so that there might be no deception, no more than for buying a horse at a fair. Isn't all that marvelous? And how about their social organization? No one owns anything for himself, not even a single object: that is the principle of principles according to our sailor-philosopher. Everyone goes to bed at the same hour and sleeps at the same rhythm; all go to meals in common to the sound of the trumpet; all of them take a break at the same moment, and according to accepted forms; each lives under the gaze of the others, under the surveillance of the Syphograntes and the censure of the priests; one can leave the city only with the permission of the Tranibores and others, by means of a pass from the Prince. . . . Who wouldn't like to live in Utopia? And how would a Christian not see the best of societies, or, as this half-mad Hythlodeus puts it, "institutions so wise and so holy," in a place where priests marry, women become priests, marriages break up, sufferings are shortened, children are distributed. Lucian argues that Plato had to go alone into his Republic, since no one wanted to follow him. I'm afraid to be hardly more successful, and, for myself, I'm out of the game. In short this Utopia is crazy, even if it's not merely that, and crazy is the man who puts his trust in it.

I may be wrong, I confess. I haven't taken enough precautions to enlighten the good reader. Here is one. Do you remember the letter to my friend Pierre Gilles of Anvers, my foreword to this little book? I go from one scruple to another, or, better put, I go from one tall story to another, and these reveal themselves for what they are. I reach the point where I seriously question my friend Pierre as to what Hythlodeus said exactly, on the length of the Amaurote bridge (the absent-city), on the Anydrous (or waterless) river. I am all the more entitled to question myself because the answer is given further down in the story of our navigator, which I took so many pains to report. And this answer is not in keeping with my memories.[10] Am I not right,

---

[10] The question is to know whether, according to the reports of Hythlodeus, the Amaurote bridge is five hundred yards long, as More the narrator

on that same page, to boast of an excellent memory? And then I close
the question which, as you see is not an unimportant one, by this sentence which would perhaps deserve to be coined as a maxim:

> As I shall endeavor to avoid that there should be any false-
> hood in this book, so, if a point be ambiguous, I'd rather tell
> a lie than lie, preferring to be honest [*bonus*] rather than wise
> [*prudens*].[11]

The rest of the text is of the same vintage. It isn't without a sense
of shame that I become aware of an unpardonable omission: where,
precisely, is the island of Nowhere located? I shall stop there, or rather

believes he remembers, or two hundred yards, as his page John Clement
(who is supposed to have been present at this dialogue) seems to think.
Now Hythlodeus in his narrative indicates that the river in question
"reaches facing the city a width of five hundred yards; soon it broadens
out even more . . ." The bridge, if it existed, would be clearly more than
five hundred yards wide.

[11]   This phrase has provided many headaches for translators and interpreters
alike. Here is the original text: "nam ut maxime curabo, ne quid sit in
libro falsi, ita si quid in ambiguo, potius mendacium dicam quam mentiar,
quod malim bonus esse quam prudens." With a view to coherence, a number of translators have rendered *mendacium* by "an error" (Marie Delcourt), "an objective falsehood" (Edward Surtz), "an honest mistake"
(Robert Adams). André Prévost ("I'd rather tell a lie than commit a lie")
and Elizabeth McCutcheon ("I'd rather tell a lie than lie") are more faithful to the texts.

In his letter, More does not provide the key. But in reading him, and
considering the context, it is more than doubtful that he wanted to say
something serious. All of this appears like a meaningless statement, a game
signifying that the characters are playing: 1) The question revolves around
a fictitious bridge; 2) The fictitious answer is in the text; 3) If we enter the
game and consider that More the narrator is wrong, it is a mistake, not a
lie; 4) From beginning to end it is More the author who determines what
is true and false. In short, the question of error and that of lying make no
sense. The marginal note, "Note the theological distinction between telling
a lie and lying" adds an extra dose of fantasy. Such a theological distinction doesn't exist.

stop the narrator who has usurped my name. You will find many other signs. The more I am serious, the more I joke; the more I conceal, the more I reveal.

Signor Machiavelli, do you know the French game of "Je te pince sans rire"? [I speak tongue-in-cheek; in French in the text] I dare not invite you to play it. Don't hold it against me if I play this game with my friend Gilles and a few other friends.

[2] So much for the first rule. I must evidently add this: joking can be a serious matter. Serious matters can be sinister farces (tyranny, for example). I'm still joking, or half-joking. The most illustrious Erasmus says of Dame Folly that she is not entirely mad. If I may follow this up, I would say that Raphael Hythlodeus's pipe dreams are not entirely dreams. The second rule of the game blends perfectly with the first: you must entertain people and make them think. This is not to limit the game to joking for joking's sake. The joke may conceal a serious intent, sometimes accompany it. I need not remind you that our great Ancients did not look down on this method. Socrates proceeded with irony and disguise. Lucian was ironic and told wild tales. Horace told truths while laughing. It follows that things get complicated. I will admit to you that I have taken some pains to cloud the issues. That's the game, and it has a few advantages: it arouses curiosity, it stimulates the mind. Would you like a model of this sort of writing which is a thousand times better than my little *Utopia*? Why don't you reread that *Praise of Folly* which the subtle and learned Erasmus did me the honor of dedicating to me? Rumor has it that it was written at my place. Dame Folly reasons as she should, then all of a sudden she talks nonsense as you might expect. She begins to boast—it's wise to be mad—then in the following paragraph she denigrates herself—it is foolish to be mad. Then she concludes by uttering the only foolish thing that is wise. I'll admit that the ill-advised reader feels he's losing his foothold. But the well-advised reader enjoys it and benefits greatly; and the reader with a finely tuned ear hears the voice from the depths.

As you can see, I'm in good company when I confuse the game in the manner of my illustrious friend, or in my own way. I mix, I juxtapose, I criss-cross: history and my own fantasies, tricks and object lessons, all the tones at my disposal, the dialogue, the oration. . . . There are different voices; one in particular holds the dice, but even that voice doesn't always speak in the same register. She often goes off the deep end, but she doesn't do just that. In any writing, as you know, we must consider who is talking. Dame Folly is multiple; more modestly, my explorer-philosopher is double. His name indicates that duplicity in dotted lines: first of all, he is Hythlodeus (you know the meaning of that); sometimes he can be Raphael (for the meaning of that name, ask Tobias).[12] His character, as Book I [of the *Utopia*] shows, suggests that. What a horrible character, don't you think? He is oversensitive, sometimes curt, ponderous as a Scholastic theologian; on the other hand he is upright, inflexible, with a great love of justice and truth. His laughable sides don't tell the whole story. In short, there's something wise in his madness.

[3] Do you like this method, Signor Machiavelli? I'm afraid that this mixture of genres is not to your taste. I already hear your complaints: what contortions, what nonsense, what pettifoggery, instead of going straight to the "verita effettuale della cosa" [the effective truth of things]. I owe you an answer. Let's forget, for the moment, the reader's satisfaction; I've already spoken too much of that, and I wouldn't be a good judge in any case. On your own terrain, I don't believe you've been heading in the right direction. True realism isn't where you think it is.

Let's talk about tone, if you don't mind. A touch of mockery is rather suitable for a discussion of things human. The sublime Plato, whom you fail to give credit to, has this memorable phrase told to the Athenian Stranger: "Human affairs are not worthy of much seriousness, and yet they must be taken seriously" [Laws, 803b]. It follows that it is serious not to be completely serious, and it is not serious to be completely serious. Isn't the most appropriate stylistic trope, which permits one to say serious things in an unserious manner . . .

---

[12] The name Raphael (etymologically "God cures") evokes the angel who protects and guides Tobias in the Old Testament narrative (Tb 5 and 6). He is the messenger or inspired guide.

irony itself? Another way of proceeding is to mix tones and to cover the pleasantness of a discussion with a basting of seriousness, large or small. In any case, a joke can be in good taste, especially when you don't spare yourself. Sometimes, Signor Machiavelli, we show ourselves as the stuffed shirts that we are, raising our hackles. It is then that the extravagant simplicity of the Utopians tells us how trivial our life is. Wear a precious stone, people look at you with gleaming eyes; a golden chain, your voice grows imperious; a few ancestors, and the aristocrat looks down his nose at everyone else. As soon as our vanity is pricked, the world darkens; our vanity is satisfied, the whole world is ablaze. It's good for us to see ourselves as we are. Erasmus laughs at Erasmus, More laughs at More, why shouldn't Machiavelli laugh at Machiavelli?

Forgive me, Signor Machiavelli, I'm asking too much of a courtesan of Princes like you. Let me consider those who fully deserve to be made fun of, I mean Princes themselves and all the VIPs. VIPs are fools who take themselves for VIPs. Power is a strong drink that makes them giddy. "It's a fact," says Dame Folly, "that kings hate the truth." You, wise Machiavelli, do your best not to displease them. The half-mad Raphael, if we understand him correctly, tells them some of those truths they don't like to hear: that the pomp of the mighty is nothing other than the measuring-stick of their vanity; that the kings of France are losing their way in Italy; that war makes men brutal, and not only the Pagans; that our Princes, who are always quarreling among themselves, and the Pontiffs who participate in battle, prostitute their office and their word; that the randomness of birth is a pretty poor excuse to set oneself apart and dominate others; that a conspiracy of the rich is rife in Christian lands; that the same Christendom is full of parasites and idlers; that a number of them wear the ecclesiastical habit; that all of them are deaf to the plaintive cry of a starving humanity; that all these VIPs, supposedly very Christian, are disfiguring Christianity . . .

Your new Princes, Signor Florentine, are, to be sure, not soiling the picture. What are they doing? They appear on the scene, they indulge in a frenzied restlessness, they skillfully combine cunning and force, a Machiavelli flatters them, they disappear, to be replaced immediately by other actors equally vain and ephemeral. But they bequeath to history a few bloody traces. What glory! I understand your unqualified admiration for Cesare Borgia, that crook.

Irony, surely, is not the only way of talking about the ills that man inflicts on man, and Raphael's indignation, particularly in Book I, sometimes deserves to be taken literally. But I haven't the slightest doubt that there is one way that doesn't work: yours. An icy tone does not tell things as they are. I should like to add that irony provides an extraordinary breathing space. Do you think that Erasmus would have had the audacity to denounce superstitious imbeciles, pompous theologians, disastrous dialecticians, parasitic monks, servile courtesans, greedy bishops, depraved kings, impious Pontiffs, all these VIPs reeking with self-importance, all these majestic contortions and this bogus piety if he hadn't taken refuge behind Dame Folly? The same rule applies to me. My navigator's extravagant ravings make people smile, even laugh, I hope; and the prevailing tone is, to a certain extent, a safeguard. I've said enough. You'll understand me, if you really want to.

[4] I'm running out of breath, a little. Let's take a break, if you will, and I'll recapitulate. So, as all those who have studied literature are aware, as you know better than anyone, the art of reading must submit to the art of writing. Here, if I am correct in my reading of what I allowed myself to write, the method yields the following: the tone of the dialogues tends toward gravity, but you mustn't let yourself be fooled, it conceals eccentricities and inconsistencies. The tone then turns toward the pleasant, again you mustn't let yourself be fooled to the end: it conceals things that are worth their weight in gold. It follows that Raphael Hythlodeus is greatly foolish and partially wise. He is foolish in his praise of a wise Utopia, he is wise in his denunciation of human folly. Now are we to stop there? Your objections encourage me to go a bit further in your wise company. What, really, does our hero's wisdom say, and, to begin with, what says his folly? Hythlodeus's madness reveals itself, as I have said, in the insanity of his discourse. Fundamentally it is due to this: Hythlodeus is mad to believe in the possibility of the perfect city here below, and he is still madder to believe that a social reform, however radical, is enough. He

claims to follow wisdom and, as you have already seen, he believes in political miracles: set up a community of goods, and justice and happiness will follow. In Utopia, that formula has produced industrious, zealous, hard-working, disinterested, lovable, united, benevolent men, full of joy and serenity. What an admirable stroke of magic: vices have disappeared, or almost. What a curious Christian this is, who seems to think that a reform of institutions makes original sin obsolete, and who depicts a pagan society from which the sin par excellence which the Christian spirit combats, namely pride [*superbia*] has disappeared. May Saint Augustine forgive him! Conversion of the heart is not a consequence of faith in Christ; it is the fruit of common property. It is enough, in a way, to make everyone join a philosophical monastery ! The Evil one is excluded. If my dear friend Erasmus had taken this narrative seriously, I doubt whether this man, who had hardly enjoyed life in a real convent, would have gone out of his way as he did for the reputation of this little book, which hardly deserved it.

Need I say more? The character who bears my name in this story discreetly raises a few reasonable objections.[13] To insist would have been to disobey the rules of the game. But who is so ignorant of Scripture and the Fathers to ignore the fact that the perfect city will be revealed only at the end of time?

This strange Christian is also a bogus philosopher. His chief error here is to reason about human things as if the choice were reducible to one place and its antipodes. He rails against an iniquitous and depraved society, he celebrates a just and happy society, he sees nothing in-between. That's not the way politics works. Recall the dialogue in Book I. The perceptive reader cannot fail to see the incoherence of the character. He praises Cardinal Morton, the English Chancellor, relentlessly, then he denigrates all the Princes. The keen reader too cannot

---

13   These objections are presented briefly by the "Thomas More" of the narrative toward the end of Book I, and in the last pages of Book II. The two serious objections are the classic ones: 1) Every system as such is insufficient: "since it is impossible that all should go well unless everyone is good, I do not expect to see this ideal realized for many years"; 2) This system offers no encouragement to work: " everyone shirks working [. . .] counting upon the activity of others."

fail to see his uncompromising folly: he himself is the wise man, those who govern are mad, the wise man cannot possibly be understood by fools. The only solution is this radical reform or revolution that will put an end to human folly. Otherwise put, for Hythlodeus, it's all or nothing: either the government of fools, that of the reigning Princes, or the government of wisdom, that of Utopia. Obviously this opposition is sheer madness. If this hardy navigator is lacking one virtue it is surely prudence [*prudential*], that political virtue par excellence.

And yet Raphael Hythlodeus is not without virtues of his own. This half-mad man is wise not to give in, not to set himself up in this world. This world is mad, wise Machiavelli, you should not be taken in by it. Raphael isn't wrong when he attacks the mirages that men are fooled by. Here is one of the traits that cling most to our condition: even in Italy, men mistake what is truly good for them. Nor is he wrong when, toward the end, he denounces the poison par excellence, this devious, opinionated pride which slips into everything, even in these lines, no doubt, and which is ever saying in every tone of voice: you deserve to be ahead of the other guy . How many men there are who live only by comparison! The glory which you make so much of is merely the most dazzling form of this misery. Raphael would tell you that what you advise the new Prince holds in these few words: put all of your *virtù* into filling a leaking barrel.

What follows from all this, at least I hope so, is this rule of thumb for wise conduct: be uncompromising, be moderate. What Hythlodeus doesn't know is that he must hedge his bets. In my letter to my friend Gilles, I end the list of his qualities with these words: "No one combines simplicity with prudence better than he does." You see what phrase of Scripture I am paraphrasing, inscribed on the engraving at the end of the volume: "Be prudent as serpents and simple as doves" [Matt. 10: 16]. There's the rule: an inflexible simplicity which makes no concessions, allied to a prudence in action which adapts to weaknesses and contingencies. That is why a well-made discourse on politics follows an oblique path [*dictus obliquus*] and gives a double vision to whoever knows how to read. Our sailor-philosopher does not understand what the oblique path is, looking only in one direction. But do you do otherwise, Signor Counselor, when you look in another direction? When we come down to it, I can boast of being more realistic than you. Behind my jokes, there is the demand without the illusion; beneath your icy comments, there are only temptations and the illusion of omnipotence. Your great enterprise consists of making a rule of corruption. You sound the retreat while shouting victory.

[6] I've almost finished, patient Machiavelli. I would not dare, in finishing, compare my modest work with your great treatise. But since I've told you my manner of writing, I am counting on you to do likewise for me. You tell me that I don't understand, I agree that your manner of writing is perhaps too deceitful for me, as mine is too facetious for you; so do me a favor, tell me your secret in turn.

While waiting, allow me to add a final word on the substance of our quarrel. And if I'm wrong about you, set me straight. What I see you always bumping up against is this: men, these ordinary men who don't have the honor of having your respect, these ordinary men who are by nature at the very heart of politics, men are not on your side. They obey willingly only if the Sovereign himself obeys this unwritten law: he isn't where he is to serve himself but to serve the people. All the Atecratoses and the Cesare Borgias of this world will be missing the foundations that make for solid states: this assent of the people which makes power legitimate. All the arms and all the lies will never make slaves behave like free men, or make a subject people say yes to whoever is subjecting them. Words may be powerful and daunting when one knows the art of lying (who knows it better than you?), but as soon as men are able to judge on the evidence, the most cunning of ruses goes up in smoke. What follows is that your laws of necessity are far less necessary than you say, and those that you object to are more necessary. This necessity that you reject, Atecratos is drawn to as are the tyrants of yesterday and today, who break with laws and are then surprised that others don't feel constrained by them. The end of the story (which you never speak of, I understand why, it ruins your grand political scheme) is that the tyrant causes not merely the misfortune of his people, but his own. How many of them come to a disastrous end! Atecratos is wrong to complain of ill-fortune.

The root of all these errors is that you are wrong about men. You say they are evil in order to justify cunning and force, you call them credulous in order that cunning might work. But they are not as evil as you say nor as credulous as you suppose. And they could never be fully both at the same time. You must choose. Forgive me, I was forgetting that you have more than one contradiction up your sleeve

I conclude, therefore (as you might say with this sense of authority that impresses people so), I conclude, O sagacious Machiavelli, not that you have bad vision but that you are short-sighted. You see with a sharp eye some things that are sadly true, but you only see a fraction of reality. Your eye shrinks the world. The owl who knows she is an owl is harmless, but what can be more misleading than an owl who takes herself for a sparrow-hawk? And what is more depressing than an owl who tries to fool you by uttering blasphemies?

I've said enough. There would be more to say. But as you know, what we say must be proportional to the receptivity of the souls we speak to. I believe I have already gone beyond the measure.

Do not be angry with me for having talked so much. You know the vanity of writers and their hopeless desire to be understood by those they esteem highly.

Be well, and watch out for the Evil One.

III.
MACHIAVELLI TO MORE
Florence, 10 November 1518

To Thomas More of London

I am grateful to you, More, for all the pains you have taken to dispel the fogs that surround your enchanted island. I will grant you that I had not really seen Utopia. But you must grant me this excuse: I had read your work with the attention it deserves. And what is hidden in no way spoils what isn't, for your wildest fantasies merely conceal other more deceptive ones. If I need another excuse, I might add that I didn't know you were so attached to childish things. I'll leave you on this playground.

Now, as to my treatise, might I say that you don't understand it for an entirely different reason, which is that you aren't one of those people capable of understanding it. To do that one needs a virtue you don't have, and which the great Erasmus doesn't have either. So I'll forgive you the commentaries you inflicted upon me at such great length. But so as not to appear uncivilized, I'd like to add a word on your work and a word on mine. Concerning your little opus, I say it will fool many of your readers, and that these deceptions were neither wanted nor foreseen by you. I have no doubt, for example, that some will see in your Utopia the best of Republics; that they will find arguments to support a foolishness that is different from yours, and that you will be the victim of your own disguises. It follows that your manner of writing is as "sensible" as your politics.

As to my treatise, let me say it will fool many a reader, but that these deceptions are a part of my design. For the naïve readers will remain at the level you both [i.e., More and Erasmus] have chosen, and that is the register I have restricted myself to in order to answer you. The readers truly worthy of me will see other things and will know they are participants in a new enterprise. It follows that my art of writing is part of my maneuver. This must give you some idea, my dear More, of everything that separates us; for you use little bits of cunning without seeing the effects, and I practice the great Cunning, with the effects always in mind. Of this noble art, you know nothing.

That's all for now. Allow me to put an end to this correspondence, which is a waste of time for both of us. I leave you to your pipe-dreams. Take care, nice guys finish last.

BOOK III
THE HIDDEN PRINCE
(1519–1525)

CHAPTER 5
Quia Nominor Princeps (1)
[For I am called the Prince]

The following document was found in a separate sheaf. It is preceded by a testament-letter written by Luigi Firenze, attributing the text to Niccolò Machiavelli and describing its story. Little is known about Luigi Firenze, except that he was one of the young followers and friends of Machiavelli and that he is thought with certainty to have attended, toward the end of the year 1510, the "Orti Oricellari," those meetings of literati which were held in the magnificent Rucellai gardens in Florence. Machiavelli took part in these reunions, and gave there a public reading of his "Discourses on the First Decade of Livy," in part or in toto. Firenze's letter is dated December 1527, shortly before his death. It was authenticated, with the help of family documents, as being from his own hand. What remains, of course, is the problem of the authenticity of the text, which Firenze claims to have been written by Machiavelli, and which he recopied. The learned works cited in the Introduction have dispelled most of the doubts. The text is not dated, but several clues lead one to think that it was written in the first months of 1519.

Here is the essential part of Luigi Firenze's long letter:

Now I want to explain how I came into the possession of this dis-course written by the most illustrious, most subtle, and most formi-dable Signor Machiavelli, whom I had as master and friend, to my enchantment and to the peril of my soul.

Master Niccolò was the most fascinating and the most slippery of men. He would instruct us in his own manner, which was indirect and often left us in suspense, not knowing where he was leading us, and whether he was playing or not. Then one of us, joined by the others, asked for a written explication of his dazzling and sinuous work ["The Prince"]. *He resisted a long time, invoking the principle that any act of confidence which places you at the mercy of others is a weakness and a sin. Finally, as we urged him on, he wrote this discourse where he removed many masks without removing them all. The style he adopted was the very same style as his treatise. Enough, he said, to il-lustrate the maneuver and to exercise the minds of the young. Con-cerning the* Discourses on Livy *which he was reading to us, he added this: whoever has understood* The Prince *will understand* The Dis-courses, *provided the addressees be kept in mind.*

Nevertheless, if he read this discourse, or gave it to be read to who-ever deserved it, in his opinion, he was careful never to leave it out of his sight. He said that if that discourse ever had the misfortune of being circulated, he would scream that it was a forgery and would never leave the forger in peace. Those papers, he would say mockingly, are meant for the stake.

I was driven by that ardor of youth the Master so enjoyed, yet he could not know that it would end up thwarting his own will. The idea that this discourse might be lost forever made my blood boil. One day, when Signor Niccolò was speaking in his manner, which has never been equaled, I took the papers from the table where he had left them and recopied the text as fast as I could. And because this discourse was known to me, and that I knew shorthand, I did it quickly. Since that time I have recopied it anew, often reread it, always kept it secret, moved to tears that I possessed this treasure, ashamed of the manner, tormented by its content.

Today, with the end of my life approaching, I want to entrust these lines to divine Providence, not knowing what to decide, and whether this way or that would add to my sins . . .

A few devout words follow, and, at the end, a postscript which the reader will find further down in the text. Machiavelli's text is comprised of two parts. We have given them in two chapters. The title is by the translator.

I.

All the works which men find authoritative have been written either with covered words, or with uncovered words. Those written with covered words can be written in different ways. A new book calls for a novel form of writing. Whoever wants to understand it must grasp the fact that to write as I do is to act. *Et facta mea, vos, sequi volo.*[1] Once the writer's intentions have been fixed, the words come easily to whoever knows how to use them. That is why one must read carefully what I say that I say, in order to understand what I do without saying it. And what must enlighten the reader who knows how to read is that I give signals through which I say in a veiled manner that I proceed veiled.

To examine this well, it is necessary to follow steps. The first step is to discern the figures of this art of writing (*arte della scrittura*). The second is to understand its reasons and its effects. One can allow oneself many things provided one knows how to write. For men are so simple, all the more so when the object is beyond the ordinary, that they easily let themselves be duped.

II.

To begin with examples, I'll take the one which, to all appearances, governs all the others, I mean that of governments. Here I pass over in silence the classification established by those who have the rep-

---

[1]   "And I want you to follow my acts," extracted from a phrase which Livy places in the mouth of an army captain (*Roman History*, VII, 32), and which Machiavelli also cites in his *Discourses on the First Decade of Livy*, III, 28.

utation of being wise, and I classify principalities in a new manner. The vulgar mob will be impressed by the appearance of a powerful logic. And you must see how illogical is this logic.

In the first chapter, and at the start of the second, I say as follows;

> (I) All States, all Seigneuries which have had a command over men have been and are either republics or principalities. Principalities are either hereditary, as when their princes have long been of the blood of their lord, or new. The new ones are either entirely new, as Milan was for Francesco Sforza, or they are like members added to the hereditary State of the Prince who acquires them, such as the kingdom of Naples for the King of Spain. These Seigneuries thus acquired are either accustomed to live under a Prince, or habituated to being free; and they are acquired either with the arms of others, or with one's own, either by fortune or by virtue.

> (II) I shall leave aside the discussion of republics, because I have discussed this at length elsewhere. I shall turn my attention only to principalities and I shall strive to follow the canvas I have said, and I shall discuss how these principalities can be governed and preserved.[2]

It appears that I make firm distinctions. First, I say that regimes

---

[2]   Machiavelli's Italian, like More's Latin, raises daunting problems of translation. In the case of the *Prince*, the chief difficulties are due to this: Machiavelli's phrase is elliptical, its construction can be slipshod, his vocabulary is often ambiguous, trenchant formulations are followed by convoluted ones. Translators are tempted to want to do too well, so they resort to logic, select among the possible meanings of the text and arrange it as best they can. But to stray from the letter in the case of an author like Machiavelli is to run the risk of distorting him. An irrefutable example is the following: a frequent usage among contemporary translators has been to render *virtù, fortuna, ordini, stato,* by different words corresponding to the meaning that the context apparently gives it. But if Machiavelli chose to use a single term when he could have used several, it is undoubtedly for good reason. A good rule to follow is to believe in the credibility of the author, especially when he gives innumerable signs of his subtlety. On the same subject, it is erroneous to translate *principe* as *king.*

are of two kinds, and only two, and of those of the second kind, I say that I will not discuss them. But whoever has good vision must see that the distinction is not as clear-cut as it appears to be, and that I'm always ready to overrule myself. The way of doing this is to confuse the ideas and to mix up the examples. Thus I say that in a Republic one lives in liberty and in keeping with its laws [V], but I also say that under a Prince, one can live according to the laws and even in a "civil" manner [IX].[3] As for examples, I take them of all sorts, and for the republican examples, I place them once in a while on the same footing as the others. In Chapter III, I contrast the errors of the King of France in Italy and the conquests, so wisely conducted, by Republican Rome. There follows the Venetian Republic, the Florentine, the Swiss Republics and other similar cases, as you will see below (or as you will not see, for what I announce I sometimes forget on the way). And you must also see that of the Republics I speak of, I speak repeatedly of their strength and say nothing that might reduce their merits or offend the Republicans.

Secondly, I distinguish the principalities according to the manner of acquiring them, in order to consider the manner of governing and keeping them. As I have said, the principalities are of two kinds: the hereditary and the new. But there is a sort of principality that is neither

On the other hand, a purely literal translation runs up against expressions or turns of phrase that cannot be translated word for word without spoiling the literary qualities of the text. Specifically, a literal translation dulls the trenchancy of the Machiavellian turn of phrase and erases its rhythm and its assonances. We have chosen to proceed as we did with More: to be as faithful as possible to the letter, except when there is too much dissymmetry between the two languages. Concerning the *Prince*, we have generally relied on translations that stick closely to the text, those of Harvey Mansfield in English and of Jean-Louis Fournel and Jean-Claude Zancarini in French. On the different translations, see the Appendix.

[3] Chapter IX is dedicated to the "civil Principate." This expression seems to be a contradiction in terms, since the adjective *civile* suggests, in the usage of the time, a republican form of government. This chapter has raised many speculations and many quarrels.

hereditary nor new. And a Prince can be new without being so. And a Prince can be hereditary or new according to the way I accommodate history. Let me give you some enlightenment as to these three points. I want them to suffice for the moment (as you know I like this manner of speaking, which impresses and sounds authoritative).

As to the first point, this sort of principality which is neither hereditary nor new, we find that in Chapter XI, where I speak of the Papacy under the title "ecclesiastical principalities," and you will find something to smile about. I take that matter up again in a digression in Chapter XIX:

> In the same manner [as the Turk], the Sultan's Kingdom, being entirely in the hands of the soldiers, he must, without regard for the peoples, keep them as friends. You will note that this Sultan's State is different from all the other principalities: for it is similar to the Christian pontificate, which can be called neither a hereditary principality nor a new principality.

Scrupulous souls will perhaps want to find in the Sultan's State the equivalent of the Sacred College, or in Rome, the equivalent of the Mamelouks.

The second point is that a Prince may be new without being so. Such, for example, is Ferdinand of Aragon, the present king of Spain, Prince by hereditary right, but who can almost be called new Prince. For "If you consider his actions, you will find them all very great, some of them extraordinary." His means of action is good faith preached but never practiced, and a "pious cruelty," with the effect that subjects are held in suspense and in great awe [XXI].

For the third point one should read Chapter XIX and what I say there about the Roman emperors. Let me pause over these emperors, who reigned successively from Marcus Aurelius to Maximinus: ten princes, eight put to death, a most unhappy sequence. I don't say why I begin here and stop there; I distribute titles and qualities in my own way. Of Marcus Aurelius, who acceded to the Empire by adoption, I make a hereditary prince; but for Alexander, who became emperor by the same way, I place him among the new Princes. Of Commodus and Caracalla, hereditary princes, I say that they had the misfortune of imitating the new Prince, Septimus Severus; but of Maximinus, himself a new Prince, I say the same thing. In short, I confuse things. It must be concluded that the way my discourse is ordered will be easy to find if the reader examines some of the examples I have mentioned and if he sees how Livy orders what he writes. To all these orders [*ordini*], I submit myself entirely.[4] (Let's pause for a moment. This last phrase is intimidating and confusing. The reader remains in suspense, then he catches on or he doesn't. Or he catches on and sees that the confusion is deliberate, and that its purpose is to give a signal to some and to disconcert others. Or he doesn't get the point, and he believes he has missed something worth noting, and he feels slightly defeated. It follows that the first reader is on the right track, and the second also, but it isn't the same track and leads him into being led by the nose. And you should see that I don't dislike this method.)

Now, for the sake of concision, I ask you to pause and consider the three great models I give of the new Prince: Cesare Borgia, Ferdinand of Aragon and Septimus Severus. The first owed his elevation to the good fortune of his father Alexander VI; the second, as I have said, acquired his kingdom by way of heredity; the third became emperor by virtue of his arms and by the favor of his army. Therefore you should see that the new Prince is not new by his manner of acquiring power but by the virtue he puts into its exercise. You will ask yourself if the "new Prince" doesn't disdain the above distinctions, and if my aim is to classify or to do the opposite.

III.

Now I want to take up Chapter V, one of those chapters about conquest. You'll find there many things that are self-contradictory

---

[4] With this last phrase, Machiavelli pastiches the phrase which closes Chapter XIII: "And the mode of ordering one's own arms will be easy to find if one reviews the orders of the four I have named above [Cesare Borgia, Hiero, David, Charles VII] and if one sees how Philip, father of Alexander the Great, and how many republics have armed and ordered themselves; and to these orders I submit myself entirely."

in a certain way, for there are many ways and many reasons for contradicting oneself. This chapter is entitled "How to administer the cities or the principalities which, before they were conquered, lived under their own laws." He says this:

> When those States which are acquired, as we have said, are accustomed to live under their own laws and in liberty, and that you want to hold them, there are three ways of doing it. The first is to leave them in ruins; the second is to go and live there in person; the third is to let them live under their own laws, exacting a tribute from them and creating within them a State composed with a few [an oligarchical State] that keeps them friendly to you. For this State being created by that Prince, it knows that it cannot last without his friendship and power, and that it must do everything to maintain him. One holds more easily a city accustomed to live free by means of the citizens themselves than in any other way, if you wish to spare it.
>
> As examples, take the Spartans and the Romans. The Spartans held Athens and Thebes by creating a State of a few there; and yet they lost them. The Romans, to hold Capua, Carthage and Numantia, destroyed them and did not lose them. They wanted to hold Greece almost as the Spartans had done, and that did not succeed; so much so that, to hold Greece, they were forced to destroy many cities of this province. For in truth, there is no sure way to possess them except to ruin them. Whoever becomes the boss of a city accustomed to live free and does not destroy it, should expect to be destroyed by it. For it always has as a refuge in rebellion the name of liberty and its ancient orders, which are never forgotten either through length of time or because of kind deeds. Whatever one does and whatever measures one takes, unless the inhabitants are separated or dispersed, they do not forget this word *liberty* nor their ancient orders; and at the least event, immediately, they resort to it. That is what Pisa did a hundred years after being reduced to slavery by the Florentines.

However, when the cities or the provinces are accustomed to live under a Prince, and those of the same blood have been annihilated, since on the one hand they are accustomed to obey and, on the other, they do not have their former Prince, they don't come to an agreement on choosing one and do not know how to live free. Consequently they are slower in taking up arms, and it is easier for a prince to win them over and secure them. But in republics, there is more life, a greater hatred, a greater desire for revenge. The remembrance of their ancient liberty does not leave them, and cannot leave them in peace. So the surest way is to annihilate them or to live among them.

I skip quickly over two points: that the principalities I speak of in the text are not those I refer to in the title;[5] and that the word *city* covers that of *Republic*. I come now to the argument and do a bit of logic. I say, therefore, that the conqueror of a free city can act in three ways: the first (A), the second (B) and the third (C). The best way is C if you want to avoid A, but the examples say that C leads to ruin and that the only sure way is A. After a detour, it follows that the best way is either A or B. From this I conclude that the author is doing what he can to lose the reader, which impresses the vulgar reader and alerts the clever one. You should also see something else. The discourse has enough to suggest to men of both camps things that flatter their ears. Reread the last sentences, which can be taken with a double meaning. I'll return to this point.

IV.

As examples, I want to take now Chapters VII and VIII and what they say about the way a new Prince must conduct himself. I say that the best way to proceed is to use several languages well, which means to alternate and mix them as one should.

First of all, it should be observed that the propositions which follow one another don't harmonize between them or are in some other

[5] The first do not know how to live free, unlike republics; the second (those of the title) live under their laws like republics.

form of disharmony. In Chapter VII, I praise Cesare Borgia and give him as an example. Of his actions, which were filled with such cunning and force, I say that they were of such virtue that "I could not give a better teaching to a new Prince." In a second step, in the following chapter, I blame those who have set an abominable example, riddled with treasons and cruelties. As examples I cite those great villains whose names were Agathocles of Sicily and, in our own time, Liverotto de Fermo. For, I say, we cannot "call virtue the fact of killing one's fellow citizens, betraying one's friends, being disloyal, pitiless, and impious." At this some readers are reassured. Others will see that the acts for which Cesare Borgia is praised are no different in nature than those for which Agathocles and Liverotto are blamed. About Liverotto, whoever knows Italian history will remember that before he was betrayed and strangled by Cesare Borgia, he was one of his mercenary chieftains. The lieutenant's infamy did not spoil the captain's virtue. The third step comes at the end of the chapter: it is allowed to talk of a good and a bad use of cruelty, according to whether it is appropriate or not. The new Prince must be wise in his cruelty: it must be dealt swiftly, to secure his power before reassuring the people, in order to secure himself even more. And you see that the art of astounding and of reassuring can also be practiced in writing.

Now I want to add that these chapters can be read differently. One could read like this: that the example of Alexander's bastard son [Cesare Borgia] is forced and should not be taken literally; that I give him honors that are belied by his reputation; that his virtue did not resist misfortune and that he collapsed with the one who was sustaining him [that is, at the death of his father]; that there is something paradoxical in glorifying something that ends up in ruin; that the place deserved by the Valentinois [Cesare Borgia] is far more that of Alexander's instrument, which I give him further down [Chapter XI]. Once again you see that whoever knows how to write can provide the reader with several discourses in the same discourse.

The second part of the writer's maneuver is to mix the two languages so as to get the compasses out of sync. Looking at matters more closely, one can see that there was in Cesare Borgia a great ferocity and a great virtue [*tanta ferocità e tanta virtù*]; that Agathocles conducted himself without virtue, but also with virtue; that Liverotto allied virtues and villainy. Further on, I attribute to the Medici Pope [Leo X] "goodness and virtues without number" [XI], and to Hannibal "an inhuman cruelty [. . .] joined to virtues without number" [XVII]. As to Septimus Severus, that he was "a most ferocious lion and a very sly fox" detracts nothing from his great virtue [XIX]. And to conclude, I'll say that, in Chapter XV, virtues are opposed to vices, but that "everything considered, we can find something that looks like virtue" in using the vices imposed by necessity.

The word *virtue*, therefore, has many virtues provided it be utilized as a box with multiple drawers. I leave aside other uses that blur things even more, and I restrict myself to what is important. Virtue can be both ancient and new; it can either oppose vice or give it a wise acceptance (in the preceding sentence, as in my little treatise, I also play with the word *wise*). I conclude, then, that the right usage of words means using the art of contradiction and ambiguity in order to skirt around defenses or aim elsewhere.

V.

It should not come as a surprise (whoever is surprised should be surprised at being surprised) if I add a few words on my manner of holding forth about our religion. This manner follows the same rules, including that of undermining the rules.

Of men and of things established and sustained by God, I say first that we must not reason, because these are lofty objects which our intelligence cannot attain. Then I reason about them to show that these are not lofty objects and that our intelligence can understand them [VI, XI]. Whoever reads with care the pages on the Roman church will easily find in those pages a dash of irony and a great Absentee. For God wants, doubtlessly, his Pontiffs to believe more in arms and perjuries than in prayers raised up to Him. In Chapter XVIII, I praise as is fitting the Borgia pope for his having known how to perjure himself and fool his people.

Of the great men of the Old Testament, I retain Moses and David. In Chapter VI, on the question of those who by their virtue and their own arms became new Princes, I say that "the most excellent were Moses, Cyrus, Romulus, Theseus and others like them." Of Moses, "who had such a great preceptor," I say that he was of another rank, then I immediately place him in the same rank as the others. In the rank of Romulus, son of the god Mars, who killed his brother and was rewarded by his elevation to the realm of the immortals; the rank of Theseus, who killed the Minotaur, slept with the queen of the Amazons and performed many other miraculous actions. You will see that this way of taking seriously the history told by the religion of the Ancients says something about how seriously we must take the history on which our Holy Church bases itself. You will equally see whether I'm not correcting this history as I should be doing, by hushing up the action of God in favor of the military feats of Moses and David.

Of the latter I have written only a few lines concerning auxiliary soldiers, mixed and one's own [XIII]. But since the reason given contains an element of surprise, you might see whether there isn't something hidden here. So I take the episode of David's fight against Goliath, where David divested himself of the arms given him by Saul to face the Philistine and decided to go into combat with his slingshot and a stick (which I transform into a knife with my pious imagination).[6] I make of this an example in favor of one's own arms, as opposed to mercenary and auxiliary arms. As for the other examples, they are Cesare Borgia, Hiero of Syracuse, Charles VIII, and Philip of Macedonia. Some will perhaps find that my biblical allegory has something amusing about it and that the connection between David and Cesare or Hiero makes one ponder a bit. From all this it isn't difficult to draw conclusions about what separates or draws together the Pope and other Princes, Moses and the imaginary founders of Antiquity, David and some tyrants.

To clarify things better, I want to add that what is helpful in this art of the writer's maneuver is the way I have of talking in profane

---

[6] See I Samuel 17: 38–51. The biblical text insists: "There was no sword in David's hand." David fights in the name of the Lord of Israel, "for Yahweh is the master of combat." The connection with one's own troops is not self-evident.

terms of religious things and in religious terms of profane things. On the first point I have said enough in the preceding pages. Concerning the second, I shall cite first as an example the use I make of the words *sin* and *redemption*. On the ruin of Italy when she was taken by the Barbarians [the French, the Spanish and the Germans], I invoke our *"sins,"* but not in the sense used by Friar Savonarola: "he who said that our sins were the cause told the truth; but these were not at all the sins he was thinking of, but the sins I have narrated; and since those were the sins of princes, they suffered the pains of their sins as well" [XII]. And the redemption I speak of further on is certainly not the redemption of sins against heaven. Read Chapter XXVI, where Cesare Borgia, without being named, appears as the man sent by God for the *redemption* of Italy, and where the rest of the text calls upon marvelous things inspired by the book of *Exodus* to invite the Medici to make themselves the *redeemers* of Italy. I leave it to you to see whether there is mockery here or not.

Now I want to finish with a passage which recapitulates many of the things said above. At the end of Chapter VI, speaking of prince-founders—Moses, Cyrus, and others like them—I distinguish between those who have recourse to prayers and those who can force things:

> In the first case, they always end badly and bring nothing to term; but when they depend on themselves and can force things, then it is rare that they perish. This is the reason why all the armed prophets triumphed and the disarmed prophets were ruined. For over and above what we've said, the nature of peoples varies, and it is easy to persuade them of a thing but difficult to keep them firm in this persuasion. That is why things must be ordered in such a way that, when they no longer believe, they can be made to believe by force. Moses, Cyrus, Theseus and Romulus could never have made their peoples observe their constitutions for a long period if they had been disarmed, as occurred in our time to Friar Savonarola. He went to his ruin with his new orders when the multitude began not believing him.

It follows that the word *prophet* can be stretched to the point of including Cyrus, Theseus, and Romulus; that Moses and Savonarola are in opposition only as armed prophet and disarmed prophet; that the laws of Moses are of the same nature as the institutions of Rome, Athens, or Persia; that religions are established, maintained or lost through coercion. It follows equally that beliefs don't really differ and that their fortune depends on the force of arms; that the truth we claim to follow at present has no other force than the force of force. We must also see that I am silent about the Founder of our religion, whose posterity belies the idea that disarmed prophets are condemned to fail. This might serve to shed some light on my new enterprise (*mi empresa nuova*).

VI.

Examples of my way of writing you now have abundantly. But to put an end to this point, I want to come back to present things and to shed some light on the discourses I am addressing to our new masters [The Medici]. I speak of the discourses where I speak to them in a live voice, the one that opens the work along with my dedication to the magnificent Lorenzo, or the one that ends it and is addressed to the whole illustrious House. I don't speak of the rest, where I abstain from citing as an example the Medici of yesteryear. I leave you to guess why.

About these discourses, I say they offer openly many words of honey or incense and say covertly that these words are so much smoke. And I take the first example, the dedication. There, addressing myself to the young Prince's Magnificence, I offer him the volume as well as my services. I do it in keeping with custom and in my own way. I flatter the Prince as I should and I flatter myself to be teaching him how a Prince must act. I solicit humbly, I promise proudly, I pay my court, I speak hardily and firmly.

I am not speaking to the Prince alone, however. I send signals to others. Let's pick up where we left off. For a moment, I boast of having "the knowledge of the actions of great men, a knowledge taught me by a long experience of modern things and by a constant reading of the ancient ones." Then I modestly suggest that this is not the presumption of a man of low condition, for:

As those who draw landscapes place themselves below in the plain to observe the nature of mountains and of high places, and to observe the nature of low places place themselves high on the mountain, so too, to know the nature of peoples well, one needs be a Prince, and to know the nature of princes well, one needs to be from the people.

Whoever reads this attentively will be compelled to ask himself how I intend to counsel a Prince who governs a people if I know just the Prince and not the people. How can I bank on my experience and my readings, then place myself in the midst of the people who have neither this experience nor these readings; if I am really convinced that the people know the Prince when I am about to advise the Prince to fool a people that is easily fooled? That is why I say to some that you mustn't confuse the spirit and the letter.

The second discourse, I mean the final exhortation, must be understood in the same manner. There I adopt a tone that contrasts sharply with the rest. Here I speak in a contrived voice and speak as a prophet. Some people might ask themselves whether this new language is to be taken seriously: for example, these marvelous events I borrow from the Bible, which I claim to be without precedent. Or these high-flown hopes placed on this family whose head is the Prince of the Church. Look elsewhere in my work. The Medici Pontiff, I kiss his fisherman's shoes as I should [XI], but I also say something that makes him look stripped naked. For among the reasons I list for our present calamities, there is that one which is to be read between the lines, which is this worldly will of the popes to be great in the temporal order. Reread me with attention and you will see: that the Church was at the origin of the division of Italy [XII]; that the popes made an inordinate use of the material profits of their state [XI]; that "as the Cardinal of Rouen [George of Amboise, minister of King Louis XII] was telling me that the Italians knew nothing about war, I answered him that, as for me, the French understood nothing about the State, for if they did, they wouldn't have let the Church rise to such greatness" [III]. You may conclude as you see fit.

VII.

Therefore, he who writes a book must never turn his thoughts away from the art of the maneuver. And I want to recapitulate the ways a good captain in writing must hold his pen. All those we have seen amount to six different matters: reasoning, words, examples, allusions, tones, signs. Reasoning I bend; words I distort; examples, ancient and modern, I arrange; allusions I multiply; and tone I play with in order to position the rest, including signs.

Concerning reasoning, I say that the simplest maneuver is retraction at a distance. The most subtle maneuver is to align the reasons so as to place things in disorder. And for this to happen, one must go fast, march with assurance, give false directions, or branch off on the sly. For there is an art of self-contradiction made in the shadow of reasons and distinctions, which is an art of telling each of the hearers what he must hear. He who wishes to be enlightened must know that contradictions can be of several kinds: either they are there to comfort those readers who get scared, or they are there to alert some others, or they are there to declassify and reclassify things, or they are there for other reasons which it is pointless to name here (for there is some virtue in leaving the reader in suspense). Of all this I have given a sufficient number of examples. I would only add this: I say that habit makes peoples well disposed toward hereditary princes [II] and that men easily change masters [III]; that hereditary principality is a natural thing [II], as is natural the desire to acquire [III]; that the Prince must gain the friendship of the people [IX] and that he must be feared by the people [XVII]; that divisions within the city are inevitable [IX] and that one must guard against them [XX].

Of words and of ways of using them to turn or dance around things I have already spoken. The careful reader will see what the rules are: never define, deregulate usage (but not always nor entirely), divert the meaning by changing the object, give preference to words with a broad meaning; in short act with *liberty, virtue, prudence and wisdom*, all things which must be understood correctly in order to master *fortune* and to found new *orders*. That is why I bestow the title of *Prince* so generously on kings, popes, consuls, emperors, tyrants, prophets, warlords, heroes and others like them or not.

Concerning the ancient and modern examples, I provide them short and numerous and I color them as I will. I contend that I am doing here what most of those who have written about the past have done; but I'm also acting in a new way. What I am doing like most of the other writers is not telling the whole truth, For many of them tell marvelous things. These and others celebrate the winners, concealing what could bring them dishonor and magnifying what brings them glory. What makes my route a novel one is that I use this tactic with far more liberty. For I treat history like a conquered land. I derive no vanity from this; it is a territory in submission. And I want to give you an example, as a supplement. As you know, I say of mercenary captains that they never commit anything except evil. To demonstrate this point, I cite the case of Francis Sforza, who was made captain of the Milanese, gave them victory and took their liberty away [XIII]. But of Francis, I said previously that he became a new Prince "by proper means and with a great virtue of his own" [VII]. I conclude from this that examples are good arms.

Concerning allusions and eloquent silences, I want to provide a few new examples. The first can be discovered without effort, but not always its double meaning. In Chapter XX, I advise the Prince whom I am addressing that "princes, and especially those that are new have found more faith and utility among men who, at the beginning of their states, were thought suspicious than among those who, at the beginning, had their confidence." If a few readers of this and what follows find that the paradox is a strong one and that I am courting the Prince too openly, let them consider that the paradox can be understood in two ways: is it the forced note of an impatient courtesan or the irony of an apparent one? Readers of whatever stripe will be getting something out of this.

For the other examples I leave you to judge. Those who are reputed wise, I treat them as they should be treated, abstaining from quoting anyone, unless it be the honorable Xenophon and his fantasies about Cyrus [the *Cyropaidea*]. I attack "things imagined" [XV] and "writers" [XVIII] without naming anyone. For their sleep must be untroubled. You will observe that I am constant in my omission of words like *tyranny* and *usurpation*; equally constant in omitting the words *justice* and *common good;* that I never mention salvation or hell; I play sleight of hand with our divine Master on occasion, and I never mention his divine Son. For our hidden God has a virtue which he shares with the sages who went into the other world: He never protests.

From all this it follows that I give many signs which make it clear that I leave things in suspension. I shall give other examples below. I want to say one thing, however, that you must have noticed already: that my enterprise reveals itself for a moment in Chapter XV, which is at the heart of my treatise. There I say that I am borrowing a new route, and that "my intention is to write something useful for whoever understands it." Only the vulgar understand nothing. But, as we say, "in the world, there is nothing but the vulgar" [XVIII].

Now to finish with this matter, I will say how I induce a state of non-understanding in the vulgar. The principal means is the tone of the discourse. On this point it should be understood that there are occasional tones, and an overall tone. The occasional tones are of two kinds: that of the Prince's courtesan, and that of the Italian who is bowled over by the present misfortunes.[7] The overall tone is a dry, grave and hardy tone whose primary object is to take in the vulgar with appearances. For the appearances are those of logic, and I manhandle logic frequently; for these appearances are those of seriousness, and I do not disdain lightness; for they are those of sincerity and I use that parsimoniously; except, perhaps to make you less of a bumpkin. I shall speak of these three points in a few words.

So, I give the appearance of rigor. I stake a claim on the "effective truth of the thing" (the *verità effetfuale della cosa*), and I adopt the tone of a Master. Everybody must notice (and if he doesn't he's a prick [*cazzo*]) how I begin my sentences (like this one) and how often I say *I*. There follow reasons, distinctions and examples which I tune or

[7] Machiavelli speaks as a courtesan in his dedication, in the final chapter, and occasionally elsewhere. He speaks as an Italian "patriot" in the final chapter, and with less lyricism in several places in the body of the text (the term *patriot* is imperfectly adequate because, very generally, it seems, he uses the word meaning Florence, or Tuscany).

untune carefully. In short I blur things with firmness. The naïve reader is impressed; he is lost but thinks he gets the big picture; and he keeps going to know how it all ends. That's where he's trapped, or in the process; for he doesn't dare admit or admit to himself that he's following his nose. And he is losing his defenses.

So I give the appearances of gravity. You've noticed that I easily dramatize things. But underneath, I indulge in mockery, as you have seen up above, and as anyone should see in the following propositions: that ecclesiastical principalities alone "are safe and happy" [XI], which nobody can deny in the days of Pope Alexander's booby-traps and Pope Jules's furies; that wherever there are good arms there are good laws [XII], and good friends [XIX], which any wise man should admit, as long as this means the law of boots and helmets and the friendship that depends on you alone; that, concerning the way princes must keep their word, the just answer is that they mustn't keep it [XVIII]. Simple people have a tin ear for irony, but whoever reads as he should cannot help seeing that I am winking. Well, a lot of things that most men hold as serious deserve to be treated lightly by those who know.

Finally, I give the appearances of sincerity. For I say things that strike and stupefy. The effect is to force people's attention and to make them think that I am speaking openly. Many will even be inclined to think that I am saying more than I think. And I help them out frequently by beating a hasty retreat. It follows that the most visible things conceal my concealing. The art of exaggerating is part and parcel of the art of confusing the issue. I conduct myself like a lion and a fox combined. Those who act only like the lions have understood nothing.

CHAPTER 6
Quia Nominor Princeps (2)

I.

So, to understand an author one must understand what he is doing. To do this, we must begin with what he says that he says and ask three questions: How does he speak? Whom is he addressing? What does he want to say?

As an example, I want to take that of this discourse, the one I am holding at this moment, compared to the one which is the object of my present discourse. Concerning my way of speaking, I say that I am not speaking here the way I speak in my little book. There, as I said, I use stratagems, I make believe, I conceal. Here if I do not say everything, I say nothing to lead you astray.

Concerning the one, or those, to whom I am speaking, I say that the discourse I am speaking of [*The Prince*] is addressed to different people; and that the present discourse is addressed only to you, my young friend, and to your peers. For you are the ones I have elected for your virtue. And I want to repeat it: these lines are destined for you alone. That is why I swore you to secrecy; that is why I give them to read, but they never leave my person.

Concerning what I want to say, I want to say here what must help you to understand what I want to say elsewhere. Speaking, finally, of what I want to do, I say that I want to test you and educate you. That is why I act like the God of our holy Mother Church, who reveals himself while remaining hidden. For what I want to tell you must be deserved. And I don't want you to be frightened if there are a few remaining obstacles to understanding what I mean to do by means of my little book.

Now, let's return to the matter at hand. I have spoken above of my manner of speaking. Now it remains to indicate whom I am addressing, and what I mean to say or suggest to different readers by the matter and the form. From this you will be able to conclude what it is I want to do, and what your role must be.

II.

So, speaking of those to whom my work is addressed, I say they reveal themselves if one knows how to make good use of two distinctions. The first can easily be deduced from the preceding. For as I've said, I put much care into marrying the force of appearance with signs that suggest that appearances are deceiving. You have understood that the addressees of my treatise are, first of all, of two kinds: those who limit themselves to appearances, and those who see something else underneath. Now you must grasp this other, more subtle distinction: I not only write in duplicate, I do it on two terrains. Concerning the first distinction, which concerns me directly, I say that I speak directly to the Medici and indirectly to their enemies [the Republicans]. Concerning the second, which is part of my great enterprise, I say that I speak directly to the vulgar and indirectly to those who are worthy of getting to the bottom of things. On these two points, I want to give you some enlightenment.

III.

On the first point, a few words will suffice. You now see that if I caress the Medici, I say *sotto voce* to the Republicans that I mustn't be taken literally. That's because I like keeping several irons in the fire. If you are offended by this it's because you haven't yet understood that between Principalities and Republics, the differences aren't as great as people think, and that you haven't yet grasped how I bear unjustly a great and continual malignancy of fortune. I mean to protect myself from these magnificent Medici by doing like Brutus,[8] and I'm waiting

---

[8]   The explanation of this ambiguous formula is provided, it seems, in Chapter 2 of Book III of the *Discourses*. Here is an excerpt: "Men of quality cannot choose to dwell apart, even though they sincerely desire to do so and have no further ambition, since no one will believe them; so that, though they prefer to be left alone, others will not leave them alone. They must then play the fool, as Brutus did, and act more or less like lunatics, admiring, talking about, attending to, and doing things in which they have not the slightest interest in order to please the Prince."

for them to get me out of my seedy condition. And the [Medici] Prince in question, if it isn't Giuliano (who has left to find fortune in the other world), it will be the young Lorenzo (who is good for nothing except hunting), or Cardinal Jules (who is good for nothing except procrastinating) or the Pontiff Leo, who thinks himself fit to liberate Italy.

Now, for your instruction, let me add this: whoever writes to the Prince in the manner I've just described must force his attention and flatter his ears. One can do it in two ways. The first is the common manner, which is to praise the Prince and extol his merits and his loyalty. (Necessity forces me to stoop to this manner at present, all the more so because I must overcome the suspicion of these Magnificences.) But there is also the second manner, which is my very own: that is, to capture the interest of the Prince with audacious remarks, to enter into his point of view by going further than he wishes to go alone, and to make an impression by speaking with power. And if I am not understood, it isn't my fault.

At the same time I give the Republicans something to think about, which must be read underneath. As examples take all the things I've said: these contradictions, or incoherencies, which are so many signs; these incidental remarks, which say good things about Republics; these forced examples, which incite those who are thus disposed to read the precise opposite; these mixtures of praise and blame where everybody finds what suits him. Reread that sentence which closes Chapter V: you can find there a counsel given the Prince to be ruthless toward the Republican cities, or you can read a praise of that Republican freedom whose memory never fades. To each his portion.

IV.

Now concerning the bottom of things and new things, I say that I am addressing myself on the one hand to ordinary men, and on the other to new men. Make up the multitude, whether it be the people, the Great, or the learned. Ordinary princes belong to this troupe. To all of these I speak so as to place them beneath the level of discourse. The intent is to disarm them so as to lead them where you want. As for the "new men," they are the ones who, whether princes or not, have

qualities that make them deserving of being so. By that I mean especially you and your peers, who have the audacity of youth and are
equipped to understand; for those who understand are rare, and those
who dare even more so. That is why I borrow oblique paths, which
only a few can follow: it is a matter of recruiting and shaping new
men. To these, I don't speak incidental words, as I do to the Medici or
to the Republicans.

To tell you the maneuver, I'll begin by saying that I position differently what is good and what is evil. You have already seen how I
blur ancient and modern [i.e., Christian] distinctions: between king
and tyrant, Pope and princes, prophet and Emperor, Bible and poetic
fables, just war and banditry, public interest and private goods, virtue
and villainy. To put it differently, I erase with one stroke everything
that our venerable tradition has said on the alleged differences between
good and bad regimes, healthy and corrupt politics, things divine and
things human, virtues and vices. For the objective, in a first phase, is
to regulate the compasses in another way, I mean those of the vulgar.
As to the new men, they must understand that the coast is clear.

Now concerning the second phase of the maneuver, which runs
parallel to the first, the method is a certain way of using contradictions. I've already spoken much about contradictions. But because this
point deserves to be understood well, I want to clarify the meaning of
the most meaningful contradictions.

My most ordinary way of proceeding is the following: propositions regulate, contradictions deregulate. On the one hand, each
proposition says that men and things are thus always and everywhere;
on the other, propositions as a whole state by their contradictions that
men and things are changing and malleable. On the one hand, the firm
tone, the dry reasoning, the definitive adverbs state in every case that
that the world is regulated; on the other hand, the contradictions say
that everything depends on occasions and on people. The simple
reader sees only the rule; the discerning reader sees the contradictions
and knows that the rule is nothing but appearance.

As a new example, I shall cite what I say about the common run
of men. For I appeal to *nature*, to the *order of things*, to *necessity*, to
what is done, to ancient and modern history, in order to say that

always men have been this or its contrary; that they are attached to
ancient things and inclined to new things; that they are ungrateful and
obligated by favors; that the friendship of the people is sure, and that
it is not sure at all; that the people ask for nothing save not to be
crushed under foot, and that men are mercenary and greedy for gain;
that they change and do not change, and other similar and opposite
things. Each proposition has the force of authority; and the complete
argument says that this authority is without authority; that nature is
a fantasy, that what is done depends on circumstances, that history
provides examples of everything, that necessity must be grabbed by
the throat. As far as the common run of men goes, we should see that
they are not made of very solid cloth.

Of the other means of contradicting oneself I shall say little. I want
to add only this: read my reasoning on the conquests of Louis [XII]
and their failure [III], and my reasoning on the conquests of Cesare
Borgia and his ultimate ruin [VII], and you will find that I contradict
myself in the same way. I speak at length of general reasons , and I
come down decisively in favor of a particular one. One reader will believe in the laws of politics, and the other will know what is to be
thought of it.

The maneuver being the one we have just seen, I recruit stupid disciples and discerning ones. Concerning the first, I lead them to think
that the new politics has the necessary foundations. And Necessity
gives the command. So they give their consent and adherence. Henceforth, they think, it is permitted to stray from the good so long as the
iron laws that govern politics make it necessary. For men and things
work that way. And those who remain attached to tradition are nit-
wits. That is my way of inviting weak minds to take themselves for
strong minds and to look down, for the wrong reasons, upon the ancient and modern ideas. When these simple-minded disciples will be
sure of themselves, I shall have made great advances in people's minds.

Concerning the discerning disciples, they must understand this:
that necessity does not have the power that I apparently give it; that
the good is not that fixed point that I preserve on the surface. Underneath, I undermine necessity and ruin the idea of the good. I follows
that I create a new freedom.

As for the reasons, they can be inferred from what I have just said. And I want to recapitulate them for your information. The first, as we have seen, is that things change and so do men. It follows that nature is either dumb or too talkative, and that no order of things is in command. It follows equally that, with times and circumstances varying ceaselessly, political action must conform to this rule: it all depends.

The second reason is that this world, so shaken by fortune, yet gives virtue its chances. Fortune, indeed, is a woman; she must either be seduced or tumbled. Virtue knows how to adapt to circumstances and how to seize the opportunity. For the means, she makes use of what is opportune. If conditions change, the truth of politics is immobile. For always and everywhere, politics is war, whether it be open or not. Those who believe in peace are the sheep, headed for the slaughterhouse.

The third reason is that men are of two species. You know which ones.

Therefore, I conclude on this point by saying that I must be understood in two ways. And simple-minded disciples will learn that the compass must be regulated differently. As for the discerning disciples, they will understand that the compass must be thrown overboard.

V.

From what has been said above, it follows that I form both plebeians and new men. The shape of my discourse plays a role here, and it isn't a minor one. In this regard, I want to add one thing. Whoever would understand just that would already be on the way to a total understanding. My way of writing indicates by itself the direction of my enterprise.

Therefore I want to speak of the language of form. I say that if I jostle the matter about so much, it is also so that form might speak and act by itself. She does it in two ways: either it corrupts and subdues simple minds (thereby also teaching you the art of the maneuver); or she teaches you to use of your own arms. I have already spoken of the first; I want now to speak of the second.

I take liberties, therefore. I also take them so as to take them. One of the reasons why I do not cease to contradict myself, is that I contradict myself in order to contradict myself. One of the reasons why I blur words and things is that I blur in order to blur. If I must say more, I'll say that my manner of saying says, among other things, this: words are serfs and must obey; grammar is a subject and must bend; logic is a good girl and must be seduced; history is a captive and must be made docile; truth is a maidservant and must be brought to heel. Which means that the discourse I use is not governed by the rules of discourse, where necessity yields to liberty. As an example, l shall remind you of this: I refrain from quarreling with my illustrious predecessors. I do not pit my reasons against theirs in a game played by the rules. I dismiss them with a word, and I undo in my own way their way of thinking. Whoever discusses in good faith is a weakling.

And I want again to say things differently. I tell the Prince that he must lie by necessity. The vulgar reader understands this to mean that necessity is law; the discerning reader grasps the fact that, speaking thus of myself, I say that I practice lying. Looking at this closely he sees that I lie well beyond the necessity of lying. For the lie is a fine and good thing in itself. It opens horizons.

I say, therefore, that the rules of discourse are not respectable. And with those rules, all the others. For among the excellent arms offered by the language of form, there is irony, provided we know how to use it. Which means that there is nothing we are unable to laugh about. Respect is good for the common run of men. Let's skip that. We see, then, the new freedom at work, which can dispense with reasons. That is what's called having a good time.

VI.

Now you cannot fail to see that my art of writing is new, and why I am not satisfied in just being called a preceptor. For I don't just talk, I act. I teach war while taking the offensive. For my own arms, I have those of the word, whose full virtue is unknown to the simple-minded. The sword must follow, used with wisdom. The simple-minded will applaud. As to the title I bear, see Hiero.[9]

---

[9]   Machiavelli is, in all likelihood, referring to the passage dedicated to Hiero

I want this and the rest to be enough for you. For you and your peers will have to take over.[10]And you must do it without fear nor trembling. God rewards those who have no fear of hell. I've said enough. Amen.

of Syracuse, which concludes Chapter VI, and particularly to this sentence: "And he was of such virtue, even in his fortune as a private man, that he who wrote about him said that 'he lacked nothing of being a king except a kingdom.'" Machiavelli repeats the same example and the same *formula* in his dedicatory letter of the *Discourses*.

[10] Cf. *Discourses*, *I*, Foreword; II, Foreword; III, 25.

CHAPTER 8
Addenda

Following Machiavelli's text, Luigi Firenze wrote a postscript. It begins like this: "Signor Niccolò told me this later, which I insist on recording. He made these comments a short time after he had brought his Florentine Histories *to our Holy Father Clement [1525]. About these bonds which tied him henceforth to the Medici House, I did not hide my embarrassment and I plied him with questions. And on these* Discourses *I also questioned him, concerned as I was to know if I was reading him in the spirit he had taught us. He answered mockingly, saying that I was no longer a virgin and that he had already told me how to take the truth of his discourses, preferably from behind. One day, however, he showed his willingness to light my lantern anew. I report these comments without cutting anything out. I am doing it from memory, and my memory is good."*

At this time Machiavelli is no longer in disgrace, or not entirely. Since around 1520, he has ceased being quarantined. But the Medici are employing him only for compromising or subordinate tasks.

In the autumn of 1520, Cardinal Jules Medici orders from him a report on the reform of the Florentine State, intended for Pope Leo X. In November, the Cardinal again orders him, through the intermediary of the officers of the University, to write "the Florentine annals and chronicles," which will become the Florentine Histories. *The following year, he is given a third-class mission to the Franciscans of Capri. The Medici graces are carefully measured, and not devoid of ulterior motives.*

In May 1525, after months of waiting, Machiavelli offers the eight books of his Florentine Histories *to Jules de Medici, now become Pope Clement VII. The books are graciously received. Machiavelli receives a hundred gold ducats.*

Here are Machiavelli's comments as reported by L. Firenze.

I.

You are pained, my good Luigi, by my new title [historiographer in the employ of the Medici]. My God! It's your pain that pains me. I'm doing today what I was doing yesterday, and as for my Masters, I'm paying them with the same coin. I see that you are striving to follow the road I have traced but that you are knocking up against the same old stones. Well, I love this ardor for learning which makes you horny, and I'm going to add a few coins to your education.

The Medici who now sits on Peter's throne always has on him his old bag of dirty tricks. A few years ago, before the tiara, he tried to entrap me. Try to remember, shortly after Lorenzo's burial, when the dynasty was in peril, he asked me to hold forth on the institutions of Florence. This cunning devil was showing interest for things that went against his own interests. But you won't catch Machiavelli when the trap is so obvious. Reread my Discourse [*Discourse on the things of Florence after the death of Lorenzo the Younger*], and you will see how well I have muddled things, and something to tickle one and all. On the regime since 1512, I remain quiet. On the regime to be established, I say that one has to choose between the white and the black [the Republic or the Principality], that the white is what Florence needs, but that the white can be black as long as the Medici live. *Suum cuique tribuere,* as old Cicero says [to each his due]. I favor the Republic, I say to the Medici that it could be a principality. To achieve this I recommend they bestow favors and practice fraud. This is enough to satisfy their appetite and reduce their credibility.

Enough said, my good man. Either you understand or you deserve to be whipped. And if you need supplementary practice, take up, or re-read *The Golden Ass* or *The Mandragola* and find the double meanings. I come now to these *Florentine Histories*, which seem to move you so much. Wait until you can read them carefully, you will see there also that, even when I write on the Medici something intended for the Medici, I slip in something to satisfy their enemies. Among the methods is the art of making other people speak. Listen carefully to what I say about old Cosimo [de Medici]. You will hear a convoluted discourse, where the truth of things is placed in the mouth of Cosimo's adversaries.[11] Listen also to the remarks that I attribute to this Prior,

---

[11] This passage confirms the testimony of the young Republican Donato Giannotti, who reported this confidential utterance of Machiavelli's: "I can-

sprung from my imagination, who teaches a lesson to the Duke of Athens [Gaston de Brienne, II, 24]. You will hear beautiful and strong words in favor of freedom, and you can easily guess who they are addressed to.

Enough said on this point. For the rest, and for the way I collide with this old strumpet we call history, put your common sense to work. I only want to add a word on the dedication. The reason is that I took considerable pleasure bamboozling his Holiness Clement. Here's the trick: : you know now that, here and there in my opus I say bad things, hintingly, about the illustrious house of the Medici. Now, take that letter I sent to the Pontiff: I defend myself like a cunning little devil, but against the contrary, I defend myself against the reproach of saying too many good things about them. You're not laughing, you ought to, let me try again. My dedication tells Clement that, knowing how he hates flattery, I took pains not to be a flatterer. If I seemed to be one, it was only out of respect of the truth of history. But the truth of my *Histories,* in fact, is that Clement takes pleasure in flattery, and that if I make concessions to it by necessity, he would also have a few good reasons to criticize me for not being a flatterer. But I'm wresting from him whatever it takes to see it or say it. Not everybody can be a fox.

II.

Speaking now of profound things, I shall be brief. You have the keys; it's up to you to use them. Remember always that those wise men who have opposed regimes are nit-wits. That is why the substance

not write history from Cosimo's assumption of power until his death as I would write it if I were free of all circumspection [*respetti*]. I shall narrate the events and leave nothing aside, but I shall not say by what methods, by what means, by what artifices one achieves such power. Whoever wants to learn that will pay attention to what I shall have his adversaries say, for what I shall be unable to say as if it came from me, I shall make them say." (Letter of D. Giannotti to Marcantonio Micheli, 30 June 1533, cited in various studies. Among them: Marina Marietti, "Machiavel historiographe des Médicis," in A. Rochon, ed., *Les Ecrivains et le pouvoir en Italie à l'époque de la Renaissance*, Paris: Université de la Sorbonne Nouvelle, II (1974): 126.) Up until now this is Machiavelli's only confidential remark on his art of writing that has come down to us.

of what I teach does not change whether I speak as Prince's counselor or as advocate for the Republic. You must infer from this that the content of the *Discourses* is of the same vintage as that of the *Prince*. For I always write to fool the simpletons, the ninnies, the suckers, and to teach virtue to the new men. This virtue, which defies all rules, is at work—you know it—in my writing. The writing of the *Discourses* provides countless examples: I reduce Livy and the Bible to what I want to extract from them; I speak of order and introduce disorder; I speak firmly in favor of freedom and occasionally give counsel to tyrants; here I praise the people, there I denigrate; I denounce our lack of religion and our religion itself; I blame the villains and justify the villainies; and a thousand other things where necessity is a dutiful daughter and which I leave to your shrewdness of perception. Yet I want to give you another magnificent example of my art of self-contradiction: I boast of the Ancients and I bring tidings of the New. You must read that the example of the Romans has many virtues, including that of pouring scorn on the Christians, but I give them to be imitated only to those who have no eyes to see nor ears to hear. My treatise, in fact, is a war machine against all authority. If you want to know more about my way of doing, read the last section of Book III attentively. There I speak of the good captain and I shift without pause from the captain to the combat to another captain to another combat.[12]

---

[12] If we follow Machiavelli's advice, we find numerous formulations appearing like so many allusions to his enterprise. Thus, to take only chapter titles: "What dangers are run by one who takes the lead in advising some course of action; and how much greater are the dangers incurred when the course of action is unusual" [XXXV]. "Of the qualities necessary in a captain to have the confidence of his army" [XXXVIII]; "A captain must be a good connoisseur of the places where he is in action" [XXXIX]. "That using fraud in the conduct of a war is a glorious thing." [XL]. "One often obtains with impetuousness and daring what we could not obtain through ordinary means" [XLIV]. . . . Let us add another passage which is no doubt the most direct allusion: "How dangerous it is to take the lead in a new enterprise, concerning many people, how difficult it is to handle it, to direct it, and once directed on its way, to keep it going, would be too long and too deep a topic to discuss here. Reserving it for a more appropriate place . . ." [XXXV].

Here, then, is what Machiavelli the writer said on what he does and says as a writer. But what about the man? The year is 1525. Machiavelli dies two years later. During these years, the former Secretary is very busy and, in spite of his age, shows much ardor in other fields besides that of writing. He is successful in the theater, he plunges into the "demi-monde" which populates the theater. He falls in love with the young Barbera girl, who plays, sings, and generously shares her talent. For her, Machiavelli scrapes up singers and writes little songs. Guicciardini scolds and mocks him. Machiavelli himself makes mockery of his behavior in creating the character Nicomaco—Nicollo Macliavelli, the libidinous old fogey of Clizia.

But politics grabs him by the sleeve. Italy is once again the battleground of Europe. The Imperial armies advance from the North. Florence is threatened. Machiavelli is given many missions. In April 1526, he is charged with inspecting and fortifying the walls of Florence. In 1526 and 1527, he is sent repeatedly to the armies, along with Guicciardini, Lieutenant General of the pontifical armies, to observe military operations. His letters, both official and unofficial, are filled with passion. He calls for prompt decisions and for surges of energy: "Now is not the time to start limping" (16 April 1527). But with marches and countermarches, the Imperial armies reach Rome, take the city and sack it. The terrible news reaches Florence on 11 May. It provokes the departure of the Medici (they will return) and the reestablishment of the Republic. There is little doubt that Machiavelli nourished the hope of a return to political affairs. According to a plausible witness, he confided this hope to his Republican friends. But on 10 June the Republican government named F. Tarugi to the second Chancery, although he had served the Medici administration. A void seems to have been created around the former Secretary, who was probably paying the price of his bad reputation. Machiavelli had probably been hedging his bets excessively . . .

That same day he fell sick. He died twelve days later at the age of fifty-eight. There are two versions of his death. The impious version, given by several witnesses, states that Machiavelli, in dying, would have scoffed still. He would have recounted this dream: on one side, a miserable and sad crowd, on the other a group of men discussing nobly, and in their midst, the great minds of Antiquity. Machiavelli asks who they are. "We are the saints and the blessed who are going to paradise," answer the first. "We are the damned in hell," answer the second, "for the science of this world is the enemy of God." And the narrator concludes that he would rather be in hell discussing politics than in heaven in the boring company of these beggars. The pious version is to be found in a letter written by one of his sons, the young Piero (to Francesco Nellio, 22 June). The letter states that Machiavelli accepted confession from Friar Matteo and that the said friar kept him company to the end. The authenticity of this letter has sometimes been doubted. As to the place where Machiavelli's soul went, we have no clear information. Please consult the epilogue.

Book IV
The Registers of Writing
(1535–1536)

Chapter 9
The Languages of Friendship

On the first of July 1535, at Westminster, Thomas More, the former Lord Chancellor, is condemned for high treason against Henry VIII, who has become supreme Head of the Church of England. According to the terms of the verdict, he has been guilty of speaking of the King "maliciously, treacherously, diabolically." On 6 July, around nine in the morning, he is beheaded.

The event caused a great sensation throughout Europe. Erasmus, that "most dear Desiderius," as More called him, his "darling," as the Lutheran Tyndale had written him ironically, contributed to that sensation in his own way. We shall see how Erasmus did so in the first of two letters collected here, both written during the months that followed More's execution. The second is a letter of praise for the "new martyr," sent to More's daughter Margaret. Friendship speaks out in both cases, but on different registers.

[1] *First, however, we must re-examine the series of events that preceded More's death. Since 1519–1520, the sky in Europe has grown dark. War has resumed in the East, the Turkish threat has grown more*

real, and, especially, Christendom is falling apart. On 1 November 1517, Luther nails his theses to the portal of Wittenberg church, and the tempest of religious conflict sweeps away Erasmus's hopes and those of his friends. Rabelais alone will react victoriously against the intellectual dreariness that weighs upon Europe (Marie Delcourt).

In that great quarrel which is tearing Christian Europe apart, Erasmus delays in taking sides. He maintains his distances with Luther, while also trying to restrain and protect him. He is far, no doubt, from Luther's intransigence and his forceful spiritual incursions, but he shares Luther's rejection of scholasticism, his hatred for the Church's abuses, and his desire to return to Scriptural sources. Erasmus then professes moderation and is reluctant to enter into what he calls "the gladiators' arena." He quickly becomes an object of suspicion on both sides.

Finally, in 1524, strongly encouraged by the Pope, by Henry VIII, by his English friends, Erasmus publishes the book so long awaited. To show his disagreement with Luther, he has chosen the terrain of free will, of nature and of grace (De Libero arbitrio). *His manner of arguing is that of the Christian humanist, who does not condemn nature out of hand, as opposed to the anti-humanism of the German Reformer who acknowledges grace alone. Erasmus proceeds cautiously, clearly not wanting to provoke a crisis; but in this case his art of maneuvering is a faulty tactic. Seen from the side of Orthodoxy, the book has neither the brilliance nor the punch required to answer their expectations. Seen from Luther's side, the measured tone is ineffectual. For the Reformer the question is a crucial one. He answers Erasmus with a terrifying violence and the force of all or nothing* (De Servo arbitrio, 1525). *There is no doubt, as Augustin Renaudet wrote, that Erasmus "buckled under the blow." He replies out of duty and without eagerness. The break with Luther is consummated, yet Erasmus remains a target of criticism and suspicion for theologians and monks. He states and repeats his fidelity to Rome, but he remains more or less marginalized, increasingly critical of the Reformed churches, but always dissatisfied with his own Church and attached to its internal reformation. Ever he continues to plead for a Christian return to unity: let no one provoke a confrontation, let the Church put an end to its abuses, let the innovators not reject traditional piety, let both sides concentrate on what is at the heart of Christianity. . . . But all of Erasmus's efforts were in vain. No doubt he underestimated the dogmatic dimension of the conflict. In any case, the oppositions hardened, the rift spread throughout Europe. The man who had been the Prince of humanists moved away from the center of history (Jacques Chomarat). Yet, the aging Erasmus did not let go: he worked without letting up, rejected none of his main ideas. True, he would speak of his fatigue and his disenchantment, but with the end in sight (1536), he was gaining in serenity.*

[2] *In Germany, Lutheran ideas spread like a trail of gunpowder. In England they filter in progressively, then spread more broadly after 1525, thanks especially to the English writings of William Tyndale. As of 1521, King Henry has made himself the champion of the Catholic cause: he writes, or orders the writing of, a work wherein, against Luther, he defends the sacraments of the Church (which earns him the title of* Defender of the Faith *bestowed on him by Pope Leo X). Thomas More is his associate in this enterprise, preparing and arranging the manuscript for the printer. In 1523, no doubt at the King's request, he replies under a pseudonym to Luther's furious response to the King's treatise on the sacraments. In 1528, the bishop of London, Cuthbert Tunstall, calls upon More to refute (no longer in Latin, the language of the learned, but in English) Lutheran writings which have appeared in that language. There follow seven polemical writings (1529–1533), written in haste, wherein More makes it his duty to make no concessions to his adversaries. He refutes their doctrinal errors point by point, denounces their deceitfulness, accuses them of encouraging political sedition. In reading these texts, one has the feeling that, being unable to speak like a prophet, the author corrects like a schoolmaster (C.S. Lewis). One also finds a surprising bitterness and violence in a pen of this quality, even if this was not out of place at the time. "As we read these controversies, we become aware that More the author was scarcely less a martyr of his religion than More the man. In obedience to his conscience, he spent what might have been the best years of his literary life on work which demanded talents that*

he lacked and gave very limited scope to those he had. It may well have been no easy sacrifice."[1]

On this burning question of the Lutheran reform, then, the two friends were out of tune. More remained unaware of Erasmus's hesitations and internal divisions, pressing him to enter the fray more deeply. A man known for his affability in personal relations, he adopted a violence of tone equal to that of his adversaries. It was a time when men felt, spoke and acted with violence (E.E. Reynolds). It's Erasmus who was an exception.

[3] The events that follow belong in part to caprices of history. Henry VIII, this so Catholic king, breaks with Rome and gives, without having wanted to, a new orientation to English history. A complicated chain of small causes, combined with the dynamics of the national monarchy, produce a great effect. The origin of the crisis is a personal and critical affair: the question of the King's "divorce," or, more precisely, of the annulment of his marriage. This affair, "the King's Great Matter," opens in 1527. It leads to the schism with Rome, which is consummated in 1534. Of this affair, Thomas More is the most illustrious victim.

So, in 1527, the King has become infatuated with Ann Boleyn and laments not having a son. Is this a punishment from heaven? He begins to have doubts as to the validity of his marriage. In 1509, he had married Catherine of Aragon, daughter of the King of Spain, who was then the widow of the King's brother, a union between two adolescents which had lasted no more than a few months. A dispensation had been necessary, Pope Julius II had granted it. Nearly twenty years later, Henry "placed his conscience in the service of his passion" (Bossuet) and invoked various arguments, including his young age at the time and the interdictions of Leviticus, in order to declare his scruples of conscience and to appeal to Pope Clement VII. He asks that both the dispensation and the marriage be annulled. The Pope hesitates, the theologians are divided, Queen Catherine is inflexible, her nephew

---

[1]   C.S. Lewis, *English Literature in the Sixteenth Century* (Oxford: Clarendon Press, 1965): 176.

Charles the Fifth has a hold on the Pope, King Henry is cunning and obstinate. The quarrel ends in a complete break. In a succession of measures, Henry VIII whittles away the rights of the Church of England, breaks the resistances of the Parliament, abrogates the Roman privileges on English soil. In 1533 he marries Anne Boleyn and has her crowned. The following year he forces the adoption of the Act of Succession and of the Act of Supremacy, which mark the break with Rome. Henceforth the King is the supreme Head of the Church of England. Henry seizes spiritual power and founds de facto a national Church.

Thomas More held to the validity of the King's marriage to Catherine. Solicited by the King from the start of the affair, he tried to disqualify himself on grounds of ignorance of the matter at hand; but pressured to take sides, he produced arguments and quotations which did not go in the direction the King wanted. Yet the King maintained his esteem and "friendship" for More. In October 1529, he named him Lord Chancellor. More inherited the charge previously held by Wolsey, now disgraced, but not his privileges. He succeeded in not implicating himself in the Great Affair, or in not being implicated too closely. He concentrated his attention on judiciary decisions and on the implementation of legislation against "heretics" (the Lutherans). In May 1532, the day following the submission of the clergy to King Henry, the King accepts his "resignation." More then retires completely from public life, says nothing about the most burning issue, and pursues his polemical work against heresy. In June 1533, he is invited to Queen Anne's coronation and doesn't go. His absence, like his silence, is unequivocal. The King's Secretary, Thomas Cromwell, brings charges against him in several affairs, including one of bribery, but the charges fizzle out. In April 1534 the Act of Succession is passed, coupled with the obligation of taking an oath. The Act officially recognizes the new Queen, giving priority to her children, retroactively uncrowns Catherine, and repudiates the authority of Rome. The union of Henry and Catherine is described as "contrary to the laws of Almighty God." More is the only layman to be ordered to come to Lambeth Palace on 13 April. He refuses to take the oath, and is imprisoned in the Tower of London, where he spends fifteenth months. The King, and Cromwell with him, apparently seek to break him or erase him from human memory. But More remains inflexible. He invokes his conscience, rejects the oath, and refuses to give his reasons. He is dispossessed of all his possessions, condemned to life imprisonment. But he remains a cumbersome prisoner. In May 1535, a new interrogation takes place, led, as always, by Cromwell. More is questioned on the Act of Supremacy that has been passed in November. He refuses to answer directly. He is a man of the Law and knows that it is an act of treason to say that the King is not the supreme Head of the Church of England; but that it is not treasonable not to say that he is. During the discussion, More, according to his own testimony, gives this reply (among the most famous ones):

> I am the King's true faithful subject and daily bedesman and pray for his Highness and all his and all the realm. I do nobody harm, I say none harm, I think none harm, but wish everybody good. And If this be not enough to keep a man alive, in good faith I long not to live. (More's letter to his daughter Margaret, 2 or 3 May)

In all likelihood, the King now wants his head. Cromwell stages the trial. More defends himself inch by inch. There arrives a witness at Cromwell's behest who relates a conversation during which More would have told him that Parliament could not make the King the Head of the Church. On the faith of this questionable testimony (or worse), More is condemned for high treason. He then rises to speak, to say what he had kept hidden so firmly but which in fact everyone knew: his uncompromising opposition to an Act of Parliament which "formally contradicts the laws of God and of his holy Church." He is beheaded on 6 July, and his head stuck on a pike or picket on London Bridge.

The internment, the trial and the death of Thomas More are a famous episode of English history. The dramatic intensity of the events, the image of a man alone, unshaken, opposing the demands of conscience to the abuse of power, the dialectical virtuosity of the accused and his striking replies, in short the grandeur of the drama and of the man, have made the glory—one of two glories—of Thomas More and *inspired many dramatic writers.*[2] *Many disputed questions still remain, however. Why did Henry VIII make More his Chancellor, knowing his reticence concerning divorce? Why, in such conditions, did More accept? Could he refuse? What were the reservations, misunderstandings, ruses, deceptions in their mutual relations between October 1529 and May 1532? What lay behind the praises addressed to More at the moment he was leaving his post? How can we explain the former Chancellor's obstinate or admirable silence, which brought him prison, a trial, and death? To be sure, he explained himself in his letters to his daughter and at his trial, but did he say everything? How are we to understand this freedom of conscience which he claims to have but denies to heretics? Any answer to these questions can only be more or less likely. "The real story is never written" (François Mauriac).*

[4] *In this chapter, then, the reader will find two letters written by Erasmus shortly after the execution of his "incomparable friend." The first is addressed, under the seal of discretion, to Boniface Amerbach, a friend of long standing, who will be his universal executor. In this*

---

[2]   The contemporary work that has contributed most to sustaining More's glory is Robert Bolt's play, staged for the first time in 1960, *A Man for all Seasons* (the French title puts it differently: A Man for Eternity). The play was brought to the screen under the same title by Fred Zinneman in 1966. The film won many awards and drew a large number of viewers. Bolt's Thomas More is largely that of W. Chambers, which is largely that of W. Roper. Roper, who was Margaret's husband and therefore More's son-in-law, is the author of a short *Life of Thomas More*. With a certain number of reservations, this is a masterpiece of the biographical genre. It has a great simplicity of tone, More's explosive words, whether recorded directly or reconstituted, vividness of dialogue, dramatic episodes pulsating with life. In 1935, W. Chambers wrote a great biography of More, which was long considered authoritative. Today a number of historians have criticized its hagiographic character. The same historians have taken their distances toward Roper's text for three reasons: the author's filial devotion, the silences on More's persecution of heretics, the late composition of the text (twenty years after the facts). The result, right or wrong, has been a change in More's image in the last twenty years. On these recent biographical works, see the Appendix.

letter Erasmus explains his public attitude in the face of the event, that is, what he intends to say and not to say. The content of this letter agrees with what we know from other sources. On the one hand, Erasmus is guarding More's memory. Very quickly, he writes a discreet but fervent homage, which he inserts in the Preface to his Ecclesiastes, *or the* Art of Preaching *(published in August). In his correspondence, Erasmus tells of his sorrow, he weaves crowns of glory for the "new martyrs," More and Bishop John Fisher, beheaded a few days earlier). He sends, or makes known a narrative of the trial and of the execution. This narrative is probably that of the* Expositio fidelis, *which is published by Froben in October [1535] and will have broad repercussions. Erasmus is then living at Froben's. It is entirely plausible that the text reflects Erasmus's editorial hand.*

On another score, however, Erasmus does not attack King Henry. Never will he condemn him, at least explicitly, whether in his works or in his letters. So far as we know, the only prickly comment against Henry VIII is this sentence to be found in Book I of his Ecclesiastes: *"There still exist potentates like Herod who turn Christ and his teaching to derision." The allusion was hardly difficult to grasp: as Herod, because of Herodias, had John the Baptist beheaded, Henry, because of Anne, had More and Fisher beheaded. However, this allusion is lost, we might say, in a dense work, "a forest," Erasmus called it, on the art of preaching. Why this restraint toward a King who is behaving like a despot? We shall see in his letter to Amerbach, among other things, the reasons he gives.*

The second letter is Erasmus's response to a letter sent by Margaret Roper, Thomas More's darling daughter. Margaret's letter and the texts appended (pages of the Tristitia Christi, *written by More while in the Tower] have never been found. Margaret was More's eldest daughter. She had been reared by her father in the cultivation of great literature and was at ease in Latin. She was also Erasmus's favorite. The reply he sends her is a letter of consolation wherein, while praising More, he lets his affection speak.*

To all appearances, this letter to Margaret was never sent. Perhaps Erasmus never found a sure means of making it reach its addressee. Perhaps he had learned of the persecutions which More's family were subject to. Perhaps his customary prudence in the face of the Powerful prevailed. There is, in times of trouble and confusion, a way to write and a way not to write.

I.

ERASMUS TO BONIFACE AMERBACH
Basel, 10 September 1535

Hail! This letter is for you alone. The young man who is bringing it to you was sent to me by X [illegible). I'm happy with him and I think him worthy of confidence.

You know what happened to the bishop of Rochester [Fisher] and to Thomas More, the holiest and best of men. I don't need to tell you how dear More was to me. What a man England has lost! And I, what a friend!

[1] Until a few days ago, I knew very little. No one dares write over there. The friends who long honored me with their letters and services don't dare budge an inch any longer, as if a scorpion were sleeping under every stone. Things are worse than before, but they are not new. For years More had been unable to write. Fortunately I could on several occasions send one of my boys [clerk or secretary] who brought the mail and returned with news. The last letters I received from More, two or three years ago, said almost nothing, I mean nothing that couldn't or shouldn't be placed under the King's eyes. More's discourse was meant to cajole the King or bridle him with the virtues he conferred on him. His departure from the high office he occupied, More justified by an illness which [he said] gave him chest pains. Nothing further, so far as he was concerned, except his regret to be unable to continue; and on the King's side, nothing other than benevolence and indulgence. Not a word about the divorce and the wrangles with Rome. So I played the game in turn. You know the high regard the King said he held me in. Not so long ago he had invited me to England, with lots of compliments and promises [18 September 1527]. I did my best to put the kind feelings of the Prince, and of all those over

there who appreciate my writings, to use as a shield for More. You remember, I wrote to various and sundry, to say and repeat what More wanted said about his dismissal. I also wrote a defense of More and sent it to the Reverend Faber [Johann Faber, bishop of Vienna, counselor to King Ferdinand of Austria, June 1532], so that it might be properly recognized. You know all that, but perhaps you don't know the full extent of my efforts and how vain they were. In this letter to Faber, then, I was giving fulsome praise for More and I was taking his defense on every point. To whom I was really addressing myself [King Henry], I said what proof he had given of his humanity and generosity by freeing More of the burden of the Chancellorship after giving it to him. I went so far as to say that in discharging the man who was begging him to do so, he was proving to be his friend [*philomorôs*]. In a word I was denying the discord, or the disgrace, in order to ward it off. I was also striving to make the Prince's concern for his reputation restrain him. You know that that is a usual tactic of mine. Alas! Nothing worked.

But listen to the rest of the story. Thomas Boleyn, Lord of Wiltshire and father of the new Queen of England, was urging me to send him *On the Preparation for Death*, which I had promised him. The man has a philosophical cast of mind, a rare thing among the nobility, and this wasn't the first time he was asking something of me. Whatever his intention was, I never knew. I had dedicated my *Christian Marriage* to Queen Catherine [1526]. It may be that the rival party, I mean the Boleyns, were egged on by some sort of rivalry. I had hesitated as to what answer I should give, and I had finally resolved to send this eminent personality a few short texts totally unrelated to the question of the divorce. But when he raised the question again, things had taken a new turn. More was now one of the last not to approve of the King's un-marriage and re-marriage, and the Sovereign's brand new and most honorable father-in-law could not be unaware of my ties with More. So here is what I did. I sent him the manuscript he had requested, with a dedicatory letter [1 December 1533]. Froben printed both [January 1534], but with a supplement: sixteen letters, two of them by More, the epitaph he had written, and my own letter to Faber. I don't know what repercussion this had in England, but I do know that the decision makers in that country didn't care a whit about Erasmus's friendship for More.

[2] As to the end of this unhappy story, what I know of it today I hold from Glocenius and an account of More's execution that was sent me.[3] I'm sending you some copies. You will see how More defended himself, and with what eloquence. This account should be disseminated in all the cities of Europe. I'm counting on young Froben. You'll probably be surprised to see that the King is not maligned. But I think this is preferable. I'll tell you why in a moment.

I'm also sending you the *Ecclesiastes,* which has just appeared. I put into the Preface something to do justice to the new martyrs. Look also at Book I and the phrase about Herod. You will understand without difficulty.

I plan to hold to this line of behavior. I defend, and I will defend, More's memory, but I will abstain from any public scene against the King. I know that Henry's counselors will tell him what I really feel. They aren't deaf, they will understand what I mean when I say that the man they have condemned for high treason had a heart purer than snow [Preface to *Ecclesiastes*]. But I am expecting the King to see also that I go no further. To put things differently, I say covertly what I think, but I also say that I will not say it openly. I think the King will see some advantage in not having Erasmus as a sworn enemy.

I know that some of our friends will say or think that I'm holding aback too much. But I believe that being too candid would be damaging. I don't feel like fanning the fury of this madman. As you know, I've always thought and always said that one mustn't anger wayward princes with bitter reproaches for fear that worse dramas follow— such is Augustine's opinion of impious princes. In this case nothing must be done that might block any return to good feeling. There is a lot of madness in this affair. This King's Great Matter, which was

---

3   The letter of Conrad Glocenius, Professor of the trilingual College of Louvain and a longtime friend of Erasmus, is dated 10 August 1535. The account in question is no doubt the *Exposition fidelis de morte Thomae Mori* which Froben published that October.

about changing wives, has led to the Church of England's changing Heads and to the Emperor's changing dispositions. Now the Church is crumbling just a bit more, Christendom is once again divided, war is threatening once more, and all this as the Turks are at our doorstep. There's nothing that the charms of Herodias cannot do!

I should add that the Pontiff Clement helped things out with his hesitations and his blunders. But when the cloth has been torn by teeth like those, one can hope it is not beyond mending.

I have two other reasons for dealing carefully with Henry. (The second is meant for you alone.) I am thinking of those friends in England who are under the King's claw. I am not entirely forgetting my English royalties, which I sorely need to assure my freedom. I fear that these will be dealt a fatal blow by my Preface to *Ecclesiastes*.

[3] Finally, I do in these matters what I've always done. I strive to choose carefully the terrain I must fight on, and not get involved on a terrain where doing battle is harmful. There are many occasions where it is better not to say everything.

You remember that it was popes, kings, and friends who urged me into the arena against Luther. Try as I might have done to invoke my age, my infirmities, my weakness, to swear by the gods that I would only be stirring up a hornet's nest, nothing mattered. I had to play the gladiator and enter the lists. God knows that I was born for other exercises than these! I began the match in the most courteous possible manner by publishing my *Free Will* [*De libero arbitrio*]. What a triumph! Luther answered by stoning me with insults: I was an atheist, a skeptic, a disciple of Epicurus, a blasphemer, what have you! On the other hand, although I was trying to rescue the theologians, they whipped me even harder. And do you remember the outcome? Since I wasn't in a hurry to answer Luther, they called me a coward and an incompetent. Friends themselves, like More and Tunstall, were pressing me to continue the fight. I may have crossed swords once more [with Luther], nothing could disarm the monks and the theologians. Their slogans were peddled about: "Erasmus is the father of Luther." "Erasmus has laid the eggs that Luther hatched." In short, both camps barricaded themselves, and I received the blows from both sides.

Yet I must admit that in this madman Luther, I sometimes felt the inspiration of an apostle. This world of ours, numbed by scholastic opinions, human constitutions, pontifical indulgences, he was waking it up to evangelical truth. What a tragedy that he spoiled everything with his violence, his pride, his revolt, with the cooperation of all those facing him who could do nothing other than keep screaming "Fire! Fire!" I kept saying at the time that in burning everything you burn the wheat with the tares. The arsonists were too busy to listen to me. I'm not sure that, on this point, my dear More himself didn't go off the deep end. You know that he was the best of men and a Christian of the purest blood. Yet (this is just between us), I never fully approved his war treatise against Luther (*Responsio ad Lutherum*, 1523). I have only a faint idea of the works that followed; they are written in that tongue of theirs [English] no one understands. But I know they are of the same vintage. I believe his scruples led him too far. A few years later, they led him to the chopping block. Would to God he had never got mixed up in these theologians' quarrels!

[4] I won't delay joining him. I've lived enough, I should say more than enough. There's nothing left for me but pain and labor. I see my friends dwindling and my enemies increasing. And importunate old age is daily more wearisome. Ah! If only the Lord would come and recall me from this crazy world and welcome me in his peace!

But I'm overwhelming you with sadness. You should know that, however decrepit and afflicted he might be, Erasmus is still able to work and even to make you smile. Listen. The new Pontiff [Paul III] has decided, in anticipation of the coming Council, to create a few particularly erudite cardinals. Among them, Erasmus, a reed among oaks. There are a few obstacles: my advanced age, my failing health and especially the thinness of my income. That is why the intriguers have gone to work to overwhelm me with provostships, even though I'm trying desperately to wiggle out of it. I enclose the Papal brief. I am most thankful for his intentions. But the ox that I am will not accept the yoke.

While waiting, be well, with all your dear ones.

II.

ERASMUS TO MARGARET ROPER
Basel, 12 September 1535

Your letter, dearest Margaret, I read with a trembling hand. I know how your heart has bled and bleeds still. Your father, the best of men in every way, I mourn him with you, my dear child. But, like you also, I rejoice that he should now be in the peace of Our Lord. I remember what he used to say about people in sorrow: there are those who struggle and those who let themselves go. I know that you will not let yourself go, Margaret. You have your father's strength, the strength you have shown during these long, terrible months. Remember, when he spoke of the future life, one felt he was expressing the depths of his soul He was vibrant with Hope. Today, his Hope is fulfilled. He has found the port after so many tribulations. He is at peace.

[1] I am grateful to you for having found the strength and the opportunity to write a few lines. I know the risks and the obstacles. I was roughly aware of most of the events, but now I can better measure all the trials that your dear father had to endure. He neither wanted nor sought martyrdom—this is as it should be—but he accepted it and lived it grandly. The light kindled by his sacrifice will shine for a long time.

You say he saw it all coming. He was preparing you for this coming adversity. He had a premonition that his silence, however unshakable it was, would not be a refuge. How could it have been? How could a Prince who wanted everybody bowing before him put up with the tacit but striking rejection of the most honest and respected of all the servants of the Kingdom? Then came those fifteen months in the Tower, which is little in the eyes of eternity but which must have seemed endless to our dear More and to all his loved ones. You tell me that at home [in England] he was alone, without help nor support, and that his equanimity was conquered, not without pain, against men's desertion and the fear of torture. Margaret, you who are such a worthy daughter of such a father, I believe you are being too harsh on yourself. You never abandoned him, none of his loved ones did. He was sustained by your affection—I know how great it was and how much it counted for him—especially that of his tender Margaret. You reproach yourself for having told him, after Dame Alice [More's wife, Margaret's stepmother], that you didn't understand his persistence in refusing the oath when all the others were taking it. But what did you do but act out of filial love and repeat everything you were hearing from the mouths of the Norfolks, the Audleys and the others, of all these Notables who had the arrogance of their groveling slavishness: What prevents him from swearing an oath? Didn't I swear it? I suspect an afterthought: this More, he isn't even born noble and he's playing the hero, waving the flag of conscience! Is he trying to teach us a lesson? Cowardice, especially when it is decorated with coats of arms and heraldry, has its pride; real nobility is an affront.

I have read, holding back my tears, what you have written me about his sufferings. You tell me that prison did not shake him, any more than the prospect of an imminent death. That's More as I knew him! No, what weighed him down was, first of all, the anxiety he felt for his loved ones. You know, my dear Margaret, that I have known human love only from the outside. But I did discover its beauty in the bosom of the More family: among other places, in seeing you, so well and tenderly united to dear Roper. I imagined what your father's torment must have been to see his wife, his children and grandchildren, all those of his household, reduced to poverty and put in danger.

And then he experienced another anxiety that I can feel in every fiber of my being. The body desperate, the body uncontrolled, which rebels, which collapses in the face of torture. I am sickly, and I shudder with my whole carcass when I think of what he dreaded and of what he was at least spared.[4] This terror of the flesh, Our Lord knew it on the eve of his Passion: his sweat became like big drops of blood which fell to the earth [Luke 22: 44]. In the beautiful pages which you sent

---

4   The irons of torture and the execution for high treason. Here was the list of tortures, as signified by the Court's President, Thomas Audley, More's successor as Chancellor, to More at the end of the trial: "Sir Thomas More, you are to be drawn on a hurdle through the City of London to Tyburn, there to be hanged till you are half dead, after that cut down yet alive, your bowels to be taken out of your body and burned before you, your privy parts cut off, your head cut off, your body to be divided in

me [*De tristitia Christi,* last text written at the Tower], we see that your dear father placed his steps in the footprints of Christ. In his prison, he was in the Garden of Olives. There he struggled, there he triumphed by following the One who accepted a terrifying death in order to save us. Then, he did not falter, he did not fail.

He failed at nothing and he defended himself to the very end. To the very end he gave his accusers a hard time, never giving them a hold. In reading you I rediscovered Thomas More, the great man of the law. They tried to pin him against the wall, prove him in the wrong, entrap him. But, however diminished, he never gave his accusers an opportunity to bring him down for high treason. He held firm with, as you put it, this gentle firmness which was customary with him. Your letter allows me to see again this rare combination that made him what he was. Every time I revisited your father, he made me commit the sin of envy.

To make him die, they needed this fake trial and these lies of the traitor Richard Rich. Your father played the game of legality by protecting himself through silence. But the law is an obedient young lady when testimony is fabricated and the jurors are at the King's orders. This sinister play was already written: a man erect facing men bending over, it is the benders who condemned him. His death he faced with the same courage. In the words you cite, we find him, facing the ordeal that makes our poor nature tremble, such as he was on ordinary days. At the foot of the gallows, he showed his usual mock courtesy: "I pray you, Master Lieutenant, see me safe up, and for my coming down, let me shift for myself." In his last words he showed his fidelity and his unswerving faith: "I die the King's good servant, but God's first." In the long procession of martyrs, I have no doubt your father holds a place of honor.

[2] The man you are mourning with all your loved ones, you knew four parts, and your head and body to be set at such places as the King shall assign." Cited by Peter Ackroyd, *The Life of Thomas More* (New York/London: 1998): 398. The King commuted the sentence to a pure and simple decapitation at the Tower. Whether this change was the result of his old "friendship" for More or of the fear of riots on the road to Tyburn is not known.

him, dear Margaret, better than anyone. Yet please permit his old friend, for whom he remains the dearest of his friends, to tell you what a friend he was, and why a part of me died with him.

First, I loved your father because he was lovable. He loved, he was loved. Need I tell you the memories I have kept of the household in which you grew up? I have known no man who loved his family so much, or formed with them such a perfect society. Who would not have been enthralled by this welcoming, warm home, where affection, piety, good books and gaiety were the very air one breathed. Never was a quarrel to be heard, never a disputatious word; never was anyone seen idle. And he who governed this little world did so with a smile. To all of you I owe more than I can say. I would also like to mention this: I owe to the education you and your sisters received to have revised my opinion on the education of girls. Up until then, I was not far from thinking with the rest of the world that the study of Letters was useless to the female sex. But I saw your father take care to instruct his daughters as well as he did his son, and I saw the results. The most accomplished of them has the name Margaret. She was her father's pride and joy.

And then there were the friends. If the family had not existed, one would have said that he was born for friendship. He cultivated friendship, with an open heart, with constancy. He wasn't, surely, the type of man who dreaded an excess of friends. What kindness he showed them! What pleasure he took conversing with those who shared his turn of mind! How he took their affairs to heart while showing so little concern for his own interests! As you know I derived enormous profit from this.

I also admired your father. The reason? I can only respond with these words: he was noble. His was that true nobility which owes nothing to a chance title but proceeds from a natural distinction, culture of the mind and perfect simplicity. He was on an equal footing with everybody, with his literary friends no doubt, but also with the common man as well as with the Duke of Norfolk. Etiquette was the least of his concerns.

But you know all this better than I. I only want to add a word on a subject with which I have some acquaintance. Those who wield power are changed by it; those who achieve power without being born to it try hard to achieve it. Your father held the highest offices of the Kingdom, but without having the ambition to achieve them, and without ever ceasing to be himself. If the King made him Chancellor while being aware of his dissent on a question so dear to his heart, it is surely because he saw the advantage of having at his side a man like this.

You see what I mean. Among those who govern, your excellent father was a man apart. No one was ever more convinced than he of the vanity of power for power's sake. I remember hearing him quote Boethius: whoever prides himself in governing other men is very similar to a mouse who would pride himself in governing other mice in a barn. I'm also thinking of Holbein's Portrait. I haven't had the fortune of seeing it face to face, but my friend Holbein has shown me sketches. Your father sits in majesty with the sumptuous cape and the Knight's collar. But have you seen his look! In his eyes, there is no desire at all to dominate others ; no, they speak of retirement, reserve, gravity. Your father observes with detachment and attention, he is not a participant. He is in power, but looks further.

Ultimately, I loved my dear More because he was who he was and I am who I am. There is a secret affinity between spirits which makes some people give you an extreme pleasure. From the first time we met [1499]—you were not yet born—we recognized each other through the eyes of the soul. How can I explain that? I can't really say. True, we are of the same race of men, that race of pious banterers who put so many people off. How I appreciated his gaiety, ever ready to laugh at human stupidity, combined with a heart so fervent for the things that count! He was the living image of what I have always pleaded for: an amiable Christianity which is not a tepid one. And then there was a charm at work which made our conversations so open and so warm!

[3] My memories follow like a string of pearls, my dear Margaret. I speak of far-off times when we had the joy of seeing one another and when all the hopes were permitted. Then came those fatal years when we had more occasions to weep than to laugh. I was following events in England from afar. During the last years, as you know, we could no

longer converse in writing, but the boys I would send to your home would return with news. I would think of your father amidst his affairs, in daily confrontation with these ordeals, where it is so difficult to combine the virtues that were his. When I learned of his fall from grace, then of his imprisonment, I did my best to make a rampart for him of Erasmus's friendship, and that of the company of lettered friends wherein he held such a beautiful place. Alas!

This, my dear Margaret, is what my affection wanted to tell you in these days of sorrow. I'll see to it that this letter reaches you as soon as I find a sure means. I know how difficult things are for you, and I especially don't want to add to your misfortune. I must urgently ask you to burn it as soon as you have read it.

May the Lord keep you all and assist you in these moments of sorrow. To your mother, the very distinguished Dame Alice, please convey my affectionate thoughts; as well as to John, whom I remember as a small boy and who is now a father in his turn; to your dear husband William, to your sisters' husbands. Please assure them of Erasmus's prayers: His abiding hope is to find himself, when the time comes—and it will not delay—at the side of your dearest father in the peace of the Lord.

CHAPTER 10
Apte Dicere, Apte Tacere
[To speak suitably, to be silent suitably]

Shortly before his death, Erasmus wrote two letters on the art of writing, intended for a young disciple who was asking his advice. Almost nothing is known of this young man except his name. In this chapter we provide a translation of these letters.

In the first letter, Erasmus the rhetor returns to ideas he had previously developed on many occasions and gives his young correspondent a few general counsels on the art of reading and the art of writing. The second letter is more original and more personal. Here Erasmus explains his own texts, particularly the Praise of Folly, *and the practice of indirect writing. Surprisingly, this man, who is so attached to his privacy, reveals himself, even though he does so only relatively. Is this the effect of age? The effect of an almost fatherly concern? Be that as it may, he does not forsake all prudence. As we shall see, he sees to it that what he confides is discreet. He opens up, but at the same time argues his case. Perhaps he doesn't say everything about his writer's tricks or their reasons? Perhaps he tends to force an artificial unity of inspiration on his entire work? In any case, and even if the letter ends on a note of disenchantment, the aged Erasmus, that veteran in the war of ideas, exhausted by illness, in combat on many fronts, remains always valiant, as he will be to the end.*

I.
ERASMUS TO JOHN X
Basel 15 March 1536

Most distinguished young man, you have asked me for advice on the correct way of writing. But your request is quite correctly written. Do you really need my advice? And you know Erasmus's writings on the matter as well as one possibly can. What more do you need?

I'm teasing you, my dear John, I know that you know that there is more to know. I would like to give you satisfaction in memory of your excellent father, and because I know you as a young man of great piety, of great passion for study, and of great promise. But old Erasmus is loaded with work and tugged at from all sides. One day I said to your esteemed father that, of all the men for whom I have trouble having pious feelings, are those who are prodigal with other people's time. I have the feeling that that species is proliferating: I mean, you see, all these importuners who take the time to waste other people's time, who make airy promises, solicit for the hell of it, squabble out of vanity—and most of the time you ignore them at your own risk. So much time lost for cultivating the devotion for the great books!

But I know that you are not cut of that cloth. You will put what you solicit to good use. For the reasons stated above, and for another, I cannot write you as long and precise a letter as you wish. But I want to compress the essentials for you, as all the rest derives from these. As for the rest, and Erasmus's manner of proceeding, I'll tell you how to satisfy your healthy curiosity without breaching my own rules.

[1] My first piece of advice is contained fully in this rule: the art of writing is learned from the art of reading. You're heaving a sigh of disappointment. I can hear you from here; but wait for the rest. First, tell yourself this: he who knows how to write has something of the magician, for he has a bag full of tricks. According to the person or persons he is addressing, he can compliment, soften, or joke with them; he can grow angry, shorten or stretch his discourse, clarify or obfuscate, promote some ideas or conceal his thinking, take detours or go straight to the point. And you know that the detours of rhetoric are more numerous than Solomon's wives or the Pope's indulgences. Think of this: the sheet of paper is a good girl; she lets herself be scribbled on, corrected, torn without ever complaining, lending herself obligingly to every form of discourse. The man of letters has more freedom than might suppose those who are not of the shop, even when the censors are on watch outside. You know that painters sometimes hide certain things in their paintings; writers are able to do the same thing with their pens. It's easier to conceal ideas from the ignorant or inattentive reader than it is to hide jewels from a thief. If you read

carelessly a work that has been carefully written, you will grasp only what the author wanted the unreflecting reader to grasp. Consequently, the heart of the matter is the author's design [*auctoris consilium*]. You must go back up from the letters and the figures to the spirit that gives them life. To do this, here are some good questions: Who is speaking? To whom? In what genre? On what tone? What is he saying? In what circumstances? For what reasons? Why do we never hear Plato's voice? What is serious beneath Horace's trivialities? What do Cicero's fake movements signify? Is there an ounce of irony in the wise comments of Jerome? What game is More playing in his *Utopia*? Why does Erasmus hide behind Dame Folly? You see what I mean? Do not put yourself above the author, assume that an apparent triviality or mistake can be a trick or a detour, read with attention, reread, reread again and pursue unceasingly what the author intends to do at the place he occupies.

I am telling you nothing here that the masters of rhetoric didn't know, and all the Fathers [of the Church] who had been to their school. But since that time, a form of thinking has been raging which inclines one to twist the texts. I have written quite often, in bold type and underlined, that there is a science which corrupts people and is fit to make them deaf. At worst, the cleverest master of that science wants to hear nothing, he just wants to win. As you know I am thinking of our Doctors from Paris, Louvain, or elsewhere, who don't know how to read Holy Scripture, or rather, who don't really want to read it, and who bite you as soon as you want to read it as one should. They come with their principles, read a few fragments in keeping with these principles, and then leave to speculate at their ease. Would that they took for their models Origen, Basil, Gregory of Nazianzus, Athanasius, Chrysostom, Jerome, Ambrose, Hilary, Augustine!

You are following me, I think. Surely I don't mean to tell you that to read Holy Scripture it suffices to do so the way we read Vergil or Cicero. First and foremost you need a pious and pure soul, fit to listen to the Word. But to grasp the hidden truths [*in figura*], what is also needed is a sustained attention to the text, seen in detail and as a whole, with always the same questions in mind: What subject is Scripture speaking of? Who is speaking? Before whom? On what occasion? In what terms? To what end? There is a divine rhetoric, which I'll speak of later; there is also a rhetoric of the sacred writers. Take Paul. His art is such that we ask ourselves if it is always the same man speaking. The old proverb, "When in the presence of a Cretan one must make oneself a Cretan" seems made for Paul. According to what he is speaking of and to whom, he turns and re-turns, ever changing shapes. Reread the Acts [of the Apostles] and the Epistles. Here Paul appears reasonable and moderate, there he wears the mask of a madman. Sometimes he caresses, sometimes he thunders; he clearly demands certain things, then suggests others as if by underground paths. You will learn how many sleepless nights and trials are needed to explain the intentions of poets and orators. You must know that Paul's discourses require still far more, in order to grasp, in ever singular occasions, what he wants, where he is going, what he is avoiding, what he is counting on. And yet, who doesn't see that he is always going in the same direction? Whether he addresses himself to the Athenians on the Areopagus or to the Jews of Jerusalem, whether he is writing to the Christians of Corinth, of Rome, of Ephesus, or elsewhere, whether he speaks in one tone or another, he never speaks except for the work of Christ. He concedes nothing, he speaks in keeping with the occasion. If you read well, you must see that if I I am speaking of Paul, I am not speaking merely of him.

[2] Now what you have learned or will learn by reading as you should must instruct you in speaking as you should. Let me put you on guard on one point: every writer can only give what he has. Marcus Tully [Cicero] is par excellence the master of eloquence. Does that mean you must swear by Cicero alone, write well in order to write well, speak like a pagan, however great he might be? I'm not urging you in that direction: you would be deserving of the rods I gave to the Ciceronians of Italy [*Ciceronianus*, 1528]. If you are looking for a compass, take Paul. He always speaks appropriately, always in the spirit of truth. These are the two pillars of the art of writing. Chain yourself to both and keep both ends of the chain as tight as you can. Believe me, that will not be easy.

Don't grumble, let me continue. The first rule, that of appropriateness, is valid for the manner, signifying that there is no other rule except, as Quintilian puts it, to speak in an appropriate manner [*apte dicere*]. It's a matter of letting your discourse be regulated by its object, its addressee, its circumstances. It's easier to do when you speak with your mouth than when you speak with your pen. The divine Plato said it once for all: "Once written, the discourse goes rolling all over the place, as much toward the people who know what it means as toward the people for whom it is not appropriate at all" [*Phaedrus*, 275]. I might add that today written things roll faster and farther, by means of this printing press which makes so many copies and gives so much ammunition to imprudent authors and tactless editors. Here is one of the great difficulties of the art of writing. To what extent, I know better today than at the time of my *Moria* [*Praise of Folly*]. I learned the hard way. That is why I suggest you be careful. Whether you like it or not, your pen is writing for people of all colors, for your friends and your enemies, to some people you know, to many you know nothing about. How, then, can you put that pen to appropriate use? You must learn to adjust the words in consequence, or to silence what must be silenced. It isn't that easy. I'll come back to that point.

So you will write appropriately. I'm not saying that you must throw overboard the rules you have learned, those rules of grammar and rhetoric which I took great pains to collate, to rank, to sift through in my treatises—those rules in particular which are proper to each oratorical genre [declamation, dialogue, paraphrase, sermon, letter]. But I want you to know that these rules are secondary or auxiliary with respect to the principle of *apte dicere*. The real orator couldn't care less about the orator.

First I'll give you the simplest example, where the art of writing comes closest to the art of saying. You've guessed it, I'm speaking of the personal letter that is destined to remain personal; a letter like the one I'm writing at this moment for you and you alone—and I trust that you will take it to heart to deserve my confidence. I am writing for you alone, and I measure what I am saying by what I know that you know. Only one interlocutor; the task is simplified. Yet what is the best way of writing a letter? If you hesitate, I'll make you stand in the corner. You should blurt out your answer: "It depends." Follow what I've said in fixing your goal and write accordingly. Don't consider what it would be pleasant to say, but what is useful, prudent, honest to say in the situation at hand. What is your objective? To solicit, to recommend, to advise, to maintain a friendship, what have you? To whom are you writing? To a Prince or to John Doe, to a man of letters or to an ignoramus, to Erasmus or to Beda [Dean of the Theology Faculty of Paris, a tenacious enemy of Erasmus]? Are you writing urgently or not, with or without support, on a dangerous question or a subject without risks? In each and every case, the manner must follow, it must be appropriate. There are a thousand ways of writing the same thing, and the way of saying it is very important.

Let me recommend this: most of the time you must spare the person you are addressing, respect his feelings, skirt around his defenses, outsmart his weaknesses, take advantage of what he knows. If you write a single word that shocks or wounds, he will lower the castle gate and block his ears. That is one of the reasons for the oblique ways that are often reasonable to take. As you know, the Powerful have ticklish ears. If you are dealing with one of them and want to straighten him out, as I've often been tempted to do, hide the criticism under a note of praise, praise the virtues he doesn't have, condemn in others the vices which are his, in short, take detours to avoid his putting his back up. At one or two notches lower, you have to use the same tactics with most of the men you are aiming to convince: hide an objection under a question, disguise a reprimand under a joke, reshuffle the deck to bury a quarrel, avoid a remark which uselessly offends, don't overpower the ignorant with your knowledge. But of course you will write more freely to a very dear friend, and you will write quite differently to a very devious enemy, or to defend yourself against calumny.

Remember this: in every case you must do what suits the occasion [*quod decet*], that is, find the words that touch. Then you will know how to comfort those who weep, awaken those who sleep, calm those who lose their temper, persuade the reluctant, and you will master that great art which is also a great pleasure: conversing with your friends. Barbarians don't realize that the right tone is the salt and the honey of human relations.

Now if you are thinking of the printed work you will write some day and which will "go rolling all over the place," you will see that things get complicated. They get even more complicated if the subject is a hot one or if the things that need to be said are things that are painful to hear. How can one write suitably in these conditions? I have already told you the cardinal rule; as for its application, old Erasmus has a long experience. He will have more to say about this some other time.

Now I come to the rule which I speak of in second place for the sake of comprehension, but which occupies the first rank: one must write, as one must speak, in a spirit of truth. But, you will say, how does the spirit of truth blend with the principle of suitability? How to practice oblique writing without lying? This raises a famous and puzzling question: is the Christian permitted to lie? Let me try to summarize the essential points for you. The first point is as follows: nothing is more repugnant to Christianity than lying, I mean hypocrisy and deceit. Christ is Truth itself; his entire teaching condemns those whose words and actions belie their hearts, especially those who pride themselves in having false virtues. As you know, every period has its own. With the Greeks it was those philosophers who were always mouthing morality and wisdom while being slaves of their bellies or of their glory. With the Jews, it was the Pharisees who wrapped themselves in sanctity with their sad faces, their scrolls and other disguises. In our day, all these façade Christians who don't know what piety of heart and true charity are. In short, it's those who wear disguises, and who often fall into the Adversary's trap: they discredit what they profess, they are victims of habit, they know not what they do.

However, and this is the second point, it doesn't follow that you must tell the truth to anyone, anytime, anyhow. You must tell it at a suitable time, and sometimes silence it. There are many reasons for practicing the pious trick, the charitable or prudent reservation. Some of these reasons flow from what I told you earlier, and are the result of common sense, or almost: must one tell the whole truth, at the risk of weakening the sick, of wounding a friend, of inflaming a quarrel, of offending a king, of losing a protector, of encouraging calumny, of arming the censors? The other reasons go deeper: must one tell the whole truth at the risk of being misunderstood, or of disturbing honest souls, of dissuading men of good will, of sowing unnecessary division? According to the times, the places, the conditions, men understand more or less well. The good teacher adapts to his student and proceeds step by step. Paul does not do otherwise. Nor does God Himself. There was a time for the Old Law, there is a time for the New. What would Abraham have understood if God had told him what his Son told the Apostles? The Spirit's dispensation of his gifts is measured by the readiness of the succeeding periods to receive them. Christ himself was made a Teacher. During his life, he concealed his divinity, he only allowed the truth to be obscurely guessed at. He dispensed his teaching with the same divine prudence, sparing the stiff necks of the Apostles, dodging the traps of the Pharisees, using parables, tracing slowly that path which is so repugnant to those who do not know it, the path leading from the carnal to the spiritual. As you see, there is a form of deceit which conspires against the truth, there is a reserve, or a form of prudence which is part of the apprenticeship of truth. Ultimately, what I'm trying to tell you is entirely contained in the word of the Gospel as recorded by Matthew: "Be prudent like the serpent and simple like the dove" [10: 16].

There you have it, my dear John: something to keep your days and your nights occupied in the times to come. If you really want to know the sequel, come visit me. I shall speak to you of the way I have tried to write in a spirit of suitability and in a spirit of truth. If I have the time, the opportunity and the strength, I'll put it down on paper. [The passage which follows, up to the final salutation, is written in Greek.] But this paper you will read in my home. I shall keep it well concealed, or I shall burn it. There are some things which it is unwise to enclose in a letter, even a letter written in Greek. Here is an additional piece of advice on the art of writing. I shall tell you things I have never written, but which are in my writings: something to put your art of reading into practice. I also want you to learn from my blunders. The magician can sometimes miss his trick.

Be discreet. Read with care. Work like a horse. Be well.

II.
ERASMUS TO JOHN X
Undated

Is there anything I wouldn't do for your instruction, my dear John? Here is the sequel I promised, and it bears upon Erasmus's indirect form of writing. As I told you, this must stay between us, and the text must remain with me. Please don't consider this a sign of mistrust; I'm just being prudent, that's all. I have learned the hard way that papers get lost, get stolen, get copied, get printed secretly—and I don't want to risk this one falling into the wrong hands. But you, I know that I can tell you things that should not be scattered to the winds. So listen attentively and remember what should be remembered.

You are not unaware that I am prolific. I give birth more often than the mother rabbit herself. I have published in every genre and on every tone. But make no mistake. Whatever be the forms or the detours I have taken, whatever my enemies have peddled about—that ill-tempered Luther who calls me an "eel," those on the other side who call me a coward when yesterday they were calling me impudent or bold—in short, whatever might be said by appearances and calumny, I have always followed the same routes in the service of Letters, of peace, of true piety. However, I have striven to do so in a spirit of suitability. Reflect on this: if I am daring here and prudent there, it is not without reason. Yet I do confess that I haven't always chosen the good way, but when I will have told you why and how, I hope you will accuse me of venial sins only.

Now here's the key which many writers have made use of, but which I use in my own way: to write suitably or prudently what I mean to write means, most of the time, writing in an indirect manner. Surely, this doesn't mean that I travesty the truth, but I tell it obliquely, or I do not tell it whole. The reasons for these detours I will tell you frankly. I am not a man of categories, as you know, but nevertheless I'm proposing three: games of wit, the art of precautions, and the pedagogy of truth. As an example I shall give you especially the *Moria*, because you will find there the three forms of indirect writing and, above all, the soul of Erasmus. In that work I wear all the masks, and I open up more than elsewhere. You have certainly grasped that these reasons are embedded together. I open up all the more freely because I open up to a mere few. Indirect writing is a way of sorting out your readers.

[1] I consider first those literary games which provide both laughter and food for thought, in the manner of those illustrious jokers of ancient times. You tell fables, you play on words, you scatter allusions, you utter paradoxes, you spice your text with irony, you speak by ricochet, what have you! Men of letters understand each other readily; reading is a conversation, a veritable feast for the mind. Beyond that circle, lightness, gaiety, banter are means of winning readers and of putting them in a mood to listen. You say something brusquely, the reader turns to ice, you've lost the game; say the same thing in a joyful and amusing manner, the reader smiles, lets himself be taken in, you've won an inning. Ancient writers tell us that Caesar himself took pleasure in sarcastic remarks directed against him, so long as they were cleverly turned. The game here becomes a means of guarding yourself. As you see, the art of saying pleasant things is more than the art of pleasing.

Of this gaiety [*festivitas*]. I have played much, and in different ways. Take the *Adages* or the *Colloquia*, I'll choose the *Moria* for you. Let me also recommend to your attention the *Utopia* of my dear More, and his facetious remarks. Let's take my *Folly* first. Who can doubt that it is first and foremost a game of the mind? Who would be so foolish as to understand it seriously from end to end? Who can fail to see that if the author took some pains, it is at least in part in order to lure, to cheer up the reader? I need not tell you that this text is a discourse, that this discourse is a declamation, that this declamation is a prosopopea, that the orator is an allegory, that this allegory is folly personified, her subject the praise of herself. Here, you will agree, is matter enough for players and pickpockets.

So Dame Folly holds the dice alone and sings her own praises. The embarrassing thing about this talkative old lady is that she isn't reasonable in her folly. She tells lies, she tells the truth, she paints falsehood more or less in the same colors as the truth; worse still, she mixes or juxtaposes wisdom and folly in the same passage or the same phrase. Finally she's all tangled up and doesn't know what she's up to:

> Would life still deserve the name of life if you take away pleasure ? . . . Your applause has answered for you. I was certain that no one among you is wise enough, or rather foolish enough, no, rather wise enough, to think so. [XII][5]

In short, if Dame Folly is the only one to speak, she speaks different languages, on different registers, without fear of self-contradiction, cheerfully.

At present, I believe you are big enough to play your game and untangle things. Here are a few exercises. I begin with child's play:

Dame Folly applauds the clown who slips mordant truths into a laugh [XXXVI]. I am much indebted to her for thus complimenting the one who plays the fool for telling the naked truth. Now it's up to you to reveal it to Fame [Erasmus, of course]. It is also up to you to reveal the character about whom *Moria* says that she shares his name [More, of course, XLV].

Here's something a bit more challenging. Dame Folly says that all mortals are fools, that everybody is faking it, that illusion is the rule and a good thing, that heroism has no other motive than the folly of glory, that all the arts are of the same vintage. Saying this, she jokes, but she isn't always joking. It's up to you to disentangle what must be disentangled.

Finally, try to see how Dame Folly interprets Scripture. She does it foolishly; she does it wisely. You sort it out. You will see Scripture misquoted [Psalm 68 in Chapter LXV], or see her read the way barbarians read to condemn letters [Paul, I Cor. 8: 1, same chapter]. You will also see Scripture understood correctly to utter the wisest of follies [the last pages on Christian folly].

I'll stop here. I don't want to succumb too much to the pleasure of game-playing. As you see, the rhetoric which I owe to my dear

---

[5]   Concerning *The Praise of Folly*, we have generally relied on the translation of Clarence Miller (see Appendix).

Greek and Latin masters, I enjoy using amicably. I must confess to you that I don't dislike playing the fool. Charge that to the account of Erasmian frivolity. But remember also that a writer who oozes boredom is like a whore who offers her syphilis free.

[2] Next comes the art of precaution. The best rule is not to expose oneself uselessly, not to give the malevolent and the censorious pretexts, arms, or opportunities. The loudmouths never sleep; they watch you like hawks at every hour, ready to spout criticism. As for the Mighty, they are mighty, remember.

As you know I have made many enemies; they never stop barking at my heels. There are times, no doubt, when I have been unguarded, but could I foresee the storms we are in now? I took many pains not to give them a hold, to keep them at bay, to assure myself support and protection: in short to temper boldness with prudence.

To get back to the *Moria*. For the accustomed reader, irony gives strength to criticism; for the unaccustomed, irony clouds the criticism; for those who feel offended, irony is an embarrassment. I take shelter behind Dame Folly and the jumble of her discourse. Since she ridicules everybody, who can complain? Since she mixes the pleasant and the serious, who can respond accurately? Since mockery frightens and takes one aback, those who are mocked in wholesale restrain their pens for fear of being mocked in retail.

This little work, as you must know, I composed on horseback between Italy and England, for my mind's amusement; then, once at More's home while waiting for my books to arrive, I wrote it in a few days—seven, to be precise, which is already too many—encouraged by the friends who then hurried to have it printed. That, at least, is what one is supposed to believe upon seeing my dedicatory letter to More and my letter to Dorp [May 1515], which I have since added to the work. Nonsense! Bullshit! This *Moria* cost me a great deal of work and application, as any perceptive reader must see, as Dame Folly intimates in an aside.[6] And I never ceased taking it up again, correcting

---

6   "As you know, these orators, even though they have labored over a speech for thirty years (. . .), will swear that they wrote it in three days, without even trying, or even dictated it" (III).

it, enriching it from one edition to the other. If I treat the work as a trifle, it is to disguise it all the better. Add to that all the appendices which are just so many precautions: the letter to More, the one to Dorp, my Listrius's commentary.[7] There I set up some lines of defense which you have seen or can guess at: Erasmus banters, he hurts no one in name except himself; his gaiety excludes any offense. His aim, moreover, is directed at only a few theologians, the bad ones; he attacks only foolish superstitions. Let's go on, you will see what follows.

To protect yourself, you must also guard against incurring wrath, and strive to gain supporters. You will remember that Dame Folly doesn't spare the Powerful, but that she names none except by allusion. I've always done this, and a bit more, not to irritate these irascible characters. Let me give you an example: I have flailed the Church's defects in every manner, but for the Pontiffs who are less impious than others, I have striven to assure their good graces while stroking them in the direction I hoped they would go. Do you see what I mean? Soon after Pope Clement's election, I wrote him two letters to assure him: of the nobility of his family, of the greatness of his gifts, of Erasmus's loyalty, of my confidence in his justice, of the misery of the Church, of our hopes for a renaissance, of the happy omen of his coming to the throne. Then I pointed to directions to be taken on the present disorders: better to remedy them than repress them. And on the decadent Church: it should be renewed in the image of the early Church [Letters of 31 January and of 13 February 1524].

---

[7]   The 1515 edition published at Basel by Froben added to the text a detailed commentary, signed by G. Listrius, to which Erasmus undoubtedly lent a hand. The subsequent editions were equally enriched with notes which are probably by Erasmus. These additions explain the erudite allusions of the text, but they also prudently restrict the range of the satire (these are the "lines of defense" mentioned by Erasmus in his letter). In the 1514 edition, Erasmus had gone a step further in his criticism of the Princes of the Church and of the theologians. In the following edition, he went a step further in matters of precaution. See in particular Clarence Miller's Introduction to his edition of the *Praise of Folly* in his *Opera Omnia*, IV-3, 1979, 34–36; and A. Gavin and Th. Walsh, *"The Praise of Folly* in Context: The Commentary of Girardus Listrius," *Renaissance Quarterly* 34 (1971): 59–84.

Do you want another example? Take war: I don't deal gently with it, but I do deal gently with the Princes who wage it. I borrow roads which criss-cross. To Charles, I have dedicated the *Paraphrase* of Matthew, to Ferdinand the *Paraphrase* of John. I addressed the *Paraphrase* of Luke to Henry, the *Paraphrase* of Mark to Francis [Charles V Emperor, Ferdinand of Austria, Henry VIII, Francis I, 1522–1523]. For the intention of each, I enclosed praises which are hardly justified and exhortations to concord which are far too justified.

I hope you haven't lost the thread of my thinking. I remain on the subject of precautions as an art and go on to a second point. You shouldn't bring up for discussion what shouldn't be brought up. To speak to the point is also to know how to keep an appropriate silence [*apte tacere*]. To Harpocrates [the god of silence], one must sacrifice anything that sows unnecessary trouble and division. Never forget how precious is concord and how fragile it is! I am thinking of the secrets of kings, which it is no doubt politically wise to hide from the greatest number. Princes preen themselves from the collar up, but their feet walk in sand. Who could possibly provide a rational basis for this "right of birth" which they wear like a crown? To be born a Prince, big deal! The noble lineage goes back to an original title which wasn't noble, and gives no assurance of the qualities that make a good Prince. The most philosophical of emperors [Marcus Aurelius] engendered the craziest [Commodus]. And yet that principle, right of birth, has the virtue of regulating succession, of extinguishing quarrels, of making peace. In these times of sedition, this virtue has no price.

I think even more of these theological quarrels which are often vain and which, even when they are not, should not leave the circle of initiates without incurring damage. But here is what their conflicting and discordant voices are screaming in the marketplace these days: "I am a Roman theologian, I am Reformed, I'm a Papist, I'm a Lutheran, I am Evangelical, I'm an Anabaptist"! We are erecting a new Tower of Babel. What a glory for Christendom! What is wrong with Luther and all those of his ilk is that they ignore every form of prudence. It is madness to bring before the people quarrels which are beyond them. If theologians often say more than they know, what can we say nowadays of those who join the debate? I see Luther's gospel corrupting the piety of simple souls without any benefit for the piety of the heart. Would that he had taken as a model Holy Scripture, which lets its language be regulated by our capacity to know! But I digress. How could Luther do this when he thinks that Scripture is as clear as day? You see? The bad reader makes the misdirected writer.

As you know, I abstained for a long time from these vociferations. But pressured from every side, I finished by producing my *Diatribe* [*on free will*]. I shouldn't have done it. I had to take my distance from Luther, I wanted neither to deny myself nor to widen the breach between us. So I chose that inextricable question which allows one to deliberate, to a certain extent. I admitted the difficulties of the question, I gave the book a very measured title [*Diatribe* means discussion], I proceeded with a thousand precautions. But wham! Luther blew up, and the other side accused me of not going far enough. When spirits are at war and the party spirit prevails, prudent writing is of no avail. It is better to be silent.

May I add this other reason, which I would gladly have avoided: there are things that shouldn't be said, so as not to give ammunition to those who will use it badly. My *Moria* was guilty in this regard, having lacked the gift of foresight [Luther wasn't yet Luther]. I'll come back to this.

[3] I've kept for the end the most important matter of all, which is the very pedagogy of truth. I've said it and repeated it: Scripture puts this pedagogy into practice, shows us how to do it. If you listen carefully to Holy Writ, you will hear, like the tolling of a bell, this cry which is intended for us: men do not hear, they do not understand, they are deaf to truth. Our spirits are thick, our hearts are hardened, our flesh is itchy. With material like this, it is folly indeed to attempt to create a new world in one fell swoop. You may constrain bodies, corrupt hearts; you cannot compel souls. Our world is carnal; it must be amended step by step and in subtle ways. Like nature, religion has its degrees.

You are not unaware that the most Herculean of my labors of Hercules was to work relentlessly to reedify or purify Christian piety; or rather, if these words mean more to you, to revive a religion "in spirit and in truth" [Jn. 4: 23]. False piety I attacked from every side; true piety I taught and defended in every register. But speaking of the former, if I put verve into my critique, I also put restraint so as not to scandalize simple souls; speaking of the latter, I didn't dogmatize, surely, I let Scripture speak as best I could; and I put the greatest art of writing in my power to make discernible what is invisible to the eyes of the flesh.

Must I explain to you what I mean by false piety? To borrow the eloquence of Saint Paul, I would say this: though I might fast scrupulously, though I might make pilgrimages without cease, though I might waste my fortune in indulgences, if I have not charity, I am but a sounding bronze or a tinkling cymbal. Though I might recite scrolls of prayers, light candle upon candle, splash myself with holy water, if I have not charity, I am nothing; though I might wear a hood or a miter, celebrate in pomp and magnificence, if I have not charity, it serves me nothing. Christ did not come to change ceremonies, no, he came to renew our souls and restore our lives. But what are we seeing but legions of Christians who make much ado about externals and think themselves released from their obligations? A few observances and everything's in order! I won't even mention the fake miracles, the magic prayers, bones and ashes on the altars [relics], Anthony [Saint Anthony of Padua] who returns stolen objects, Erasmus [Saint Erasmus] who attends women in labor, and other fables. Against these pharisaic practices and these nests of superstition I have written much, railed much, but always, or almost, while restraining my pen. Look at my *Colloquia:* you will see that I criticize and moderate. Look at my *Moria:* You will see that I satirize abundantly but prudently.[8] God is my witness that I never intended to rush things, be ahead of my time, or trash custom in one sweeping blow. But calumny always finds matter for self-satisfaction. Consider now not those who derive glory in being Christian, but those who live in Christ. Their piety goes to their

---

[8] Erasmus goes no further on this matter. Among the possible examples in the *Colloquia* where he mixes daring with prudence, we could cite *Miles et Cartusius* (on monastic rules), or the *De Utilitate colloquium* (on fasting, on pedagogical writing by the author). In the *Praise of Folly*, Erasmus directs his aim principally at "superstitions."

very depths, where words strain to follow. Real spiritual things can only be stammered. How achieve understanding when most men see here only strangeness, quirkiness, folly? Perhaps the best suited is Dame Folly herself.

Take up my *Moria* again and reread the final pages. I speak there of the folly of Christianity, this wonder of true Christians which likens them to madmen, this rapture of some among them which resembles delirium. The madness of God! The madness of Christians! Some take offense, take fright upon hearing this! Yet Paul spoke of it before me: "We who are foolish because of Christ," "What is God's folly is wiser than men" [II Cor. 11: 17 and I Cor. 3: 18]. So you will see that I proceed with prudence and by degrees. Up to that point, Dame Folly capers about in every direction. When she takes Holy Writ as witness to the "universal folly" [LX sq.], she still capers about but she has the wisdom to confess that she doesn't always cite "with perfect exactitude." A little further on, as soon as she has "donned the lion's skin,"[9] she capers about no more. The tone remains pleasant—why shouldn't it be when one is speaking of the felicity of Christians?—but Dame Folly no longer talks nonsense. Look closely. I send Plato as an avant-garde on successive occasions, and what follows speaks of the opposition between Christian folly and the world's folly: I mean that opposition between this new life where liberation from self leads to spiritual intoxication, and ordinary life where concern for self acts as a tyrant. You must see the care with which I distinguish the types of folly, so as not to cheat with words. Further back in the text, I have warned the reader: "Do not protest against the words; examine, rather, the bottom of things."

[4] The bottom of things stated in my little work, you are henceforth prepared to grasp. Now reread the text from beginning to end and

---

9 If we follow the Erasmus of the *Adages* (266), the expression signifies: to undertake a task beyond one's capacities. In his *Letter to Dorp* [XXIII], he indicates that the proverb is there to "soften" the fact that Folly is disputing a mystery such as the felicity of Christians. Unfortunately Erasmus goes no further. Perhaps the expression is also meant to anticipate the change of tone which follows.

lend an ear. Be attentive to the tone, sift as needed, follow the movement of the discourse.

Now what do you hear? What should you hear? If you are hard of hearing you hear nothing but banter or you aren't sure what you hear. Let's go on, I know that you aren't deaf. If your hearing is somewhat finer, you hear beneath the banter a few tonal changes which blend in with objective changes. There is, of course, much disorder in this extravagant conversationalist, but it isn't necessary to have a musician's ear to distinguish the chief subjects she speaks of and the intonations which follow. You see what is going on: in a first phase the discourse mocks the ordinary folly of men; secondly it makes rough satire over the scandal of a Christendom that is so un-Christian; finally, and briefly, it preaches that extraordinary folly which is life in Christ. Let's look at this a bit more closely. The first part has the colors of lightness and cheerfulness, and, at first sight at least, only those colors. The author banters, makes fun of the laughable traits of mortals. Dame Folly is not an evil woman; she is carefully not to be identified with those furies who lead to crime or light stakes or burning. Her domain is that of illusions, errors, those small deceptions and flatteries which nourish the comedies of everyday: in short, all those ordinary follies which it is permitted to laugh at and, apparently, to do nothing but laugh.

When I reach the second point, you must understand that the tone is no longer the same. It is hardly, or no longer, good-natured; its irony becomes drier, colder, more biting, and you have no trouble understanding why. Erasmus intends to show the extent of this scandal of all scandals, Christianity betrayed, soiled by the Princes of the Church, its scholars and its monks. Read the text again and look at the passage where Folly says how much the Sovereign Pontiff would have to lose by imitating Christ:

> So much wealth, so many honors, so many victories, all these offices, all these dispensations, all these taxes, all these indulgences, so many horses, mules, guards, so many exquisite pleasures. You see what a market of good things, what a harvest of benefices, what an ocean of goods I have displayed in a few words! In their stead, one would have to put vigils, fasts,

tears, prayers, sermons, studies, sighs, a thousand boring in-commodities of that sort. [. . .] [What else?] Instructing the people? That's tiring. Explaining Scripture? That's an occupation for the School. Praying? That's a waste of time. Shedding tears? That's miserable, good for women. Practicing poverty? Degrading. To be conquered? Shameful, and unworthy of one who hardly allows even the greatest kings to kiss his blessed foot. Finally, dying is unpleasant. Being crucified? Disreputable. [LIX].

You see, irony is an armor, it can also be a sharp sword. It permits seeing more than any other figure of speech, it veils the author's indignation which could be a screen, it strips the scandal naked. I force myself to remain icy so as to better shake minds up.

Now, concerning the final pages, I have told you how different the tonality is. Enough joking, enough irony, Folly has transformed herself. Henceforth she will speak seriously of profound things that must be attained by the soul. This point is treated in a few pages only, and with a few detours. Those who read fast, who judge what they read by the pound, who are taken in by all that glitters, will fail to notice. It follows that you must grasp what is said by its underside, for it narrates a progression. The subjects I have just been telling you about have not been placed here in disarray; they trace a route which Dame Folly suggests that we travel with her. Folly does not speak to us in solemn immobility from the heights of Olympus; no, she advances with us on an equal footing, a fool among fools. She plays her part, which is also ours. She plays the fool no doubt; but she also goes forward, transforms herself, becomes a new folly. To those who can hear, she beckons them to follow: turn in upon yourself, see your own folly, notice something else. Among all these fools, who can fail to identify himself? You see the method: Dame Folly doesn't pontificate from the height of a pulpit, she doesn't give a string of reasonings; rather, she presents her equals with a mirror and invites them to share an experience. Logic isn't her strong point, but she knows rhetoric. For your information, I'll repeat my main points. Concerning the ordinary follies of men, what does Dame Folly do if not lift the veil of appearances while saying how beneficial it is that appearances should be veiled.

She says: "men cheat or make mistakes, they benefit from it, we mustn't set them straight." And she sets them straight in saying this. In so doing, she breaks the pretense, lends a voice to the unexpressed maxims of the world: give chase to pleasures, idolize money, turn a blind eye to your condition, put on an act. Is she saying anything other than this: men fall victims to vaporous illusions, they live out of tune? Beneath the laugh, Folly digs a breach in the benighted conscience of men. She undermines the tranquil certitudes of the worldly, of the carnal who believe only in what they see or touch, of the well-established here below who take the baubles of the world seriously, of mortals, in short, who live like sleepwalkers. From the world's point of view, Dame Folly isn't wrong: you mustn't wake them up. But isn't that what she does—wake them up —when she tells all of their miseries? Isn't that what she does when she goes on to detail the corruption of our religion before their very eyes? Isn't that what she does, finally, when she strives to awaken them to invisible realities which are so foreign to them and which they don't really believe in?

Draw your ear yet closer: this is the final effort . . . almost. This progression of the spirit to which Erasmus invites us—do you think it foreign to him? Do you think him foolish enough to say that all are fools and to think that he alone is wise? Do you think that an author who knows what he is doing can give an account of a game that commits all of mankind while placing himself out of that game? I'll leave that for the Doctors.

Erasmus makes fun of Erasmus, I needn't repeat that to you. Who knows if he doesn't also call Erasmus to witness? When Dame Folly jeers at writers who blacken page upon page for a pointless glory, are we to think that Erasmus is referring only to others? When she boasts of this *philautia* [self-love] which governs the world, are we to suppose that Erasmus is speaking only from the outside? When Dame Folly's itinerary opens onto a spiritual intoxication, are we to presume that Erasmus is speaking of it only through hearsay? You will see whether it is so, and whether, behind the curtain, Erasmus isn't sometimes speaking of his soul's own tribulations.

I don't want to beat this point into the ground; but perhaps this isn't all that must be understood in reading this book. Who knows whether what Erasmus says in confidence about Erasmus through Folly's voice doesn't tell us something about the reasons why Erasmus wrote his *Folly*? These do me no credit, but they are not foreign to my glory. Writers are men, my dear Jean, they can tell human foibles in a manner which reveals their own. I should add for my defense that what is vain when desired for itself is less so when it is desired for what it authorizes, which is not vain.[10]

[5] Enough said about Dame Folly's ulterior motives , and the divine Erasmus's muddled thoughts. There remains, however, something I have to tell you about the art of writing, which isn't negligible. You have seen that the *Moria* speaks fast and quickly about pious folly. Among the reasons for this is the following: these are things which the pen has difficulty expressing. How to make the truth graspable, I mean the living and palpable truth, and how to make graspable the least graspable of all, the living truth of spiritual things? Logic is incapable of it, a soulless rhetoric even less so; only that rhetoric which is animated by an authentic feeling can go further by indirect ways, while knowing that her speech is a mere stutter.

Remember, I have told you that the writer at his work table had something of the magician. With regard to the innocent reader, without the slightest doubt, but to say profound things he is a crippled

---

[10]   What does this elliptical passage mean? If we understand correctly, Erasmus means that among the intentions which led to the composition of the *Folly* was the author's desire for glory. If such is the case, the text's extraordinary virtuosity is somehow related to Erasmus's desire for success with a relatively large public. The last sentence might be interpreted this way: Erasmus sought renown only to achieve the means of his great designs. In other words, the *Praise of Folly* would, in part, be a means of acceding to an intellectual position that would be favorable for future action, a strategy that is not unique in its genre. In this sense, we can note that for Erasmus the writer of 1511 who had only modest titles and no established position in any university, literary fame was one means of gaining the authority he didn't yet have. A literary success also allowed him to lighten his "damned poverty." The revenues from his writing were all the more welcome because they did not infringe upon his independence.

magician. Do you understand? What we can live up to is at best to suggest, to evoke, to speak in images so as to dilate the meaning, as it were; to make one see, feel, breathe what mere naked words are unable to express. On the subjects which engage the soul or the heart, all good writing is pregnant with unexpressed meanings. Poets know this.

[6] I'm taking unfair advantage of your patience, my dear Jean. You wanted Erasmus to explain himself, and Erasmus is much like those preachers who know very well that no one can interrupt them. A last word, and I will stop. This word I am telling you in spite of myself, because you should also learn about Erasmus's setbacks.

See the present situation. The Lutherans lean occasionally on my writings to foment revolt. Tyndale has cited me as a witness against More: "You have changed," he told him, "you have betrayed! See your darling Erasmus: you spare him because he wrote the *Moria* in your home." On the other bank, I am accused of having kindled the fire, unless it be to keep it secretly burning. You know that I am withdrawing nothing of what I have written, but I should have been more careful. If I had suspected the disturbances that were coming, I would have written many things differently, or I would have kept them silent. Remember to consider future readers, don't lay yourself open to anger or malevolence, or at least give them the least possible hold. Avoid them you cannot. Consider Scripture and the way it is denatured. I learned that my dear More responded eloquently to Tyndale, and that he took yet once more the defense of the *Moria*. He added that so great were the excesses of minds across the Channel that he preferred to burn the *Moria* and the *Utopia* rather than see them translated into English.[11]

---

[11] Here is the text of More's reply to Tyndale: the latter states that "if I go easy on Erasmus, whom he calls my darling, it is most likely because he composed his *Moria* in my home. [. . .] If I had found in Erasmus, my darling, the same cunning and the same design as I found in Tyndale, my darling Erasmus would no longer be my darling. But I find, on the contrary, that my darling Erasmus detests and abominates the errors and heresies which Tyndale teaches and in which he perseveres. That is why Erasmus

I shall stop here. May this, my dear Jean, not discourage you. It is our fate here below to push the rock of Sisyphus. And so never give up, live as if you were to die tomorrow, but work as if you could live forever. Avoid false problems, don't talk for nothing, go straight to the truth, tell the truth as needed, correct yourself if necessary, bear witness by what you say and are. Fare thee well and pray for old Erasmus, who has lived long enough and places all his hopes in the one love that cannot deceive.

ADDITION

A little story comes to mind, which I give you as a supplement in order to amuse you after so many austerities. As you now know, Dame Folly says in a high voice the maxims which tacitly govern the world. In this register she recites in passing the hidden gospel of the strong, or fragments of this gospel: fortune favors the plucky [LXI]; he who abandons all scruple and can dare all derives immense profit [XXIX]; this great powerful beast which is the people, you lead it by the nose [XXVI]; you capture the human spirit more easily through lying than through truth [XLV]; you can obtain anything with nice shining crowns [LXII]. Well, imagine, a Florentine writer has apparently taken these maxims literally and complimented me about them. This man was a demon of a rare species, even in Italy. To his missive he joined a manuscript which was enough to make my little Folly faint with hor-

---

my darling will remain my darling. And, of course, if Tyndale had never taught them, or if he had had the courage to renounce them, well! Then Tyndale too would be my darling. But since he clings to his heresies, I cannot consider as my darling a man whom the devil considers his own." In the rest of the text, More denies that he thinks differently today than at the time of the *Moria*. But he adds: "If someone today wanted to translate the *Moria* into English, or a few of the works that I myself have written before today—they find nothing wrong with this, but people today take anything good the wrong way—I would with my own hands aid in the burning the books of my darling Erasmus, and my own to boot, rather than see people derive any evil from them [. . .]." *Confutation of Tyndale's Answer* (1532–1533), in Thomas More, *The Complete Works*, ed. L. Schuster et al. (New Haven, Conn.: Yale University Press, 1973): 8–1: 177–179.

ror. By comparison she was an innocent lamb. To what excesses will Folly not go! This character had the most venomous pen I have ever known. Thank heavens, he remained in an obscurity as black as his soul, unless his soul at present is glowing red in hell fire. And yet when I think of this episode, I see anew how vulnerable my *Moria* is to prejudice and superficiality. I should prefer that it fall into oblivion. But, enough illusions, she will be delivered defenseless into future times. To be used how? I know the offhand treatment of the living toward the dead.

* * *

A few months later, Erasmus died in Basel in the night of 11–12 July 1536, one year, almost to the day, after his dear More.

In the years that followed, their works were mishandled or mistreated, no doubt well beyond their greatest fears. In England, More's writings were ostracized, except during the intermezzo when the Catholic Mary, daughter of Henry and Catherine of Aragon, was on the throne. This ostracism extended throughout the reign of Elizabeth. In 1559, the daughter of Henry and Anne Boleyn gave a definitive triumph to the Anglican compromise, and therefore the schism with Rome. More belonged to the camp of the defeated without right of appeal. One work, however, escaped the common fate, this singular Utopia *which More would have rather consigned to the flames than to see it translated into English. It was translated, however, in 1551, under the reign of Edward VI, even while its author was held a "traitor" and a "papist." In his dedication, the translator, Ralph Robinson, deplored More's "blind obstinacy." Why then, this publication? The reason, or one of the reasons, is probably the following: the innovators found in their enemy's work something to sustain their cause (the abuses of Pontiffs and monks, divorce authorized in Utopia, as well as the marriage of priests).*[12]Utopia *was once again slipping out of its author's intentions, awaiting even more.*

[12] In agreement with the official spirit, Robinson skips certain delicate phrases and translates *pontifex* by *bishops*. See Andre Prévost's edition of the *Utopia*, 253–254. Correlatively, the Catholic authors of the first biographies of More, written during the period but published later, tend to

The fate of Erasmus's works was no happier. As long as he was alive, the protection of popes, sometimes of kings prevented any effective measures from being taken against his books. But after his death, the blade of the guillotine fell. The Roman Index of 1559, the Index of Paul IV, condemned all of his works en bloc. Less severe, the Index of the Council of Trent (1564) condemned six of his works, among them the Folly *and the* Colloquia. *But he remained a condemned author of the first class (*primae classis*), along with Machiavelli.*

On the other hand, across the Channel, the translations were many, some of them more or less inflected so as to make of his writings a war machine against Rome and Roman Christianity. Cromwell, the King's man, put Erasmus to use serving the break which he condemned.

In his Life of Sir Thomas More, *William Roper, More's son-in-law, reports the following dialogue:*

> *So, on a time, walking with me along the Thames side at Chelsey, in talking of other things he said unto me: "Now would to our Lord, son Roper, upon condition that three things were well established in Christendom, I were put in a sack, and here presently cast into the Thames."*
>
> *"What great things be those, Sir," quoth I, "that should move you so to wish?"*
>
> *"Wouldst you know what they be. Son Roper?" quoth he.*
>
> *"Yea, marry, with good will, sir, if it please you," quoth I.*
>
> *"In faith, son, they be these," said he. "The first is, that whereas the [most] part of Christian princes be at mortal war, they were [all] at an universal peace. The second, that where the Church of Christ is [at this present] sore afflicted with many errors and heresies, it were settled in perfect uniformity of religion. The third, that where the kings matter of his*

disregard *Utopia*. William Roper had nothing to say about it. See James J. Greene, "Utopia and Early More Biography," *Moreana* 31–32 (November 1971): 199–207.

*marriage is now come in question, it were to the glory of God
and quietness of all parties brought to a good conclusion."
Whereby, as I could gather, he judged that otherwise it would
be a disturbance to a great part of Christendom.*[13]

*None of these wishes was fulfilled. During the same period,
Erasmus feared that the religious division would lead to an "atrocious
carnage." What he feared, and what overwhelmed him, in fact happened. It follows that More appears like a defeated figure of history,
Erasmus even more so. The Catholic reform he had called for and prepared slipped away in favor of a Protestant Reformation which denatured his message, and of a Catholic Counter-Reformation which
transformed it and threw Erasmus overboard. "Historically speaking," wrote Lucien Febvre, "Erasmus appears as one defeated; Luther
and Loyola appear like winners, it's a fact."*[14] *If we extend that per-
spective, it is More, Erasmus, Luther and Loyola who appear like the
vanquished of history. Who is the winner? Machiavelli?*

---

[13] William Roper, *The Lyfe of Sir Thomas Moore, Knighte,* ed. Leslie
  Vaughan Hitchcock London: Early English Text Society, Humphrey Mil-
  ford: Oxford University Press, 1935), 197: 24–25(corrected to modern
  English spelling).

[14] *Le Problème de l'incroyance au XVIe siècle, La Religion de Rabelais*
  (Paris: Albin Michel, 1942; Nelle ed. 1974: 28.

EPILOGUE

The final letters are separate. They come from beyond the grave by ways that have been untraceable with precision. These are the only letters whose authenticity has been doubted by certain scholars of little faith. Arbitration here is impossible, yet these are the same voices expressing themselves as in previous letters.

I.

MACHIAVELLI TO THOMAS MORE
Downstairs (undated)

[1] I learned, esteemed More, of your falling out with the Prince, and that the executioner had cut through the affair. I must admit to you that I had a hearty laugh. Here is a fine and good example of the salary that your paternosters deserve, and those of the Reverend Erasmus.

All these tribulations, I trust, have knocked some sense into that head you have lost. For, my good More, brains are of three kinds: one understands by itself, a second discerns what the first understands, a third understands neither alone nor through others. And since your prejudices placed you way at the bottom, I restrained myself from saying what you could not understand. I'd like to think that I can now explain things to you without your slamming the door in my face immediately. Up there, on earth, they will know nothing about it.

So you will find, joined to this missive, the textual explication which you were aspiring to, and which I wrote for a few who knew its price [*Quia nominor Princeps*]. And since I'm alone in this place, and since they're letting me rot with boredom, let me take the time to add a few words.

[2] As you must know, this nastiness of Fortune overwhelmed me with insults when I was alive. But I'll have my revenge. For I want to teach you something: the New World, blessed More, you dreamed of it, I am inaugurating it. If yours is new at a cheap cost, mine traces a radical break in the history of the world.

I sense that your soul is shivering; get over it, here's something to warm it up. First, take my explication, which will tell you the words and the things, and all the newness they contain. Second, consider the place I am speaking from in this text, and which is the most extraordinary of conquests. For I am speaking not as philosopher who makes the nature of things speak, nor am I speaking as a prophet who makes himself the echo of another word; no, I am speaking of my own authority. As for the others, yourself, your darling Erasmus, you are mere commentators. Myself, I comment only for show, I speak without crutches, my own arms are sufficient. You people are merely the servants of a truth that you go and find higher than yourselves; for me, truth is something that I say and make. For my Word is a Beginning. And nothing can ever make it possible that what I have done might not have been done.

That, my dear More, is the news I wanted to bring you. The breach has been made; and the new men will know that nothing can hold them back, that the world is theirs. The action of men upon men: I have opened a magnificent space to it, for the benefit of those who have the intelligence to understand and the virtue to act. As you see, that forbidden tree of the Garden of Eden, I have done more than crunch its apples; I have attacked it at the root. Might I add, to add to your remorse, that those apples are the best in the world?

[3] But I feel that I have distressed you. Here is another matter which might allow your pious soul to seek some consolation. I have revealed to you my mind as an author, but this doesn't mean that I

have revealed to you my mind and my heart as a man. Whoever would think he knows me after reading these lines would be as presumptuous as a Capuchin friar. For it may be that I have lived several lives on several planes. As examples, I'll give you these: I didn't spare my strength in the service of my country [Florence]; but I shan't tell you whether it's out of a taste for action, or for the love of my city. Of the pleasures of Venus I had my quota; as for the torments of the heart, I'll keep that to myself. And as for Heaven I made much fun of it; I'll leave it to you to guess whether I've relegated it to outer darkness. Now I want to tell you two things. The first is that I've always thought that an excellent man has but two ways of killing boredom: the first is to fuck the ladies with the means of nature; the second is to play with men with the means of politics. The second thing is that I've always known that desire is insatiable, that success is fleeting, and that life is short. I leave it to you to guess which of these is the true proposition, or whether they are both true. I'm playing, perhaps, but perhaps we are all playing? What are you playing at?

[4] I'm bored here. No one to talk to. I don't even know where I am. In Purgatory? At the door of Hell? In the antechamber of Nothingness? I have written to Cyrus, Romulus, Theseus, Cesare, and even syphilitic old Jules, who, according to your friend Erasmus, should be around here somewhere. Perhaps are they now no more than shades, perhaps some censor from above has done his duty. Oh well, Intercede with your divine Master, if you ever bump into Him, not to leave me to rot in this rat hole. I salute your beautiful soul and beg her not to bear a grudge against me. If I have sullied her, it's for her own good.

II.
MORE TO MACHIAVELLI
Upstairs (undated)

I answer in haste, dear Niccolò, I'm waiting for a call. Don't hold it against me if I speak curtly. I'm not in the mood for subtleties.

[1] You laughed, you say, at my tribulations. I've a hard time be-

lieving it, you are playing even now. For myself, I didn't laugh, surely not, but I did unload, disencumber myself, got rid of those vain things you make such a fuss about. You see, I have put down my load. If I hadn't trembled for my loved ones, if my poor body hadn't screamed with fright, I would have felt myself the freest of men.

Don't worry, I'm not inviting you to knock at the door of the Tower of London, it's too late. But please, Niccolò, relax and drop the mask. I feel it from here, your soul is tense from top to bottom. The remedy is in this quotation recorded by Matthew: "The Kingdom suffereth violence, and the violent bear it away" [Matt.11: 12]. This quotation, you know it, Niccolò, you used it for your own ends for the pleasure of the maneuver and for the pleasure of impiety. What it really signifies, I know all too well, and I don't doubt that you know: you must do violence to yourself and divest yourself of the old man. And who is your "new" man if not the old man par excellence?

[2] The rest of the story, if you don't know it, is that your blindness about yourself is nothing short of a miracle. What you must divest yourself of first and foremost, of course, is pride, that insensate pride which oozes from every line of your prose, or almost. You are making too much of yourself, Niccolò, and you invite these poor people who will believe in you to do the same. Who are we on this earth, if not mendicants of truth? What are you glorying in, if not treasures of counterfeit money? The passions you kindle devour those who fall into your trap. They dry up, like deadwood.

[3] Enough said, let's drop our weapons. It's no longer time for quarreling. We shall, both of us, appear before the Sovereign Judge. You tell me that I cannot know you fully. You are right, a thousand times right. God alone knows our souls. At the end of our letter, you play the clown again; I pass, don't hold it against me, I'm no longer in the game. I'm too busy with my soul, I feel I know it (I'm wrong perhaps), we shall see very soon. But down there, among the living, who will ever know what my torments were, my temptations, my falls and my remorses? And who will ever know Machiavelli's?

That is surely why we know so badly the reasons for the actions of men; but the reasons which should make them act we know far better. And thinking you know the former and wanting to disqualify the latter, you are going the wrong way, beyond the shadow of a doubt. But I'm quarreling again. Forgive me, I'm an old man of the law, incorrigible in these matters. Let me return to the only thing that counts. I have only poor words to offer you but I know that divine mercy is offered to each one of us. I might add. . . . But I hear a rattling of keys. I'm sure they are Saint Peter's. Enough, I am filled with hope. Farewell, Niccolò, farewell, with all my heart.

APPENDICES

Appendix I

THOMAS MORE, THE UTOPIANS, THE HERETICS, AND THE RIGHTS OF CONSCIENCE

In his different official duties, and especially as Lord Chancellor, Thomas More pursued the Reformers actively and, on certain occasions, approved their execution. More precisely, but allowing for a few uncertainties, he was personally implicated, during his three years as Chancellor, in three or four of the six cases of heresy which led the condemned heretics to the execution block. In doing so More was merely applying the law, but it is beyond doubt that he approved it fully. He would strive first to convince the dissidents of their error, without hatred, he said, toward their person,[1] but if they persisted, the chastisement had to follow. In his eyes, the Lutherans were not only unfaithful to the true faith, they were also conspirators who opened the way to civil disorders. On both terrains, heresy was treason.

In this, More thought no differently from his times, which did not dissociate political and religious unity. But he experienced this shattering of Christendom with an extreme intensity. His polemical works show the extent of his passion. So many pages, so much haste, so much

---

[1] In his *Apology* (1533), More writes: "As touching heretics, I hate that vice of theirs and not their persons, and very fain would I that the one were destroyed and the other saved." *The Complete Works*, vol. 9: 167.

vehemence, a number of these texts written at night after overburdened days—all of this cannot be explained without a sense of crisis and urgency. A drama is in the offing. The most profound reason for his attitude is probably the result of his attachment to the unity of Christendom, the unity of the Church, the unity of Europe. His fears could only be intensified by the troubles in Germany (the Peasant War of 1524–1525), the sack of Rome (1527), his King's quarrel with the Pope. No doubt he saw on the horizon the risk of the wars of religion; perhaps he foresaw the appropriation of religion by the princes; perhaps he experienced the feeling of a world coming to an end. In any case, the persecutor of the Lutherans does not fit well, apparently, with the author of the *Utopia*, who favored, or seemed to favor, religious tolerance. Nor does he fit well with the prisoner of the Tower, who appealed to his conscience to refuse the oaths imposed by the Acts of Parliament of 1534 and 1535. How can we interpret these apparently irreconcilable attitudes? Must we distinguish between several Mores? Here are a few attempts at an answer, which seem to us the most convincing.

[1] Concerning the *Utopia*, our answer derives from the interpretation given in Chapter V. The passages concerning the religion of the Utopians are similar to the rest: a mixture of genres where fantasy and satire dominate. The satire (by contrast to what is done in Utopia) is directed notably against lazy, hedonistic monks, against the excessive number of priests, many of them without a vocation, against the attitude of ordinary Christians toward death. The fantasy is expressed through general description (diverse religions but a common practice), through crazy details (the faithful falling to their knees at the priest's entry as a gesture of adoration, the women kneeling for confession before their husbands prior to great ceremonies . . .), lastly through multiple contradictions.

What can be said of that famous *tolerance* which reigned in Utopia? More does here what he does elsewhere: he aligns propositions which cancel one another out. He evidently does it with subtlety. Here is the passage concerning religious freedom in Utopia. Leaving aside the embellishments and the secondary developments, there emerges a chain of propositions which takes care of the incoherencies:

1. One of the most ancient laws of Utopia forbids harming anyone in matters of religion. Each can believe what he wishes. So decided Utopus, the founder.
2. Utopus, however, decreed a severe and inviolable law which forbids not believing in the immortality of the soul and in Providence. The guilty cannot even be counted among the men, and their rights as citizens are revoked.
3. Nevertheless, no penalty is inflicted upon them,[2] since everyone in Utopia is convinced that man is incapable of believing whatever he wants.
4. They are not even asked to hide their feelings.
5. But they are obliged to be silent in public.
6. It being understood that there is nothing more guarded against in Utopia than to pronounce oneself lightly on this or that form of religion.

The passage on the power of priests is of the same crafting. These priests, we remember, are fiendishly ecumenical, since they are the same for all and officiate for several cults at the same time: the sun, the moon, a shooting star, a hero, "the Being that engenders." Their power takes the following form:

1. They exercise a form of censure on morals.
2. But they are present only to exhort and blame. The magistrates alone decide.
3. Nevertheless, they exclude the guilty from the ceremonies, and if the latter do not repent promptly, they are arrested by the Senate and punished for their impiety.

To crown the whole matter, Hythlodeus speaks repeatedly of the feeling of fear or religious terror which exits in Utopia. He nonetheless

---

[2] The text reads that they are inflicted "nullo supplicio." Marie Delcourt and André Prévost translate *supplicium* by "corporal punishment" to eliminate an incoherence which is nonetheless in the text. *Supplicium* means punishment, chastisement, torture. Robinson is more exact: "They are not punished in any way." And Adams: "Yet they do not afflict him with punishments."

continues to boast of the freedom which reigns there in matters of religion.

It therefore seems difficult to oppose the tolerance of the *Utopia* to the intolerance of the Chancellor. It cannot be denied, however, that the last years changed his tone concerning the affairs of the Church. The misfortunes of the time were surely a factor. First of all, the critical audacities he thought salutary in 1516 were no longer in season when the unity of the Church was in danger. Secondly, in his combat against heresy, and no doubt because of this combat, he appears more attached to exterior forms of piety than in his younger years, and generally more uncompromising (or less Erasmian). And yet one can't speak of a reversal.

[2] Concerning the "rights" of conscience refused to the Lutherans by More the Chancellor but claimed for himself by More imprisoned, the question is more uncertain. The most researched and most precise analysis of this question, it seems to us, that of Steven D. Smith, reaches the conclusion that it is difficult to conclude.[3] The interpretation he submits with prudence, however, appears until further notice the most likely. It can be presented as follows: there is no contradiction between More's attitude facing the Lutherans and his own attitude facing Henry VIII and Cromwell, because the authority of conscience he is claiming to refuse the oath cannot be confused with the authority of conscience in the modern sense. In the longest development he devotes to this point, which lies at the heart of his defense (as reported by his daughter Margaret in a letter to Alice Arlington of August 1534), More distinguishes between the Christian truths which are clearly established and questions which are not resolved with certainty. The established truths are those which have been so established by a general Council, or which belong to the common faith of Christendom. In this case, conscience would be guilty of not acquiescing. In the second case, on the other hand, it is permitted to take one's conscience as a guide. Consequently, the apparent contradictions

---

3   "Interrogating Thomas More: The Conundrums of Conscience," *University of St. Thomas Law Journal* I,I (Fall 2003): 580–609.

between More the persecutor and More the persecuted dissolve, at least in part: the validity of the marriage between Henry and Catherine of Aragon is one of those unresolved questions about which one can judge in conscience, while recognizing someone else's freedom to judge differently; but the same freedom of judgment cannot be recognized for Luther or his followers, who attack established truths. It is difficult to think, however, that More considered Henry's separation from Rome as one of those questions open to the judgment of conscience. Perhaps one should also allow for tactics on More's part, or on his reluctance to place his loved ones in danger?

In a second sense, the rights of conscience More was claiming had only a limited range and did not extend to the Lutherans. From his point of view, the Lutherans were encouraging sedition with their proselytizing. He, on the other hand, silences his disagreement and reiterates his loyalty to the King. What More is claiming is the right to be silent, the right not to pronounce the oath which he abhors. Political power can legitimately force him to be silent, nothing more. W. Chambers, who submits this argument, concludes: "In Burke's words, he took his idea of liberty low, and stuck to it [. . .]. A low ideal, you may say. Anyway, it was too high for More to hold it and live, in the days of Henri VIII."[4] If this interpretation is correct, Thomas More, by his death, is certainly a hero of conscience, but he remains a man of his time by his restrictive conception of the rights of conscience.

---

[4] *Thomas More, op. cit., 368.* See also Louis L. Matz, "Thomas More: The Search for the Inner Man," in *Miscellanea Moreana: Essays for Germain Marc'hadour*, ed. Claire Murphy et al., *Moreana*, XXVI.100 (1989): 397–416. For another viewpoint, see esp. G.R. Elton, *Policy and Police: The Enforcement of Reformation in the Age of Cromwell* (Cambridge University Press, 1985), esp. 416–418.

Appendix II

EXPLICATION DE TEXTE

May the shades of Erasmus, More, and Machiavelli forgive us this offhand manner we have of writing apocryphal works! In certain respects these three writers are players. We have taken a leaf from their book, while attempting to see through their game. It's only fair, perhaps, provided our own game is not disloyal. We have taken pains not to do them violence.

1. We have taken no liberties with dates, places, facts, works. Unless we are mistaken, everything set down here is in keeping with history, or at least with the history of the historians. However, the letters from the other world ["Downstairs" and "Upstairs"] are a separate matter, and in this particular case we beg permission not to reveal our sources.

The only liberty we have taken concerns Erasmus and his knowledge of languages. So far as we know, Erasmus had only smatterings of Italian, even though he had made one long sojourn in Italy. For the present need, we have assumed that he knew more.

The familiar letters exchanged here between Erasmus and More on the one hand, and Machiavelli and Vettori on the other, closely follow the authentic correspondence, from which we have taken excerpts. Machiavelli's crude language is in tune with what he writes elsewhere, which can be obscene (see the famous letter of 8 December 1509 to Luigi Guicciardini on the old stinking and emaciated whore).

Concerning the quarrel on political and religious questions, our intention has been to make Erasmus, More, and Machiavelli speak in the line of their writings. The texts on which these developments are based are indicated in Appendix III.

2. As to the interpretation of the works, the method we have tried to follow and to illustrate is based on the following principles:

– A work cannot be understood, all the less so a great work, without taking the author's art of writing into consideration. The text can be written plainly; it can be written obliquely. In any case, the first objective is to grasp the author's intention, beginning with the hypothesis that he knows what he is doing.

As Erasmus, More, and Machiavelli make clear, and many other political writers as well, there are many ways of writing obliquely, and many reasons to write that way: gaming, prudence, pedagogy, self-respect, strategy, etc. To grasp what is written between the lines, one must take the entire text, not just make a selection, as has so often been done for Machiavelli. (A commentator reads a single passage and concludes immediately: "Machiavelli thinks that . . ." whereas prudence dictates one's saying "Machiavelli says here that . . .").

One of the key questions is the interpretation of contradictions. Take the example of the Florentine: 1) these contradictions are multiple: on the people, the Prince, men, arms . . . ; 2) they can be inserted into the reasoning itself. These are not ordinary contradictions. They must not be forgotten along the way, but taken head on. How can one doubt that they are deliberate?

– In order to do this, much depends on one's attitude facing the text. One must "put himself in a state of readiness to comprehend" (Etienne Gilson), that is to say, suspend one's judgment, be ready to listen, eschew any method which prejudges the rest, finally, recognize this: it is the author who is the chief, not the interpreter. This rule, of course, is not easy to follow when we are dealing with works which come to us overloaded with interpretations. To this may be added other current obstacles: 1) the "democratic" spirit, in Tocqueville's sense, which leads the interpreter to assume power, as it were, to place himself above the text, otherwise said to posit as an *a priori:* I am in a position to understand this author better than he understood himself. The historicists err in this direction. 2) the spirit of seriousness, which has struck so many translators and commentators of More, Erasmus, and Machiavelli. But the great minds are allowed to joke or play in their own way.

– For the rest, it all depends. Explication by the intentions does not necessarily exhaust the meaning of a work. It all depends. It may be that the author does not know the full meaning of what he is doing. But concerning the greatest minds, it seems reasonable to trust their credibility, at least as a first step.

One ought, therefore, to be wary of the systematizing spirit, and particularly to avoid these two opposite mistakes: 1) attributing as a matter of principle or reflex, to authors distant from us, sentiments or ideas similar to ours; 2) enclosing them in a time forever foreign to ours. Lucien Febvre eloquently condemned the first attitude; Leo Strauss stated forcefully how erroneous the second could be. All this depends on the men: the greater their minds, the farther they see, the more they transcend their time. All this depends on the subjects: the more profound or elevated they are, the more they are detached from time.

Now our three authors are great minds and they see far. They pursue their thinking to the very end —to the affirmation of a radical freedom with Machiavelli, to a conversion to the radicalism of the Gospel or to "Christian folly" with Erasmus and More. Only More and Erasmus temper the express of their thinking by a practical prudence, and Machiavelli through the esoteric writing of a conspirator.

3. Concerning these rules of method, concerning also the interpretation we have proposed of Machiavelli, we owe much to Leo Strauss. We have traveled on the road he has opened with his *Thoughts on Machiavelli* (Glencoe, Ill. Free Press, 1958), and more generally on the road opened by his analyses and commentaries on the great political philosophers.

Strauss's teaching has renewed the history of political thought and has liberated the great thinkers from the chains of historicism. Revised and corrected, this history appears more profound and enigmatic than was once thought, and it can hardly be understood without finding a niche for that forgotten art of writing: esoteric writing (see in particular Strauss's *Persecution and the Art of Writing*, University of Chicago Press, 1952). Perhaps, however, Strauss's analyses are at times too systematic (they fail, it seems to us, to account for all the diversity of rhetorical strategies, they can underestimate the role of history). On the other hand, it is possible to pay homage to Strauss without adhering to his political philosophy, which reserves truth, and life in the truth, to a few "real" philosophers.

We are equally indebted to the works of Harvey Mansfield, which lie, as it were, within the Straussian sphere, and in particular to that collection of penetrating analyses entitled *Machiavelli's Virtue* (University of Chicago Press, 1996). Finally, Claude Lefort's powerful work, *Le Travail de l'oeuvre. Machiavel* (Paris: Gallimard, 1972) was immensely helpful to us. Though we do not share his interpretation, we have benefited greatly from his fine and penetrating analyses of the texts, and, foremost, that of the *Prince*.

4. As far as Erasmus is concerned, the interpretation we have given of the *Praise of Folly* is largely inspired by these two *explications de texte*:

– M.A. Screech, *Ecstasy and the Praise of Folly* (London: Duckworth, 1980). This is an extraordinarily erudite work, shedding light on the genesis of the text and its successive versions, and showing that the theme of Christian folly is in no way an incidental one and that it holds a choice place in Erasmus's thinking.

– Marc Fumaroli, "*L'Eloquence de la folie*," in *Dix Conférences sur l'Eloge de la Folie [Ten Lectures on the Praise of Folly]*, texts assembled by Claude Blum (Paris: Champion, 1988): 11–21, a dazzling lecture which illustrates the importance of the status of the orator (Dame Folly) to understand the text.

The first letter of Chapter X, where Erasmus speaks as a professor of Rhetoric, is based in large measure on the monumental thesis of Jacques Chomarat, *Grammaire et rhétorique chez Erasme* (Paris: Les Belles Lettres, 1981), 2 vols.

Appendix III

THE SOURCES, THEIR RESOURCES, THEIR LIMITS

I.

The Primary Sources

The essential sources are, of course, the works and the letters of the three protagonists. Fortunately, there usually exist magnificent scholarly editions. All praise to the scholars!

1. The excerpts of letters cited in the texts of presentation are taken from:
– Erasmus, *Opus epistolorum*, ed. P.S. Allen (Oxford University Press, 1906–1958), 12 vols. French translation: The *Correspondance d'Erasme*, under the direction of A. Gerlo (Brussels: Presses Universitaires, 1967–1984), 12 vols. English Translation: *The Correspondence of Erasmus*, ed. and transl. R.A.B. Mynors and al. (University of Toronto Press, 1974 et sq.), 8 vols.
– Thomas More, *Selected Letters* (in the original English or translated from the Latin, ed. Elizabeth Frances Rogers (New Haven, Ct.: Yale University Press, 1967); *Erasme et Thomas More. Correspondance*, French translation by Germain Marc'hadour and Roland Galibois (Sherbrooke: Centre d'Etudes de la Renaissance, 1985).
– Machiavelli, *Lettere*, ed. F. Gaeta (Milano: Feltrinelli, 1964); *Machiavelli and His Friends: Their Personal Correspondence*, ed. J.B. Atkinson and D. Sices (DeKalb, Ill. : Northern Illinois University Press, 1996); *Toutes les lettres officielles et familières de* Machiavel, ed. Edmond Barincou (Paris: Gallimard, 1955), 2 vols. Unequal translation.

2. The *explications de texte* of the *Folly,* of the *Utopia,* and of the *Prince* given by their authors are based, clearly, on the texts. The editions utilized are the following:
– *The Praise of Folly:* the edition of reference is that of Clarence

Miller in: *Erasmus, Opera Omnia* IV.3 (Amsterdam: North Holland Publishing Co., 1979). English translation by Clarence Miller, The *Praise of Folly* (New Haven, Conn.: Yale University Press, 2003) [includes Erasmus's letter to Dorp]. French Translations: Jacques Chomarat, ed. and transl., in *Erasme. Oeuvres choisies* (Paris: Livre de Poche Classique, 1991); Claude Blum's translation in Erasme, *Oeuvres*, ed. Jean-Claude Margolin et al. (Paris: R. Laffont/Bouquins, 1992). The translation by Pierre de Nolhac, which was long considered definitive in French, is very elegant and has maintained many of its virtues, but it has its share of inaccuracies. On the vicissitudes of the French translations, see J. Chomarat, "L'Eloge de la folie et ses traducteurs français au XXe siècle," *Bulletin de l'Association Guillaume Budé*, IV.1 (March 1972): 169–188.

– As we have seen, the *Utopia* is undoubtedly the work that has been the most maltreated by the translators. The original text is reproduced in Volume IV of the *Complete Works of Thomas More* (Yale University Press, 1965), with an English translation revised by Edward Surtz (the notes are scholarly and very rich, the translation is close to the text but it sometimes prefers logic to grammar). The Latin text is also reproduced in André Prévost's handsome edition (Paris: Mame, 1978), with a French translation. This translation seems to us the most faithful French translation by far (unfortunately the commentaries are not up to the same standard). The other English or French translations cited in the notes are the following: Ralph Robinson (1551), reedited Ware, Hert (Wordsworth Editions, 1997); Marie Delcourt (1936), re-ed. Geneva: Droz, 1983); R.M. Adams (London: Norton, 1992). The translation by Elizabeth McCutcheon of the introductory letter to Pierre Gilles can be found in the annex of her work, *My Dear Peter* (Angers: Moreana, 1983). See also the important critical edition of G.M Logan, R.M Adams and Cl. Miller, *Utopia*, translation by R.M Adams, (Cambridge University Press, 1995).

– The *Prince*: N. Machiavelli, *Il Principe*, ed. G. Inglese (Torino: Einaudi, 1995) (one of the most authoritative Italian editions). The old edition of L. Arthur Burd, *Il Principe*, with Italian text, commentaries and notes in English (Oxford: Clarendon Press, 1891) is a monument of erudition. It remains very useful, even if Burd's interpretation

Appendix III

(which argues that Machiavelli writes with a flawless clarity and simplicity) is a model of incomprehension. The most dependable English and French translations—because they are as literal as possible without betraying the text—are, it seems to us, the following: *The Prince*, ed. and transl. Harvey Mansfield (University of Chicago Press, 1998); *Le Prince*, ed. Jean-Louis Fournel and Jean-Claude Zancarini, Italian text and French translation (Paris: PUF, 2000). See also the French translations of Christian Bec, *Oeuvres, op. cit.*, of Marie Gaille-Nikodimov (Paris: Le Livre de poche, 2000), and of Jacqueline Risset (Paris: Actes du Sud, 2001).

It remains true, of course, that in matters of translation it is easy to criticize and foolhardy to compete.

4. For the quarrel over political and religious questions, we have based ourselves on the following texts:

– Erasmus: *Institutio Principis Christiani*, English translation by N. Cheshire and M. Heath, entitled *The Education of a Christian Prince* (Cambridge University Press, 2003); *Querela Pacis* and other pleas for peace, collected and translated by Jean-Claude Margolin under the title *Guerre et Paix dans la pensée d'Erasme* (Paris: Aubier, 1983). Certain *Adages* are political essays: see in particular "Il faut naître Roi ou bouffon," "Le scarabée au pourchas de l'aigle," "Le sort t'a remis une Sparte, fais la resplendir," in *Oeuvres*, ed. Jean-Claude Margolin et al., or *Oeuvres choisies, ed. J. Chomarat*. In English, see *The Essential Erasmus,* ed. J.P. Dolin (New York: New American Library, 1964), and *Selected Writings*, ed. J.C. Olin (New York: Harper & Row, 1965

– Thomas More: the *Utopia*, first and foremost, and then the criticisms against tyranny in the *Epigrams* in Latin (*Latin Poems*, C.W. III.2, ed. Clarence Miller and al., 1984) and in *History of King Richard III* (C.W. II. Ed. S. Sylvester, 1963). To this may be added notations or developments scattered throughout the work. See in particular, on the theme of pride, *The Last Things* , in C.W. I (ed. A. Edwards and al., 1997).

– Machiavelli: besides the *Prince,* we have based ourselves on the *Discourses*. The best edition of the latter work in French is unquestionably that of Alessandro Fontana and Xavier Tabet, *Discours sur la première décade de Tite-Live* (Paris: Gallimard, 2004). Best Italian edition: Discorsi, ed. F. Busi (Rome/Salerno: Edizione nazionale della opera di Niccolò Machiavelli, opera politiche, v. 2, , 2001), 2 vols. English edition: *The Discourses*, ed. and transl. Leslie J. Walker (London: Routledge and Kegan Paul, 1950).

5. The two letters of Erasmus written on the occasion of Thomas More's dramatic end (Chapter IX) are based on the following sources: the correspondence of 1535–1536; the letters wherein Erasmus has sketched the portrait of his friend (the two most famous ones are the one addressed to Hutten 23 July 1519, and the one addressed to J. Faber in June 1532); finally the narratives written at the time on the trial and execution of More. On these diverse narratives, see Henri de Vocht, *Acta Thomae Mori. History of the Reports of His Trial and Death* (Louvain, Institute for Economics of the University, 1947), and the two principal narratives themselves: the one in French (the "Paris Newsletter," reproduced in *Harpsfield's Life of More*, ed. E. Hitchcock and R.W. Chambers (London: EETS, 1932): 258–266; and the "Expositio Fidelis," published in the *Opus epistolorum*, ed. P.S. Allen, Vol. XI (1963): 368–378.

We have also made extensive use of that most useful research tool which is the detailed chronology established by Germain Marc'hadour, *L'Univers de Thomas More. Chronologie critique* (Paris: Vrin, 1963).

The first letter of Chapter X, where Erasmus teaches his young disciple the art of reading and the art of writing, attempts, while borrowing extensively from the works of J. Chomarat (1981), to effect a synthesis of the abundant developments which this master of rhetoric dedicated to this subject. In particular:

– On reading the Scriptures, see the Prefaces to the *Novum Testamentum*, French translation by Yves Delègue (Geneva: Labor et fides, 1990); the *Annotations* and the *Paraphrases* of the New Testament (partial translations are found in the *Oeuvres choisies*, ed. J. Chomarat).

– On education and the art of reading, the principal work is the *De Ratione studii* (*Opera Omnia* I.2 , 1971); partial translation in the

Oeuvres, ed. J.C. Margolin and the *Oeuvres choisies,* ed. J. Chomarat).

6.Varia.

– Erasmus: *Vies de Jean Vitrier et John Colet,* ed. and transl. André Godin (Angers : éditions Moréana, 1982); *Les Colloques,* ed. and transl. E. Wolff (Paris: Imprimerie Nationale, 1992), 2 vols. *The Colloquies of Erasmus,* transl. C.R. Thompson (Chicago, 1965); *La Langue,* ed. and transl. J.P. Gillet (Geneva: Labor et Fides, 2002).

– Thomas More: *Supplication of Souls* (C.W. , Vol. 7, ed. F. Manley and al., 1990); *A Dialogue of Comfort Against Tribulation* (C.W. Vol. 12, ed. L.L. Martz and al., 1976); *De Tristitia Christi* (C.W, Vol. 14, ed. and transl. Cl. Miller, 1976). Thomas More. *Histoire, Eglise et Spiritualité, Collection of Texts,* ed. and transl. Michel Taillé (Paris: Bayard, 2005).

II.

Secondary Sources

1) History

1. On the historical period, there is no lack of works of synthesis and great books. Let us mention only those which have been particularly useful: Ludwig von Pastor, *Histoire des Papes depuis la fin du Moyen Age,* French translation, Vols. V-VIII (Paris: Plon, 1898–1909), a work which remains irreplaceable because of its documentary richness and its mastery; Joseph Leclerc, *Histoire de la tolérance au siècle de la Réforme* (Paris: 1955; reed. Albin Michel, 1994); Marc Fumaroli, *L'Age de l'éloquence. Rhéthorique et "res litteraria" de la Renaissance au seuil de l'âge classique* (Geneva: Droz, 1980); *De la Réforme à la Réformation* (1450–1530), Vol. VII of the *Histoire du christianisme,* under the direction of Marc Vénard (Paris: Desclée, 1994); Christian Bec, Ivan Cloulas et al., *L'Italie de la Renaissance. Un Monde en mutation* (Paris: Fayard, 1990).

2. On the history of political thought, the two works considered as works of reference are: Pierre Mesnard, *L'Essor de la philosophie politique au XVIème siècle* (Paris: Vrin, 1969); Quentin Skinner, *The Foundations of Modern Political Thought* (Cambridge University Press, 1978). These two "Summas," undoubtedly, have many virtues, but, in our opinion, they misunderstand the true meaning of the works of Machiavelli and More. The chief reason in both cases is inattention to the rhetorical strategies. In the second case, the particular reason is an *a priori* historicism.

2) Erasmus

1. On the" Republic of Letters" and its adversaries: Marc Fumaroli, "La République des Lettres redécouverte," *in Il Vocabulario della "République des Lettres*," ed. M. Fattori (Florence: Olschki, 1997); Jean-Claude Saladin, *La Bataille du Grec à la Renaissance* (Paris: Les Belles Lettres, 2000).

2. The biographers are in disagreement about Erasmus's qualities of character. The most critical biography is J. Huizinga's, *Erasmus of Rotterdam* (1924), English translation by F. Hopman (London: Phaidon Press, 1952). The most balanced work is undoubtedly Leon Halkin's *Erasme* (Paris: Fayard, 1987). See also the very lively biography of Marie Delcourt, *Erasme* (Brussels: Ed. Libris, 1945).
Stefan Zweig's work (*Erasmus*, 1934; English translation by E. and C. Paul [London: Cassell (Hallam Edition), 1951]) raises mixed reactions. Zweig's talent and "hand" are clearly present in this work, but he maintains the dated and false image of an Erasmus more skeptical than pious.
On the friendship between Erasmus and More, see in particular E.E. Reynolds, *Thomas More and Erasmus* (London: Burns and Oates, 1965); Marie Delcourt, *op. cit.*, Ch. III; Yvonne Charlier, *Erasme et l'amitié selon sa correspondance* (Paris: Les Belles Lettres, 1977; and the commentaries on this work in *Moreana* 17 (65–66): 155–157 (Cornélia Comorovski); and (66–67): 151–154 (Germain Marc'hadour).

3. On ways of reading the *Folly*: the interpretations of M. Screech, Marc Fumaroli, L. Halkin, are developed in the books and articles cited above; Pierre de Nolhac's reading is found in the Introduction to his 1936 translation (re-ed. Paris: Garnier-Flammartion, 1964); Clarence Miller's reading is in his Introduction to Erasmus's *Opera Omnia* IV.3, *op. cit.*; Joël Lefebvre's reading is in *Les Fols et la folie* (Paris: Klincksieck, 1968).

4. On the art of reading and writing according to Erasmus (besides the work, already cited, of Jacques Chomarat): André Godin, "La Bible et la philosophie chrétienne," in *Le Temps des Réformes et la Bible,* under the direction of Guy Bédouelle, *La Bible de tous les temps* (Paris: Beauchesnes, 1989), vol. V: 563–586. Jean-Claude Margolin, "L'Apologie de la rhétorique humaniste (1500–1536)," in *Histoire de la rhétorique dans l'Europe moderne,* under the direction of Marc Fumaroli (Paris: PUF, 1999): 191–258.

On Erasmus's rhetorical strategy, his ambiguous or changing attitude toward the printing press, the precautions taken in and around the *Moria,* see David Weil Baker, *Divulging Utopia* (Amherst, Mass.: University of Massachusetts Press, 1999), Ch. 1.

5. Other studies: A. Renaudet, *Etudes Erasmiennes* (1521–1529) (Geneva: Droz, 1939); A. Renaudet, *Erasme et l'Italie* (Geneva: Droz, 1939); Jean-Cl. Margolin, *Recherches Erasmiennes* (Geneva: Droz, 1969); André Godin, *Erasme, lecteur d'Origène* (Geneva: Droz, 1982).

3) More

1. On the life and the personality of Thomas More, modern studies are numerous and contrasted. Among those where admiration for this important figure is dominant, the most accomplished is still the biography of R.W. Chambers, *Thomas More* (London: Jonathan Cape, 1935. E.E. Reynolds's biography, *The Field Is Won* (London: Burns and Oates, 1968) is also a work that has been long matured and it offers a useful complement to Chambers on the terrain of religious sentiment.

At the opposite end are the "revisionist" historians who, for the past thirty years or so, have been providing an entirely different picture of More: ambiguous, passionate, tormented. This critical point of view is developed with moderation by G.R. Elton, "Thomas More, Councilor (1517–1529)" in *St. Thomas More: Action and Contemplation*, ed. R.S. Sylvester (New Haven, Ct.: Yale University Press, 1972): 85–122; "The Real Thomas More?" in *Reformation Principle and Practice*, ed. P.N. Brooks (London: Scholar Press, 1980): 23–31. The critical viewpoint is developed with a manifest bias by Richard Marius in his ample and controversial biography, *Thomas More* (New York: A.A. Knopf, 1984). The portrait provided by Marius intends to lift the veil: behind the stained-glass image lies a man deeply divided, racked with hidden passions (worldly ambition, sexual frustration), and one underestimated passion (religious fanaticism). Marius's demonstration is filled with uncertain or improbable assertions. Supposing it were just, More's reputation in his time would have been a masterpiece of hypocrisy; and Erasmus would have erred completely in his judgment of a friend of so many years (unless he himself were also an inveterate hypocrite).

Peter Ackroyd's biography, *The Life of Thomas More* (London: Chatto and Windus, 1998) is more balanced and written very vividly. Its contribution to More studies, however, is slight.

2. On the readings of *Utopia*. Since the end of the nineteenth century, the interpretations of this work have proliferated. See in particular George Logan, *The Meaning of More's Utopia* (Princeton, N.J.: Princeton University Press, 1983), Introduction. On recent interpretations: George Logan, "Interpreting *Utopia*," *Moreana*, XXXI, 118–119 (June, 1994): 203–258.

The principal articles dedicated to *Utopia* since the middle of the last century can be found in *More*, "Great Political Thinkers" Collection, ed. J. Dunn and I. Harris (Chestelham, UK: E. Elgar, 1997), 2 vols. (more than fifty articles, at least twenty on the *Utopia*); *Essential Articles for the Study of Thomas More*, ed. R.S. Sylvester and G. Marc'hadour (Hamden, Conn.: Archon Books, 1977). The analyses which, in our opinion, set into highest relief the satirical dimension of the *Utopia* are those of C.S. Lewis in *English Literature in the Sixteenth Century* (Oxford University Press, 1962): 167–171, and A.R. Heiserman, "Satire in the *Utopia,*" *Publications of the Modern Language Association of America* 78.3 (June 1963): 163–174.

Among recent studies, see also: *Moreana,* Special Number "Utopia Revisited," 118–119 (1994); Norbert Col, "Lire l'*Utopia* de Thomas More," in *Liberté politique* 16 (Spring-Summer 2001): 11–124; Jean-Yves Lacroix, *L'Utopie de Thomas More et la tradition platonicienne* (Paris: Vrin, 2007).

3. Other studies: G. Marc'hadour, *Thomas More et la Bible* (Paris: Vrin, 1969); G. Wagemer, *Thomas More on Statesmanship* (Washington: The Catholic University of America Press, 1996).

4) Machiavelli

1. Writing a biography is always a daunting enterprise. In Machiavelli's case the exercise is enough to make the most enterprising give up the attempt: the man is enigmatic, his works ambiguous, whole sections of his life are unknown. Those who embark on this adventure greatly risk succumbing to two temptations: 1) fill in the gaps and say more than they know; 2) believe at his word on occasion the only available witness, while much leads you to believe that he is an unreliable witness, Machiavelli himself. The most notorious example is the biography reputed to be the standard one, Roberto Ridolfi's *Vita di Niccolò Machiavelli* (Florence: Sansoni, 1978) 2 vols., English translation by C. Grayson (University of Chicago Press, 1963). Ridolfi undoubtedly knows all that can possibly be known, but his "love" (declared) for Machiavelli makes him account for uncertain things with uncertain explanations which always redound to the honor of his hero. Ridolfi is also prone to accept Machiavelli's pleas *pro domo* with full and unswerving faith. His analyses of Machiavelli's works are superficial, and he concludes that "the general coherence and the logic of his thought cannot possibly be doubted." Love is blind.

We have therefore used the biographies with reservations. Here are those which seemed to us the most prudent, or the most solid, or the richest in information or in enlightening insights.

– Among the ancient biographies: Artaud de Montor, *Nicolas Machiavel, son génie, ses erreurs* (1883), 2 vols.

– Among recent biographies: Marie Gaille-Nikodimov, *Machiavel* (Paris: Taillandier, 2005); Sandro Landi, *Machiavel* (Paris: Ellipses, 2008); Marina Marietti, *Machiavel. Le Penseur de la nécessité* (Paris: Payot, 2009).

On Machiavelli confronting the Medici and on the strategic context of his works, see the highly researched study of Marina Marietti, "Machiavel historiographe des Médicis," in *Les Ecrivains et le pouvoir en Italie à l'époque de la Renaissance*, under the direction of A. Rochon (Paris: Université de la Sorbonne Nouvelle, 1974): 2: 81–148.

2. On readings of Machiavelli:

– On the posthumous history of Machiavelli: Albert Chérel, *La Pensée de Machiavel en France* (Paris: l'Artisan du Livre, 1935); Charles Benoist, *Le Machiavélisme après Machiavel* (Paris: Plon, 1936); Sydney Anglo, *Machiavelli. The First Century* (Oxford University Press, 2005). A vast panorama of the multiple interpretations of Machiavelli can also be found in Sir Isaiah Berlin's *Against the Current: Essays on the History of Ideas* (Oxford: Clarendon Press, 1979): 25–39.

– On the modern or contemporary interpretations, see in particular the studies collected in Machiavelli, coll. "Great Political Thinkers," eds. J. Dunn and I. Harris (Cheltenham: E. Elgar, 1977), 2 vols. (more than fifty articles). See also *L'Enjeu Machiavel,* under the direction of G. Sfez and M. Sellenart (Paris: PUF, 2001).

– On the Straussian reading of Machiavelli, see notably the very clear, masterful presentation of G. Sfez, *Leo Strauss, lecteur de Machiavel* (Paris: Ellipses, 2003), and the critical analyses of Claude Lefort in *Le Travail de l'Oeuvre. Machiavel, op cit.*, 295–305.

Among the studies situated within Strauss's sphere of influence, we should cite, besides Harvey Mansfield's work already mentioned:

Paul Rahe, *Against Throne and Altar* (Cambridge University Press, 2009); Nathan Tarcov, "Quentin Skinner's Method and Machiavelli's Prince," *Ethics* 92 (1982): 692–709. Also by Harvey Mansfield is " L'Education du Prince de Machiavel," in *Le Savoir du Prince,* under the direction of Ran Halévy (Paris: Fayard, 2002): 69–79. Pierre Manent's brilliant analyses are closely related, but they are also based on the works of Claude Lefort: *Naissances de la politique moderne* (Paris: Gallimard/Tel, 2007), Première partie; also *Enquête sur la démocratie* (Paris: Gallimard/Tel, 2007), Ch. XIII-XV.

– On a historical or historicist reading of Machiavelli: A. Renaudet, *Machiavel* (Paris: Gallimard, 1956); F. Chabod, *Scritti su Machiavelli* (Torino: Einaudi, 1964); J.G.A. Pocock, *The Machiavellian Moment. Florentine Political Thought and the Atlantic Republican Tradition* (Princeton, N.J.: Princeton University Press, 1975); Quentin Skinner, *Machiavelli* (Oxford University Press, 1981).

3. Varia:

– On Machiavelli and Cesare Borgia: G. Sasso, *Machiavelli e Cesare Borgia: storia di un giudizio* (Rome: Ateneo, 1966); J.J. Marchand, "L'Evolution de la figure de Cesare Borgia dans la pensée de Machiavel," *Revue Suisse d'Histoire* 19.1 (1969): 327–355; John Larner, "Cesare Borgia, Machiavelli, and the Romagnol Militia," *Studi Romagnoli* 16 (1966): 253–268.

– On Machiavelli and his "friends": Louis Passy, *Un Ami de Machiavel: François Vettori* (Paris: Plon, 1914), 2 vols.; Felix Gilbert, *Machiavelli and Guicciardini* (Princeton, N.J.: Princeton University Press, 1965).

ACKNOWLEDGMENTS

First of all I wish to express my gratitude to M. l'Abbé Germain Marc'hadour, whose great learning and kindness were major assets in the course of our research on Thomas More. He was kind enough to accept in his review *Moreana* More's letter to Machiavelli, reproduced here in Chapter V, wherein More explains to Machiavelli how to read the *Utopia* ("L'Utopie expliquée par Thomas More," *Moreana* 159 [September 2004]): 5–25. For the translation of the excerpts cited from the *Utopia*, his help, as well as that of M. Alain Foulon, were of great help to us.

Thuriane Séveno read the manuscript with a sharp and perspicacious eye. The final version of the text owes much to her.

Concerning this edition in English, I wish to express my gratitude to Paul Archambault. The art of translation, as we noted in our discussion of our authors, is a perilous enterprise. It is all the more perilous when the text uses irony, allusion, or *double entente*. P. Archambault made light work of these difficulties, and he translated the French text with a master's hand.

This edition would not exist were it not for Daniel Mahoney and his generous friendship. Ralph Hancock's contribution was also valuable. From both, as well as from James Ceaser and Tilo Schabert, I received advice and encouragement of the most precious kind. Finally, Bruce Fingerhut proved to be the ideal editor: friendly, efficient, and judicious. To all, old friends or new, I say a hearty thank you. Thomas More was right: friendship is a thing worthy of our worship.

INDEX

Abraham, 208

Abranski, C, 9n

Achilles, 68, 73–74, 76

Ackroyd, Peter, 197n

Adams, Robert M, 133n, 139n, 234n

Agamemnon, 73

Agathocles, 49, 158

Alceste, character of Molière's *Le Misanthrope*, 16

Alberti, Leon Battista, 61

Alexander, Roman Emperor, 154

Alexander VI (Cardinal Rodrigo Borgia), Pope, 33, 74, 155, 159

Alexander the Great, 74, 76, 80

Ambrose, Saint, 32, 203

Amerbach, Boniface, 188–190

Anne of Brittany, Queen of France, 65n

Anthony of Padoua, Saint, 216

Aretino, Pietro, 39

Aristophanes, 32

Aristotle, 32, 39, 54, 80, 82

Arlington, Alice, 235

Athanasius, Saint, 203

Audley, Thomas, 196

Augustine, Saint, 32, 76, 192, 203

Averroes, 54

Bacon, Francis, 6

Baglioni, Gianpaolo, 94

Barbera : Raffacani, Salutati Barbara, 23, 26, 180

Baron, Hans, 41

Basil of Caesarea, Saint, 32, 203

Bathsheba, 81n

Bausi, Francesco, 26

Bayle, Pierre , 6

Bebel, August, 9

Bec, Christian, 61

Béda, Noël, 206

Beerbohm, Max, 13

Berghes, Henry de, 29

Bible, *passim*. Books of : *Acts*, 204 ; *Corinthians*, 211, 217; *Deuteronomy*, 95n; *Exodus*, 39, 95n, 161; *John*, 216; *Leviticus*, 185: *Luke*, 127n, 196; *Matthew*,130n, 145, 208, 230; *Numbers*, 95n; *Psalms*, 211; I *Samuel*, 160n; *Tobias*, 141

Boccacio, Giovanni, 32, 61, 87
Bodin, Jean, 6
Boethius, 199
Boleyn, Anne, Queen of Henri VIII, 185, 186, 189, 224
Boleyn, Thomas, 191
Bolt, Robert, 188n
Borgia, Cesare, Duke of Valentino, 22, 30, 39, 48, 73–74, 83, 90, 105–107, 111–115, 126–127, 143, 146, 155, 158, 160, 161, 229
Bossuet, 185
Boucheron, Patrick, 48
Brion, Marcel, 33
Brutus Lucius Junius, 90–91, 169
Brutus, Marcus Junius, 91n
Bubenicek, W, 10n
Budé, Guillaume, 52, 97, 128
Buonaccorsi, Biaggio, 22
Busleiden, Jerome, 128n

Cabet, Etienne, 47
Caesar, 74, 91n, 210
Callisthenes, 80
Calvin, Jean, 39
Campanella, Tommaso, 9
Castiglione, Balthasar, 39
Catherine of Aragon, Queen of Henry VIII, 185–186, 224, 236
Cervantes, Miguel de, 14
Chabod, Federico, 12
Campanella, Tommaso, 9
Caracalla, Roman Emperor, 154

Charles of Burgundy, see Charles V
Charles V, Holy Roman Emperor, 35, 36, 52, 75, 78, 88, 186, 214
Charles VII, King of France, 114, 155n
Charles VIII, King of France, 35, 65n, 77, 92, 160
Charles the Bold, 35
Chambers, R.W, 9, 10n, 13, 188n, 236
Chesterton, G.K, 6, 13
Chiron the centaur, 68
Chomarat, Jacques, 14, 23, 44n, 184, 240
Chrysostom, Saint John, 32, 203
Christ, passim
Cineas, 76
Cicero, 23, 32, 177, 203, 204
Cioran, Emil, 7
Clava, Antoine, 12
Clement, John, 139
Clement VII (Cardinal Giulio or Jules de' Medici), Pope, 27–28, 170, 176, 178, 185, 193, 213
Colet, John, 17, 37
Columbus, Christopher, 39
Commodus, Roman Emperor, 154, 214
Corella, Miguel, 22
Copernicus, Nicolaus, 39
Croce, Benedetto, 6
Cromwell, Thomas, 186–187, 225, 235

Cyrus, founder of the Persian
  monarchy, 76, 160–162, 165,
  229

Darius I, King of Persia, 48
Dante Alighieri, 32, 37, 60
David, 80, 83, 95, 114, 127,
  155n, 159
De libero arbitrio, see Erasmus,
  On Free Will
Delcourt, Marie, 14, 133n,
  139n, 183, 234n
Democritus, 62
Dilthey, Wilhelm, 14
Dominic, Saint, 96
Dorp, Maarten Van, 43n, 212
Duke of Valentino, *see* Borgia,
  Cesare
Dürer, Albrecht, 16, 38

Edouard VI, son of Henri VIII,
  King of England, 224
Elizabeth I, daughter of Henri
  VIII, Queen of England, 224
Elton G.R, 236n
Engels, Friedrich, 8
Epicurus, 24, 64, 193
Erasmus, Desiderius, *passim*.
  Works: *Adages*, 23, 75, 210,
  217n; *Christian Marriage*,
  191; *Ciceronianus*, 204;
  Colloquia, 23, 210, 216, 225;
  Complaint of Peace, 23, 75;
  Ecclesiastes, 189, 192, 193;
  *Education of a Christian
  Prince*, 81, 88; *Julius*

excluded, 33; *New Testa-
  ment*, 23, 54–56, 97, 99; *On
  Free Will*, 183, 193, 215; *On
  the Preparation for Death*,
  23, 191; *Paraphrases*, 214;
  Praise of Folly, *passim*, explained by Erasmus, 209–223
Erasmus, Saint, 216
Euripides, 32

Faber, Johann, Bishop of Vienna,
  191
Febvre, Lucien, 28, 226, 239
Ferdinand of Austria, 214
Ferdinand II of Aragon and V of
  Castille, also Ferdinand the
  Catholic, who unified the
  kingdom of Spain, 73, 78,
  92, 126, 154, 155
Ficino, Marsilio, 37
Fichte, Johann Gottlieb, 11
Fisher, John, Bishop of
  Rochester, 9, 57, 189, 190
Fournel, Jean-Louis, 153n
Fourier, Charles, 47
Francis I, King of France, 35–36,
  52, 65n, 75, 77–78, 85, 92,
  214
Francis of Assisi, Saint, 95
Frederick II, King of Prussia, 6,
  10
Froben, Johann, 54, 213n
Froben, Jerome, 191, 192
Fumarolli, Max, 14, 24, 240

Garin, Eugenio, 40

Gaston of Brienne, Duke of Athens, 178
Gavin, A, 213n
Gentillet, Innocent, 11
Giannotti, Donato, 177n
Gilles, Pierre, 43n, 46, 138, 145
Gilson, Etienne, 238
Glocenius, Conrad, 192
Godin, André, 14
Goliath, 95, 114, 160
Greene, James, 225n
Guicciardini, Francesco, 22–23, 34, 37, 180
Guicciardini, Luigi, 237

Halkin, Léon, 14
Harpsfield, Nicholas, 12
Hegel, Georg Wilhelm Friedrich, 6, 11
Henry VIII, King of England, 10, 19, 29, 35, 52, 53, 78, 125, 182–193, 214, 224, 235–236
Heraclitus, 62
Herder, Johann Gottfried, 11
Hermansz, W, 29
Herod, 189, 192
Herodatus, 98
Herodian, 32
Herodias, 189, 193
Hexter, J.H, 13
Hiero II of Syracusa, 114, 155, 160
Hilary, Saint, 203
Holbein, Ambrosius, 54n, 133n
Holbein, Hans, 16, 19, 54n, 133n, 199

Holy Scripture, see Bible
Horace, 31, 44n, 55n, 66, 140, 203
Homer, 32, 44n, 55n, 68
Hythlodeus, Raphael, 46, 47, 100, 102, 131–145

Institutio principis Christiani, see Erasmus, Education of a Christian Prince

Jeroboam, 95
Jerome, Saint, 32, 52 55, 203
John the Baptist, 189
John Paul II, Pope, 10
Julius II, Pope, 33, 78–79, 185, 229
Justin, 32
Juvenal, 32

Kamenev, Lev, 6, 8–9
Kautsky, Karl, 6, 13
Kirov, Sergei, 8

La Boétie, Etienne de, 18
Latimer, Hugh, 56
Lefebvre, Joël, 14
Lefèvre d'Etaples, Jacques, 37
Lefort, Claude, 12, 48, 240
Lenin, Vladimir Illyich, 8
Leo X (Cardinal Gionvanni de' Medici), Pope, 17, 27–28, 52, 54, 83, 97–98, 159, 163, 170, 176, 184
Leonardo da Vinci, 39
Lewis, C.S, 13, 25, 184, 185n

Listrius, G, 213

Liverotto de Fermo, 158

Livy Titus, 32, 98, 151n, 155, 179

Logan, George, 13

Louis XII, King of France, 22, 35, 65n, 77–78, 92

Loyola, Ignatius of, Saint, 39

Lucian of Samosata, 12, 31, 44n, 46, 138, 140

Lucretius, 32

Luther, Martin, 24, 28, 38–39, 183–184, 193–194, 214, 236

Lycurgus, 94

Machiavelli, Marietta, 22

Machiavelli, Niccolò, *passim.* Works: *Art of War*, 26, 29 ; *Clizia*, 26, 180; *Decennali*, 26, 33, *Discourses on the First decade of Titus Livy*, 11, 22, 26–27, 127n, 149–150, 151n, 169n, 175n, 179; *Discourse on the things of Florence after the death of Lorenzo the Younger*, 177; *Florentine Histories*, 27, 176–178; *Golden Ass*, 26, 177 ; *Mandragola*, 26, 177; *Prince,The*, *passim*, explained by Machiavelli, 151–175

Machiavelli Piero, 181

Madeleine de la Tour d'Auvergne, 85

Manent, Pierre, 49

Mansfield, Harvey , 12, 153n, 239

Marcus Aurelius, Roman Emperor, 144, 214

Margolin, Jean-Claude, 14, 24

Marietti, Marina, 178n

Mary I, Queen of England, 224

Marlowe, Christopher, 6

Marx, Karl, 8–9

Matz, Louis, 236n

Mauriac, François, 188

Maximilian I, Holy Roman Emperor, 53

Maximinus, Roman Emperor, 154–155

McCutcheon, Elizabeth, 139n

McClung, William, 133n

Medici family, 20–22, 26–27, 30, 37, 40, 49, 61–63, 65, 82–83, 85–86, 98, 161–162, 169, 170, 176–178, 180

Medici, Catherine de', Queen of France, 85

Medici, Cosimo de', 177

Medici, Giovanni de', *see* Leo X, Pope

Medici, Giulio or Jules de', *see* Clement VII, Pope

Medici, Giuliano de', 30, 61, 85, 170

Medici, Lorenzo the Magnificent, 30

Medici, Lorenzo de', Duke of Urbino, 22, 30, 37, 39, 63, 85, 98, 170, 177

Meslier, Jean, 9

Metsis Quentin, 16
Michelangelo, 38, 39, 63
Micheli, Marcantanio, 178n
Miller, Clarence, 14, 213n
Montaigne, Michel de, 6, 18
More, Alice Middleton, 196, 200
More, John, 200
More, Margaret, *see* Roper, Margaret More
More, Thomas, *passim*. Works: *Apology*, 232n; *Confutation of Tyndale's Answer*, 223n; *De Tristitia Christi*, 189, 197; *Dialogue of Comfort against Tribulations*, 25; *Epigrams*, 25; *History of Richard III*, 25, *Responsio ad Lutherum*, 194, *Utopia*, *passim*, explained by More, 131–147
Moria, see Erasmus, *Praise of Folly*
Morris, William, 6, 13
Morton, John, Cardinal, 144
Moses, 48, 83, 94–95, 159–162
Mussolini, Benito, 6

Nagel, Alain F., 133n
Nathan, 80
Nazianzus, Saint Gregory of, 203
Nellio, Francesco, 181
New Testament, *see* Bible, and Erasmus, New testament
Nolhac, Pierre de, 14, 36
Norfolk, Duke of, 196, 198

Novum Testamentum, *see* Erasmus, New Testament

Old Testament, *see* Bible
Oncken, H, 13
Origen, 32, 203
Orwell, George, 42
Osinovski, Igor, 10n
Ovid, 32, 60

Paracelcus, 39
Parel, A, 38
Pastor, Ludwig von, 52
Paul, Saint, 204, 208, 216
Paul III, Pope, 194
Paul IV, Pope, 225
Péguy, Charles ,7
Petrach, 32, 37, 60–61
Philip of Macedonia, 155n, 160
Pius XII, Pope, 9
Plato, 32, 46–47, 49, 67, 71, 138, 141, 203, 205, 217
Plutarch, 32, 72, 77
Pocock, J.G.A, 12, 40–41
Polybius, 32
Pomponazzi, Pietro, 39
Prévost, André, 132n, 133n, 139n, 224n, 234n
Proudhon, Pierre-Joseph, 9
Pyrrhus, King of Epirus, 76
Pythagoras, 80

Quintilian, 23, 205

Rabelais, 45, 57, 183

Raphael (Raffalleo Sanzio da Urbino), 39

Raphael (Hythlodeus), see Hythlodeus

Renaudet, Augustin, 12, 35, 40, 183

Reynolds, E.E, 185

Rich, Sir Richard, 197

Riccia, 87

Ridolfi , Roberto, 30, 85

Ritter, G, 13

Robinson, Ralph, 224, 234n

Romulus, 94, 160–162, 229

Roper, Margaret More, 182, 187–189, 195–200, 235

Roper, William, 19, 188n, 196, 200, 225, 226n

Rouen, Cardinal of (Charles d'Amboise), Minister of Louis XII, 163

Rousseau, Jean-Jacques, 6, 11

Sainte-Beuve, Charles-Augustin, 6, 14

Sallust, 32

Salviati, Alamanno, 22

Savonarola, Girolamo, 21, 32, 38, 40, 161–162

Screech, M.A, 14, 240

Seneca, 31, 76, 84

Septimus Severus, Roman Emperor, 73, 119, 155, 159

Sforza, Francesco, 152, 165

Shakespeare, William, 14, 25

Smith, Steven D, 235

Socrates, 22, 140

Soderini, Piero, 22, 26, 88

Solomon, 95

Solon, 94

Spinoza, Baruch, 11

Skinner, Quentin, 12–13, 41

Stalin, Joseph, 8

Strauss, Leo, 12, 239

Suleiman the Magnificent, Sultan of the Ottoman Empire, 36

Surtz, Edward, 132n, 133n, 139n

Sylvester, R.S, 13

Swift, Jonathan, 6, 47

Tacitus , 32

Tarugi, F, 180

Tchernychevski, Nikolaï, 9

Terence, 32

Teresa de Avila, Saint, 39

Theseus, 83, 160–162, 229

Thomas Aquinas, 32

Thucydides, 32

Tito, Sandi di, 20

Tocqueville, Alexis de, 238

Tunstall, Cuthbert, Bishop of London, 184, 193

Tyndale, William, 182, 184, 222

Uriah the Hittite, 81n

Vergil, 32, 65, 203

Vespucci, Amerigo, 103, 105

Vettori, Francesco, 23, 27, 43n, 60, 61, 85–87, 237

Vyshinsky, Andrey, 8

Vitrier, Jean, 17

Voltaire, 6, 14

Walsh, Th, 213n
Wolsey, Thomas, Cardinal, 29,
    35, 56, 100, 125, 186

Xenophon, 32, 83, 165
Xerxes, King of Persia, 76

Ximenes de Cisneros, Cardinal,
    52

Zancarini, Jean-Claude, 153n
Zinneman, Fred, 188n
Zinoviev, Gregory, 8
Zoroaster, 80
Zweig, Stefan, 6, 16